Debates in English Teaching

Edited by Jon Davison, Caroline Daly and John Moss

Routledge
Taylor & Francis Group

LONDON AND NEW YORK

First published 2011
by Routledge
2 Park Square, Milton Park, Abingdon, Oxon, OX14 4RN

Simultaneously published in the USA and Canada
by Routledge
711 Third Avenue, New York, NY 10017

Routledge is an imprint of the Taylor & Francis Group, an informa business

© 2011 Jon Davison, Caroline Daly and John Moss for selection and
editorial material; individual chapters, the contributors.

Typeset in Galliard
by Pindar NZ, Auckland, New Zealand
Printed and bound in Great Britain
by CPI Antony Rowe, Chippenham, Wiltshire

British Library Cataloguing in Publication Data
A catalogue record for this book is available from the British Library

Library of Congress Cataloging-in-Publication Data
    Davison, Jon, 1949-
    Debates in English teaching / Jon Davison, Caroline Daly, and John
Moss. — 1st ed.
        p. cm. — (Debates in subject teaching series)
    Includes bibliographical references and index.
    1. English language—Study and teaching. 2. English teachers—
Training of. I. Daly, Caroline. II. Moss, John, 1957- III. Title.
    LB1631.D28 2011
    428.0071—dc22   2010032396

ISBN13: 978-0-415-56915-6 (hbk)
ISBN13: 978-0-415-56916-3 (pbk)
ISBN13: 978-0-203-83144-1 (ebk)

Debates in English Teaching

What are the key debates in English teaching today?

Debates in English Teaching explores the major issues all English teachers encounter in their daily professional lives. It engages with established and contemporary debates, promotes and supports critical reflection and aims to stimulate both novice and experienced teachers to reach informed judgements and argue their point of view with deeper theoretical knowledge and understanding.

Key issues debated include:

- the professional identity of English teachers
- attitudes to correctness in grammar and Standard English
- the importance of the media and new technologies
- social class and literacy
- the nature of the dialogic classroom
- the role of wider reading
- the politics of early literacy.

With its combination of expert opinion and fresh insight, *Debates in English Teaching* is the ideal companion for all student and practising teachers engaged in initial training, continuing professional development and Masters level study.

Jon Davison has been Professor of Teacher Education in four universities including the Institute of Education, University of London, UK, where he was also Dean.

Caroline Daly is a Senior Lecturer in Education at the Institute of Education, University of London, UK.

John Moss is Dean of Education at Canterbury Christ Church University, UK.

Forthcoming titles in the Debates in Subject Teaching Series:

Debates in History Teaching
Edited by Ian Davies

Debates in Religious Education
Edited by Philip Barnes

Debates in Citizenship Education
Edited by James Arthur and Hilary Cremin

Debates in Art and Design Teaching
Edited by Nicholas Addison and Lesley Burgess

Contents

List of illustrations   vii
Notes on contributors   viii
Series editors' introduction to the series   xi
Acknowledgements   xiii

Introduction: educational discourses in *Debates in English Teaching*   1
JOHN MOSS

1 Becoming an English teacher: identity, self-knowledge and expertise   18
ANDY GOODWYN

2 Promoting a dialogic pedagogy in English teaching   36
FRANK HARDMAN

3 A new theory and model of writing development   48
RICHARD ANDREWS

4 Living language, live debates: grammar and Standard English   63
DEBRA MYHILL

5 The politics of early literacy   78
KATHY GOOUCH

6 'Whatever happened to the Literacy Hour?'   89
JO WESTBROOK AND HAZEL BRYAN WITH KAREN COOPER,
VICKY HAWKING AND SEAN O'MALLEY

7 Access, choice and time: a guide to wider reading in schools   104
   JO WESTBROOK

8 From *Beowulf* to Batman: connecting English and media education   117
   ANDREW BURN

9 The 'real world' of technologies: what kinds of professional
   development are needed for English teachers?   131
   CAROLINE DALY

10 Creativity in English teaching and learning   142
   SUE DYMOKE

11 English and inclusion   157
   JOHN YANDELL

12 Literacy and social class   169
   JON DAVISON

   Bibliography   188
   Index   211

Illustrations

Figures

3.1	The position of a theory and model in relation to writing practices	49
3.2	A model for writing	57
3.3	A model for writing development	58
8.1	Screengrab from Year 9 computer game adapted from *The Tempest*	127
8.2	Ariel's song as a game pop-up	128
8.3	Objects from Ariel's song as pick-ups in the game	129
9.1	The ICT CPD landscape	138
12.1	Versions of English	178

Tables

0.1	Chapter 1 discourses	3
0.2	Chapter 2 discourses	4
0.3	Chapter 3 discourses	5
0.4	Chapter 4 discourses	6
0.5	Chapter 5 discourses	7
0.6	Chapter 6 discourses	9
0.7	Chapter 7 discourses	10
0.8	Chapter 8 discourses	11
0.9	Chapter 9 discourses	12
0.10	Chapter 10 discourses	13
0.11	Chapter 11 discourses	14
0.12	Chapter 12 discourses	16
4.1	A range of definitions of Standard English	67

Contributors

Richard Andrews is Professor in English at the Institute of Education, University of London. His previous publications on writing include *Narrative and Argument*, *The Problem with Poetry* and *Teaching and Learning Argument*. More recently he has published *Re-framing Literacy: Teaching and Learning in English and the Language Arts*, which looks at one particular aspect of the model proposed in his chapter in the present book: framing. He is currently working on a book on writing development with Anna Smith of New York University.

Hazel Bryan is Head of the Department of Professional Development at Canterbury Christ Church University. Her research interests include education policy, constructs of teacher professionalism and learning and teaching at Masters and doctoral levels.

Andrew Burn is Professor of Media Education at the Institute of Education, University of London. He has researched and published work on many aspects of the media, including media literacy in schools, the semiotics of the moving image and computer games and young people's production of digital animation, film and computer games. He previously taught English, drama and media studies in comprehensive schools for over 20 years. He was a head of English and an assistant principal at his last school, Parkside Community College in Cambridge, where his main role was to direct the school's media arts specialism; it was the first specialist Media Arts College in the country. His most recent book is *Making New Media: Digital Literacies and Creative Production* (Peter Lang, 2009).

Caroline Daly is a Senior Lecturer in education at the Institute of Education, University of London. Her research areas are in English teaching, gender in education and teachers' professional development in e-learning contexts. Publications include chapters in *Issues in English Teaching* (Routledge, 2000), *Gender in Education* (ATL, 2004), *Enhancing Learning through Technology* (Idea Group, 2006) and articles in *Changing English, Journal of In-Service Education, E-Learning* and *Teaching in Higher Education*. She is co-editor of *New Designs for Teachers' Professional Learning* (Bedford Way Papers, 2007).

Jon Davison has been Professor of Teacher Education in four universities including the Institute of Education, University of London, where he was also Dean.
His research interests include sociolinguistics, citizenship education and the
professional formation of teachers. He has published extensively on the teaching and learning of English and teacher education – most recently, *Learning
to Teach English in the Secondary School*, 3rd edition (Routledge, 2009). He is
Fellow of the Royal Society of Arts and Chair of the Society for Educational
Studies.

Sue Dymoke is a Senior Lecturer and University Teaching Fellow in the School
of Education at the University of Leicester where she leads the PGCE English
and MTL programmes. She is editor of the international academic journal
English in Education. Her publications include *Teaching English Texts 11–18*
(Continuum), *Reflective Teaching and Learning* (Sage, co-edited with Jennifer
Harrison), *The New Girls* – new and selected poems (Shoestring Press) – and
Drafting and Assessing Poetry: A Guide for Teachers (Paul Chapman).

Andy Goodwyn is Professor of Education and Head of the Institute of Education
at the University of Reading. He began his career as a secondary English teacher
working in schools in the Midlands and London as Head of Department. He
joined Reading University and ran English PGCE and MA programmes for
20 years. He has undertaken a number of research projects and published
widely in English education over that period and contributed to many national
and international conferences. His most recent book is *The Expert Teacher of
English* (Routledge, 2010).

Kathy Goouch is a Senior Lecturer at Canterbury Christ Church University. She
has worked for many years with children, teachers and early years practitioners.
Her research interests are in play, children's early interactions and storying.
Her published work ranges across early literacy and early years education. She
co-authored the review of literature for the Birth to Three Framework and is
currently researching the nature of professional interactions and relationships
in baby rooms in nurseries.

Frank Hardman holds the Chair in Educational Studies at the University of York.
Previously, he held the Chair in Educational Studies at La Trobe University,
Melbourne, Australia. He has written extensively in the language and education area. Recently, his research has focused on classroom interaction as a tool
of pedagogy across various phases of education in national and international
contexts.

John Moss is Dean of Education at Canterbury Christ Church University, Kent.
A former head of English, Drama and Media Studies in a large comprehensive
school, he has taught undergraduate English and drama at university level and
Secondary PGCE courses for ten years. He is co-author of *Subject Mentoring in
the Secondary School* (Routledge, 1997), co-editor of *Issues in English Teaching*

(Routledge, 2000) and series editor of a series of books on citizenship in the secondary curriculum.

Debra Myhill is Professor of Education at the University of Exeter. Her research interests focus principally on aspects of language and literacy teaching, particularly writing and grammar, and talk in the classroom. She is the author of *Better Writers* (Courseware Publications, 2001), *Talking, Listening, Learning: Effective Talk in the Primary Classroom* (Open University Press, 2005) and co-editor of the *Sage Handbook of Writing Development* (2009). Her latest book is *Using Talk to Support Writing* (Sage, 2010).

Jo Westbrook is a Senior Lecturer in Education and Director of Taught Programmes in the School of Education and Social Work at the University of Sussex. Her research interests revolve around comprehension and wider reading in English secondary schools, and learning to read in schools in developing countries, particularly sub-Saharan Africa, through her work with the Centre for International Education at Sussex. She has written widely on the teaching and learning of English – most recently, *The Complete Guide to Becoming an English Teacher* (Sage, 2009).

John Yandell leads the Secondary PGCE English and English with Drama courses at the Institute of Education, University of London. He is the co-editor of *Critical Practice in Teacher Education: A Study of Professional Learning* (2010). Recent publications have appeared in the *British Educational Research Journal*, the *Cambridge Journal of Education*, *Changing English*, *English in Education* and *English Teaching: Practice and Critique*. He is currently engaged in research on how literature is read in English classrooms.

Series editors' introduction to the series

This book, *Debates in English Teaching*, is one of a series of books entitled *Debates in Subject Teaching*. The series has been designed to engage with a wide range of debates related to subject teaching. Unquestionably, debates vary among the subjects, but may include, for example, issues that:

- impact on Initial Teacher Education in the subject;
- are addressed in the classroom through the teaching of the subject;
- are related to the content of the subject and its definition;
- are related to subject pedagogy;
- are connected with the relationship between the subject and broader educational aims and objectives in society, and the philosophy and sociology of education;
- are related to the development of the subject and its future in the twenty-first century.

Consequently, each book presents key debates that subject teachers should understand, reflect on and engage in as part of their professional development. Chapters have been designed to highlight major questions, and to consider the evidence from research and practice in order to find possible answers. Some subject books or chapters offer at least one solution or a view of the ways forward, whereas others provide alternative views and leave readers to identify their own solution or view of the ways forward. The editors expect readers will want to pursue the issues raised, and so chapters include questions for further debate and suggestions for further reading. Debates covered in the series will provide the basis for discussion in university subject seminars or as topics for assignments or classroom research. The books have been written for all those with a professional interest in their subject, and, in particular: student teachers learning to teach the subject in secondary or primary school; newly qualified teachers; teachers undertaking study at Masters level; teachers with a subject coordination or leadership role, and those preparing for such responsibility; as well as mentors, university tutors, CPD organisers and advisers of the aforementioned groups.

Books in the series have a cross-phase dimension, because the editors believe that it is important for teachers in the primary, secondary and post-16 phases to look at subject teaching holistically, particularly in order to provide for continuity and progression, but also to increase their understanding of how children and young people learn. The balance of chapters that have a cross-phase relevance varies according to the issues relevant to different subjects. However, no matter where the emphasis is, the authors have drawn out the relevance of their topic to the whole of each book's intended audience.

Because of the range of the series, both in terms of the issues covered and its cross-phase concern, each book is an edited collection. Editors have commissioned new writing from experts on particular issues, who, collectively, represent many different perspectives on subject teaching. Readers should not expect a book in this series to cover the entire range of debates relevant to the subject, or to offer a completely unified view of subject teaching, or that every debate will be dealt with discretely, or that all aspects of a debate will be covered. Part of what each book in this series offers to readers is the opportunity to explore the interrelation-ships between positions in debates and, indeed, among the debates themselves, by identifying the overlapping concerns and competing arguments that are woven through the text.

The editors are aware that many initiatives in subject teaching continue to originate from the centre, and that teachers have decreasing control of subject content, pedagogy and assessment strategies. The editors strongly believe that for teaching to remain properly a vocation and a profession, teachers must be invited to be part of a creative and critical dialogue about subject teaching, and should be encouraged to reflect, criticise, problem-solve and innovate. This series is intended to provide teachers with a stimulus for democratic involvement in the development of the discourse of subject teaching.

Susan Capel, Jon Davison, James Arthur and John Moss
December 2010

Acknowledgements

A book like this does not spring fully formed from the mind of the editor to the bookshop or library shelves. This volume is the result of the work of many people. Thanks are due to the academics whose finely written and thought-provoking contributions make up this collection. I am grateful to my co-editors for their endeavours in producing this book. Many thanks must also go to the team at Routledge, Taylor & Francis, and, in particular, to Helen Pritt, Claire Westwood and Catherine Oakley for their help, hard work and forbearance. Lastly and most sincerely I should wish to thank Anna Clarkson, Editorial Director of Routledge, Taylor & Francis, for her unfailing support, guidance and friendship over the past 15 years.

Jon Davison
November 2010

Introduction

Educational discourses in *Debates in English Teaching*

John Moss

The editors of this series and this book debated possible titles for it for some time. The title *Debates in English Teaching* for the book (and Debates in Subject Teaching for the series) was settled on because of the editors' shared belief that many issues in subject teaching are contested, that rigorous debate is needed to take the discussion of them forward and that, in the context of the increasing recognition by the global education community, and not least by some influential stakeholders in England, that teachers' work should be supported by high-level academic engagement: teachers undertaking Initial Teacher Education and practising qualified teachers should be supported in taking part in those debates.

There are, of course, some problems associated with the representation of complex issues in the form of the kinds of debate which set up binary oppositions between positions in order to discuss them. This practice may, for example, give credibility to positions which should have none: the case is known to me of a teacher who proposed to include a debate on 'the pros and cons of apartheid' in a sixth-form general studies course.

The contributors to this book generally avoid setting up this kind of simplistic and dangerous opposition. Instead, making the assumption that what readers of this book will be primarily concerned with is how to teach English well, and that this can only be defined with primary reference to the interests of pupils, they characteristically demonstrate that debates about good practice in English teaching are embedded in a complex set of overlapping debates about the philosophy of English teaching, the politics of English teaching and the role of schooling in society, among others.

The manner in which contributors to this book typically construct the debates they engage in is, with varying degrees of explicitness, as a set of overlapping discourses, where a discourse is a self-contained collection of utterances made in connection with an identifiable purpose and controlled by an individual/group who has/have, or at least assert(s), the authority to take forward that purpose in the way that it affects the lives of others, who may or may not have opportunities to contribute to that discourse.

The discourses which contributors to this book are most concerned with are those which relate to research into subject teaching and subject teaching policy.

Some characterise subject teaching as a single discourse which government and other education policy makers assert their authority to control, while this is challenged or contested by researchers and practitioners. Others see official policy directives as a single discourse which takes more or less account of a separate discourse which might be defined as subject teaching research.

However, no matter how they choose to represent this, a view which appears to be shared by the book's contributors is that the acknowledgement of complexity in the debates about English teaching is anything but stultifying or disempowering. In particular, separating out, on the one hand, what policy makers have said to which audiences with what effect and why from what, on the other, research indicates, is the means by which many of the contributors work towards identifying a direction for the debate with which they are concerned. In other words, understanding both who has had the power to direct that subject teaching moves in practice, in what direction, with what authority, and understanding what recommendations for practice researchers make, based on their interpretation of the research evidence: while noting their possible motives for interpreting the evidence in particular ways, is a precondition for determining whether and how pupils will benefit from one or more of the implementation of existing policy in practice, challenges and/or changes to policy, and/or further research.

In Chapter 12 of this book, Davison argues 'the importance of discursive practice in the social construction of knowledge and the need to make educational discourses *visible* to pupils'. The contributors to this book have demonstrated that it is just as significant for teachers and other educational practitioners and researchers to make visible the educational discourses that contribute to the social construction of knowledge about subject teaching.

Book introductions or opening chapters often provide a critical review of the contents of the rest of the volume. In what follows, my intention is to carry out this task while making as visible as possible the discourses to which the contributors make either implicit or explicit reference, beginning with Chapter 1.

Chapter 1

Goodwyn's chapter on the professional identity of English teachers offers a characterisation of them that makes most reference to overlapping discourses concerning the professional identity of teachers in general, the particular professional identity of English teachers and the philosophy of English teaching.

He first constructs a binary opposition between the public perception of teaching as safe work and teachers' own view of it as a challenging vocation. He notes that a number of models of teaching and teacher behaviour exist but that, while conceptions that focus on competence and reflective practice dominate the discourse, there are some tensions between these not entirely compatible constructions. He also demonstrates that teaching has most of the characteristics shared by major professions, while noting that its status in this group is still contested to a degree.

Most significantly, he regards conceptualising teachers as participants in communities of practice as offering valuable potential in taking this discourse forward.

His examination of the particular professional identities of English teachers centres on the ways in which the formative experiences individuals have as students, typically both as readers and as learners who have experienced good English teaching at school themselves, influence the way in which they define and teach the subject, also typically finding language more challenging to teach just as it is more marginal to their experience. Goodwyn also describes the process by which they become pedagogic readers of all texts, reading them in relation to the teaching and learning opportunities they present.

This process of formation is related to a characteristic favouring of the personal growth model that features in the discourse concerned with the philosophy of English teaching, and a sense of embattlement when policy initiatives prevent this model from having a substantial influence on practice (see also Chapter 12 for discussion of models of English teaching).

Since Goodwyn finds a degree of inertia in the processes through which English teachers are formed which results in them defining themselves as teachers and the subject in ways which relate to their own experience, there is a sense in which they are the dominant authority in the discourses concerned with their professional identity and with the subject. Nevertheless, this authority is challenged by policy

Table 0.1 Chapter 1 discourses

Discourse	Authority	Status	Future
Professional identity of teachers	Educational theorists	Complex and developing: the teacher constructed as a participant in community of practice may provide a new direction for this discourse	The influence of communities of practice in this discourse could be secured by policy which promoted them
Professional identity of English teacher	English teachers themselves	Challenged: orthodoxies arising from repeated patterns of formative experience are challenged by incongruent policy initiatives	Communities of practice involving English teachers could develop professional identity, practice, and the subject's philosophy if they were enabled to play a significant role in policy development
Philosophy of English teaching	English teachers themselves	Contested: while the personal growth view is dominant, there are multiple conceptions of this, and teachers' preferences can be destabilised by policy	

initiatives which promote different identities for the subject, especially those concerned with a limited view of literacy.

Goodwyn consequently proposes that English teachers would benefit from engagement with strong professional associations such as the National Association for the Teaching of English, capable of providing the supportive characteristics of communities of practice, as a strategy for managing their responses to these challenges and for taking practice forward.

Chapter 2

Hardman's chapter on dialogic pedagogy begins by establishing a binary opposition in the discourse concerned with the pedagogy of talk in English teaching, between recitational and dialogic discourse. He characterises dialogic discourse as collective, reciprocal, supportive, cumulative and purposeful, and notes the influence of Vygotsky and Bakhtin in providing the theoretical justification for the significance of this kind of talk in learning. While dialogic discourse is highly valued by theoretical contributors to the discourse concerned with the pedagogy of talk, Hardman provides comprehensive evidence that recitational discourse dominates classroom practice.

He then suggests that teachers whose practice has a strong theoretical grounding, and who therefore have a strong professional conviction in the value of dialogic talk, are more likely to incorporate it in their practice. As a result it is by influencing the discourse concerned with the professional development of teachers that Hardman sees a means of bringing about change. He argues that teacher development programmes should create safe spaces in which teachers can reflect on their intentions and beliefs, model practice and experience coaching and video feedback interventions which are then used as a resource to enter into dialogue with them about their practice. Noting Alexander's view that dialogic principles

Table 0.2 Chapter 2 discourses

Discourse	Authority	Status	Future
Pedagogy of talk	Theoreticians, researchers and practitioners	Stagnating: the theory of dialogic pedagogy is orthodox but not dominant in practice	Strengthening dialogic practices in teacher education could provide a means for accelerating this practice in classrooms
Professional development of English teachers	Teacher educators	Developing: a range of strategies for including dialogic andragogy in professional development programmes are used	The strategies adopted to promote dialogic practices would require monitoring and evaluation

should inform professional learning, in effect he argues that experiencing dialogic andragogy would provide the most effective means of encouraging teachers to use dialogic pedagogy.

Chapter 3

Andrews' chapter proposes a new theory of writing development. He first establishes that this theory must be founded on a theory of writing, which takes account of the fact that writing is a cognitive, conceptual, emotional and political act. In other words, he indicates that we need to know why we write as well as how we write in order to understand better how to teach it. As is the case in a number of chapters in this book, the author insists that clarity about what it is that is being taught and learned and why must be achieved before any useful observations can be made about how to teach it.

In this case, Andrews positions his new theory of writing in relation to established overlapping discourses about writing. He defines his position in relation to rhetorical theory; reconsiders how writing relates to genre, which results in a distinction between dynamic processes of 'framing' and the mechanical adoption of 'writing frames'; recognises the significance of multimodal choice, especially in the context of the opportunities available to us to write and, indeed, not to write in contemporary society; and he asserts the significance of understanding writing as composition, and reconceptualises what is meant by writing processes. There is a thread throughout the discussion concerned with ways in which political and some educational drivers have sometimes led to practices which have restricted the choices of learning writers and by doing so, Andrews believes, limited the extent of their writing development.

It is not surprising then that the theory of writing development Andrews offers is founded on a pedagogy which makes explicit and promotes these choices. In the discourse of writing development theory, he challenges in particular practices which do not take account of our reasons for writing, constrain the thought processes through which we choose when to write, how to frame writing and to engage in the collage-like activity of composition.

Table 0.3 Chapter 3 discourses

Discourse	Authority	Status	Future
Writing theory	Researchers and practitioners	Complex and contested, including through the theoretical propositions in this chapter	The influence of this chapter's propositions on the key discourses should properly be determined through rigorous investigation of their value
Writing development theory	Researchers and practitioners	Under development	

Since his theory of writing is a new formulation it is also not surprising that the theory of writing development derived from it is recognised as being under development and requiring testing through research and practice. However, uniquely in this book, Andrews engages in formal debate by considering counterarguments to those his theories of writing and writing development advocate.

Chapter 4

Myhill's chapter on debates about language, and, most specifically, debates about Standard English and grammar, makes a particularly helpful distinction between a discourse concerned with language, identity and power, and therefore what it is that the teaching of language should set out to achieve, and a discourse that is concerned with the efficacy of particular approaches to teaching and learning. She points out that these different debates are often conflated in debates about language teaching without this being acknowledged.

By proposing the development of a new discourse in which those aspects of established ideological positions on language teaching are accepted when the evidence about how language works supports them, Myhill is able to propose a way forward in the debate. She proposes a pluralist approach to the teaching of Standard English which acknowledges the linguistic fact that no dialect is intrinsically better than another, but that, since the non-standard dialects people use can be fundamental to their sense of their own identity, it follows that, while Standard English is a privileged dialect, the use of which can contribute to the empowerment of pupils, the entitlement they should have is to learn and learn about both Standard and non-standard English.

Similarly, she demonstrates that language is, as a matter of fact, both rule-governed and susceptible to change, so that neither of the extreme ideological views – on

Table 0.4 Chapter 4 discourses

Discourse	Authority	Status	Future
Language teaching philosophy	Government and policy advisors positioned within the academic debate	Contested: by proponents of 'linguistic purity' and 'language variety' views	Extreme views linked with ideological positions which may result in stalemate in entrenched positions
Language teaching pedagogy		Contested: by proponents of prescriptive and descriptive models	
Coherent investigative language teaching philosophy and pedagogy	Academics and teachers exploring both/and solutions	Complex: under development through research and teaching	Research and practice carried out and tested

the one hand, that 'bad grammar' is an attack on necessary linguistic purity, or, on the other, that language varies so much that it is irrelevant to identify patterns or rules – is entirely defensible. Getting to this point of clarity about the relationships between the ideological and linguistic issues provides a more stable context for teachers and researchers to investigate what curriculum content and pedagogy really does develop young people both as students and users of language.

Chapter 5

Goouch's chapter on early literacy quotes Alexander: 'The vein of dichotomous discourse runs deep' (2010: 22). However, while she demonstrates, herself, that deeply contested, mutually exclusive positions are taken in the debate about early literacy, she also shows, more subtly, that internationally there is a range of varied policy discourses which pay attention to different parts of the spectrum of research findings in the discourse of early literacy theory and to different extents. What

Table 0.5 Chapter 5 discourses

Discourse(s)	Authority	Status	Future
Early literacy policy/ies	Governments informed by research	Contested: this is demonstrated through the comparison and contrast of policy in England, New Zealand and Scandinavia	Likely to depend on international comparisons and how successes in early literacy development are accounted for by governments
Early literacy theory	Researchers and practitioners	Contested: especially the role and efficacy of synthetic phonics in early literacy	The influence of developing understandings of early learning will be significant
Early learning: how children and babies learn	Researchers and practitioners (including parents and carers)	Developing: new insights from neuroscience, research into informal and home learning	A key focus for research and development
Early years practitioner development	Governments informed by research	Contested: opposed positions suggest effective practice is based on either transmission of simple models or deep understanding of complex ones	Policy will be determined by the outcomes of current strategies adopted internationally and the interpretation of their outcomes

else influences these policy discourses also varies, and includes in particular the way government understands the relationship between its targets for early years learners and what is known about learning in this phase of life.

Goouch also engages with a discourse concerned with practitioner development, recording that this is contested between those who tend to see practitioners as technicians implementing what is essentially simple policy and those who would insist on the need for practitioners to base their own decisions about teaching and learning on deep academic understanding of the complex processes through which literacy is acquired, and the different learning journeys children experience.

Without using these terms, she describes how the early experiences of children formulate a 'primary Discourse' (see Chapter 12) which will make particular kinds of 'secondary Discourses' experienced in formal early learning settings or school more or less accessible. A simple strategy for developing literacy, promoting one means of access to reading, cannot meet the needs of all children if they are all expected to engage with it at the same time and in the same way.

Goouch also establishes that the discourse of early literacy theory needs to take account of current developments in a broader discourse concerned more generally with early learning. New insights from neuroscience and research into what really happens in children's brains, in the home and in informal learning experiences have to be considered by early literacy theorists.

Chapter 6

Westbrook and Bryan review developments in literacy policy and practice in England in the last ten years, also considering the influence of practice from England and other Western countries in the teaching of literacy in the developing world. They describe the way in which the introduction of the National Literacy Strategy (NLS) in England reflected the confidence of a new government in a specific methodology, and marked a point in the literacy policy discourse at which those with authority imposed policy through a non-negotiable directive.

They demonstrate that this approach disrupted a broader discourse of teacher development by imposing what they call a palimpsestic set of pedagogical texts on the profession. Analysis of the pedagogy that was imposed, and the strengths and weaknesses within it, is clouded by the divisive effect of this mode of implementation. At the time, headteachers had a particularly important role as the authorities for the curriculum in their schools in mediating the policy directives.

They argue that the discourse concerned with the philosophy of English teaching, which had previously been dominated by an emancipatory social theory, was overwhelmed when the 'scientific' rigour attributed to NLS practice was imposed.

However, in the context of current recognition that the NLS was not completely successful (measured by its own standards, in terms of literacy targets) and was never fully implemented (partly because of the rigid approach to its implementation), newer formulations of English allow for greater pedagogical variety, even if this is because '[t]he pressure on students reaching baselines . . . has become the dominant discourse' and because the value of more individualised approaches is better understood.

Westbrook and Bryan also describe the opportunity for literacy practice now to be influenced by a richer discourse of literary theory which includes, among other things, recognition of multimodal literacies in contemporary society and the possibility of adopting pedagogies derived from critical literacy theory.

However, what is most striking in the chapter, because of its inclusion of teachers' voices, is the extent to which teachers were disempowered by their limited influence in the discourse concerned with literacy policy.

Table 0.6 Chapter 6 discourses

Discourse(s)	Authority	Status	Future
Literacy policy/ies	Governments informed by research	Contested: the limited success of the imposed NLS has reinitiated discussion	The focus on attainment still dominates this discourse and is likely to continue to do so
Literacy theory/ies	Researchers and practitioners	Contested: recognition of contemporary multimodal literacies and the opportunity to use critical literacy pedagogy can provide new direction	The opportunity to influence policy through richer versions of literacy will be limited by the extent to which it is demonstrated that standards will be raised by this approach
Philosophy of English teaching	Governments through statutory curriculum; researchers and teachers	Developing: an emancipatory social vision was replaced by a 'scientific' approach designed to raise standards, but new initiatives recognise the need for a more varied and individualised pedagogy to do this	It is implied that the fundamental question about what English is for needs to be revisited
Literacy teachers' professional development	Governments informed by research; moderating authority resting in headteachers	Contested: teachers constructed as 'clean slates' may find confidence from being directed or feel completely deprofessionalised	It is implied that a new model is needed

Chapter 7

Westbrook's chapter on reading articulates a theory of reading and a related theory of reading development, and, like Andrews' chapter on writing, demonstrates that ideas about pedagogy need to be derived from an understanding of what it is that is being taught. In essence, her position in the discourse on reading is that reading should be regarded as a complex activity, in terms of both its purposes and its processes, and that, consequently, a rich repertoire of strategies for teaching reading is needed.

In considering her key question, which is concerned with the ways in which schools can promote sustained and wide reading in pupils, Westbrook identifies the characteristics of successful and unsuccessful readers, using these as a context for identifying the features of pedagogy that work against and then for reading. In effect she sets up a binary opposition between those practices which are likely to undermine progress in reading and those which will support it.

Among the latter, she includes recognition of the contexts in which reading takes place inside and outside of school, the need to engage pupils in opportunities to read material which is of intrinsic interest to them and, among many other things, a whole school commitment to reading which is represented by exciting special events as well as a relentless determination to ensure that opportunities for sustained reading are provided regularly, structured and supported by effective teaching.

Like Andrews, Westbrook does not consider what likelihood there is of her vision becoming dominant in the discourse of reading development, but rather than voicing and combating the counterarguments to her position in a formal debate she presents the set of practices which she argues work against reading development in schools as part of the validation of her position in the discourse.

Table 0.7 Chapter 7 discourses

Discourse(s)	Authority	Status	Future
Reading theory	Researchers and practitioners	Contested: including through the theoretical propositions in this chapter	Westbrook points out that research can identify correlations between pedagogy and reading success, although causality is difficult to prove
Reading development theory	Researchers and practitioners	Contested: this chapter argues that a rich and complex view of reading points to a complex pedagogy for reading development	

Chapter 8

At the beginning of his chapter, Burn argues that English and media, in their formulations as school education disciplines, have set up competing discourses seeking to control ways in which pupils should interact with texts as productions of culture. While he recognises that school English is itself contested, he argues that a Leavisite concern to protect aesthetic engagement with a selective tradition of high-culture texts continues to dominate the National Curriculum for English in England, and that this limits the extent to which the blurring of the boundaries of English and media that he calls for can be achieved.

However, while the educational discourses of media and English retain this degree of irreconcilable rigidity, Burn points out that another discourse – concerning the real-world production of, and engagement with, texts by their generators and receivers – already demonstrates this blurring. Making reference to some very telling examples of textual and intertextual history, as well as classroom practice which draws on insights about contemporary outside-of-school engagement with texts, Burn demonstrates that how texts are regarded culturally shifts in time and according to their appropriation by different audiences, and that these audiences, through both critical and creative practices and responses, demonstrate an interest in both their aesthetic qualities and the concerns about them as texts that are associated with critical literacy and media.

While the logic of the argument seems to point towards a new formulation of the school curriculum in which the traditional definitions of media and English

Table 0.8 Chapter 8 discourses

Discourse	Authority	Status	Future
English: its identity as a school curriculum subject	English educators	Contested: but dominated by Leavisite protection of high culture	Proposed redefinitions should take account of the challenge to current competing discourses from the discourse defined below
Media: its identity as a school curriculum subject	Media educators	Challenged: its radical critical literacy agenda needs modification	
Textual production and reception across time and place	Current generators and receivers of texts (from multinational companies to individuals)	Highly complex – but analysis by teachers should inform curriculum and pedagogy	Changing: particularly under the influence of intertextual cross-referencing and development of new forms of textual generation and reception through globalisation and technology

might be absorbed into a new synthetic discipline of textual creation and response, Burn settles for identifying a modified agenda for media. Interestingly, he also finally asserts that it is only teachers who can carry the debate forward, whereas other contributors to this book have maintained that teachers' power to bring about the futures that the authors would commend is limited by the influence of other, often political, authorities.

Chapter 9

Daly's chapter on the professional development needed to improve the use of technology in English teaching points out that whereas a discourse about the relationship between schooling and society, which is used to influence educational policy, has recognised dramatic changes in the uses of technology in pupils' lived experience, another discourse about the professional education of English teachers has failed to engage effectively with the implications of this. She notes the MacArthur Report's finding that 'notions of expertise and authority are being turned on their head': developments in technology and in young people's uses of them in their lives have disrupted the discourse about the use of technology in teaching by challenging where power lies in this discourse.

Turning to another debate within which it appears a solution to this problem might be available, Daly nevertheless finds another discourse, about the professional development of teachers as users of technology in teaching, problematically

Table 0.9 Chapter 9 discourses

Discourse	Authority	Status	Future
Schooling: how it should relate to changes in society	Official and commissioned reports (intended to influence policy)	Problem-defining for education: technology is advancing rapidly outside of classrooms	Uncertain: depends on policy priorities
English teaching: how it should make use of technology	Academics, professional organisations	Challenged: conventional positions take insufficient account of pupils' lived experience	Uncertain: will be determined by policy power holders
Professional development of teachers in the use of technology	Government and/ or 'marketplace' professional development providers, and teachers and schools	Contested: no clear evidence about most effective practice	Uncertain: as above

contested: neither systematic centralised approaches to professional development nor the more varied and individualised ones available to schools and teachers through a fragmented market have achieved the quality of teaching and learning, even through the forms of technology, such as electronic whiteboards, more commonly available in schools, that most contributors to the debate about this consider desirable.

Daly indicates how this debate stands, and concludes that while the understandings about the principles of teaching and learning are available to educators, and that this should allow for teaching with technology to develop, those who have the power to determine what pedagogy and technologies are promoted may limit progress. However, while earlier in the chapter she has acknowledged the extent to which pupils are taking matters into their own hands, by determining and extending how informally inside and beyond the school they use technology to learn, she does not go on to consider the impact that giving them an authoritative voice in the debate about teachers' professional development could have.

Chapter 10

Dymoke's chapter on creativity in English takes into account the challenge that education faces in adopting a concept which is sometimes so closely associated with exceptional acts of originality that a place for it in the school curriculum would appear to place impossible demands on teachers and their pupils. She provides an account of a discourse about creativity in education, nevertheless, which demonstrates how educators have appropriated the word to describe particular qualities in educational experiences and outcomes which are achievable but which still reflect

Table 0.10 Chapter 10 discourses

Discourse	Authority	Status	Future
Creativity in education	Academics and authors of reports	Resolved, to the extent that the case for creativity has been robustly made	Status of creativity as a legitimate priority appears secure
Creativity in the English curriculum	Curriculum and assessment agencies	The position of creativity has been strengthened in the English National Curriculum, but its status is still insecure	Confirmation of a more privileged position may depend on review of benefits of this, and demonstration that assessment processes are sufficiently robust
Pedagogy of creativity in English	Teachers and educators	Under development	Research and development in practice is needed to inform this discourse

a commitment to the generation of these through comparable kinds of processes. However, when she returns to this theme at the end of the chapter, she does point out that there is a tension between education's attempts to achieve more radical versions of creativity and the constraints of any kind of curriculum, pedagogy or assessment designed to promote it.

She goes on to demonstrate that creativity has had a relatively low status in most versions of the National Curriculum in England, and more particularly so in the interpretation of this in public examination syllabuses, specifications and schemes of assessment. While the latest version of the National Curriculum highlights creativity as a key concept, there is a sense in Dymoke's chapter that it is only fully endorsed in the governmental discourse about what English should be, for the earlier stages of educational experiences, where rigour might appear less significant (i.e., at Key Stage 3 more than Key Stage 4 and in AS rather than A2 work at A level).

Dymoke also explores the extent to which there is an established pedagogy for creativity in English, including in speaking and listening, reading and writing. Although she reports evidence of good practice, it is clear, for her, that in general teachers' confidence needs to be built up, and that there is considerable scope for research and developmental work to be undertaken to further the status of creativity in English.

Table 0.11 Chapter 11 discourses

Discourse(s)	Authority	Status	Future
Philosophy of English teaching	Theorists including critical theorists	Contested: the notion of the democratic negotiation of meaning has a significant place in the discourse but does not dominate it	Yandell offers his proposals for an inclusive English curriculum as a vision as his last sentence – 'Now that really would look like an inclusive version of English!' – suggests. It is clear that government's influence in the discourse concerned with the purposes of schooling is paramount, and likely to determine how far the positions Yandell advocates in the other discourses can be realised
Pedagogy of English teaching	Learning theorists	Contested: the proposition for a more ethnographic pedagogy offers a distinctive model for inclusion	
Purposes of schooling	Government, sociologists and educators	Contested: between the views that teachers should transmit an established body of knowledge and that they should address a broader social inclusion agenda	

Chapter 11

Yandell's chapter on inclusion starts by demonstrating that the discourses concerned with the philosophy and pedagogy of English teaching are affected by positions taken in a broader discourse about the purposes of schooling.

In this broader discourse, Yandell sets up a binary opposition between the conservative view that education will achieve its objectives, including those which are inclusive in the sense of creating opportunities for all pupils, through the transmission of high-status subject knowledge by experts, and a broader view of schooling related to the objectives of *Every Child Matters*, that the teacher's role includes all the responsibilities associated with the fulfilment of that policy and which contribute to social inclusion.

He argues that the way forward in this debate is to be found in another discourse, one which is concerned with the pedagogy of English teaching. His position in this discourse is in turn derived from adopting broader Vygotskian principles of teaching and learning, which place the English teacher as an ethnographic researcher, devoting time and close attention to pupils, and what they bring to the classroom as learners, and indeed as experts in their own right, and using this deep knowledge as the foundation of the pedagogy that is adopted.

Finally, Yandell suggests that this approach is supported by the insights about meaning that come from critical theory, which is a major influence on his position in the discourse concerned with the philosophy of English teaching. His concluding argument is that both Vygotskian pedagogy and critical theory point towards the significance and value for teaching and learning in English of the negotiation of meaning at all levels, from the selection of texts and materials for study, to the interpretation and creative responses made to them.

Chapter 12

Davison's chapter argues that the discourse about the curriculum, its teaching and assessment is controlled by policy makers from the higher classes, who preserve their own cultural values and attitudes through processes of cultural reproduction which disadvantage those from less privileged classes and contribute to the maintenance of the social divide which is currently widening rather than narrowing in England.

He demonstrates that in the more localised discourse concerned with English teaching, versions of English which have privileged cultural heritage and Standard English at the expense of popular culture and dialect, and which have promoted pupils' knowledge of literary tradition and skills, rather than developing personal growth and critical literacy, have dominated the contested debate about English teaching to the disadvantage of pupils from less privileged backgrounds.

With reference to discourse theory, he demonstrates that pupils whose language, values, attitudes and beliefs are highly valued by education will be able to engage more effectively in the kind of learning required for success than those whose

Table 0.12 Chapter 12 discourses

Discourse	Authority	Status	Future
The curriculum, its teaching and assessment	Higher-class policy makers	Problematic: higher-class policy makers promote 'cultural reproduction' privileging their own classes through the curriculum	Likely to be determined by political considerations, especially the classes whose interests are most privileged by government
Philosophy of English teaching	Government, challenged by some academics and teachers	Problematic: English as skills/literary tradition dominant against English as personal growth/critical literacy	Critical literacy is increasingly recognised as of value for all pupils in versions of the official curriculum in England
Discourse theory	Discourse theorists, teachers applying the principles of critical literacy in the classroom	Problematic precisely because discourse theory is not a privileged discourse in policy making	Likely to depend on recognition by the controllers of the discourses outlined above of the benefits for all pupils and society

'primary Discourse' is constructed differently, making access to what is for them a 'secondary Discourse' far more difficult. He goes on to suggest that exploratory talk and a repertoire of activities which enable these pupils to explore, define and challenge those things that are valued in this secondary Discourse could provide a means by which they acquire a critical literacy which will not only enable them to compete with pupils whose primary Discourse is valued more in school but also to control their engagement with the range of discourses they encounter. He also argues that the development of this capacity is something that would raise the educational attainment of all pupils.

Conclusion

At the beginning of this introduction, it was suggested that recognising the presence of different educational discourses in the debates about English teaching in this book is an empowering process for taking those debates forward. Nevertheless, contributors have broadly taken two approaches to this task.

Some contributors have chosen to put forward as clearly as possible the argument for a particular philosophy of English teaching or pedagogy for English by suggesting what research or good practice indicates will most benefit pupils, without choosing to discuss the likelihood of these approaches being adopted as policy:

in a sense they offer visionary solutions to the problems identified in a particular debate. Andrews, Hardman and Westbrook are examples of this.

In the second, larger group, those who have made strong reference to the discourses concerned with educational policy in England often suggest that it is by moving out of the policy discourses into discourses which are concerned with evidence from research and practice about what is known about the matter in hand, that the knowledge and understanding that should dominate the policy discourse is located.

Interestingly, two chapters in particular provide a clue towards a new dynamic for debates about English teaching. First, Goodwyn proposes that English teachers should locate themselves in communities of practice to provide a means of support for taking practice forward. Making an argument that complements this, Hardman suggests that not only should dialogic discourse prevail in the classroom but also in the discourses concerned with teacher development and school improvement.

Extending this point a little further, there is clearly an argument that if we really believe that the social construction of knowledge discussed by Davison becomes possible in conditions that foster dialogic discourse, which include those made available to us in communities of practice, those principles of learning should apply in the debates that take place to develop English teaching and become prime influences in the discourses that determine policy.

International evidence suggests that this is achievable. One example of curriculum development which incorporated a dialogic approach is that which brought about the Australian New Basics/Rich Task curriculum in which teachers were directly involved and which has embedded critical literacy throughout it. The policy to develop teaching as a Masters level profession in England is an example of an initiative which could provide the learning spaces that, as Hardman suggests, are necessary for teachers to gain confidence in adopting dialogic discourse in the classroom. There is scope within such an initiative for the outcomes of teachers' learning to inform national policy. This would redefine the boundaries of those discourses concerned with research into subject teaching and policy for it, in such a way that teachers, researchers and politicians could share authority in those discourses. It seems certain that the learners whose interests all stakeholders claim to have at heart would benefit.

Chapter 1

Becoming an English teacher
Identity, self-knowledge and expertise

Andy Goodwyn

Introduction

In considering the nature of professional identity it is necessary to generalise about teachers (for a recent overview see Rodgers and Scott, 2008) and by the nature of this chapter, especially to generalise about teachers of English. It must be stressed that this does not suggest that all English teachers are simplistically the same or that the profession is not full of unique and remarkable individuals. The value of generalisation in relation to professional identity is essentially twofold. First, it allows readers to recognise that they are comfortably part of a significant professional group who face similar challenges and experiences and who, therefore, have much in common that is of value and that can be shared and understood. Second, this allows each individual reader to calibrate how these generalised themes and patterns necessarily a part of becoming an English teacher do, or do not, resonate with their own sense of identity as a person and as a professional.

The term 'identity' can be extremely problematic and there has been much debate about whether identity is ever stable and, indeed, whether it disguises an amalgam of many and contradictory identities. For the purposes of this chapter the term is treated in a grounded and deliberate way as essentially the idea of the evolving self interacting with the environment and therefore generating ongoing experiences that modify the self both consciously and unconsciously. There is an inherent but productive tension between the 'personal' identity and the 'professional'; this tension is explored below.

Teaching in the broadest sense is much generalised. For example, in the public's eyes teaching is a 'safe' profession, a job for life and one with a clear career structure – that phrase 'think of the holidays' still persists. As with all clichés, there is some truth in this phrase – because the public see teaching as 'safe', applications to teacher training rise rapidly during a recession; however, the quality of applications does not necessarily improve. To become an English teacher is equally to be 'pigeonholed' and one must become inured to comments about 'oh, you are an English teacher – I had better watch my spelling', 'ooh, I had better mind my grammar' and so on.

But for many, especially teachers themselves, teaching is much more than 'a job'; it is a vocation, indeed 'a job for life'. Late entrants to the profession, switching careers, often take a substantial pay cut, explaining that they have had enough of career x, it was lacking in real meaning, it was not satisfying their inner needs and they want to be a teacher to 'make a difference' and because they see teaching as exciting and dynamic, rather than safe. This vocational theme is not unproblematic as less scrupulous agencies can exploit this sense of duty as they do with other professionals such as nurses and social workers.

So what does it mean to become a teacher, especially a teacher of a subject so loosely defined as English and one that attracts such constant political and media attention? It certainly means going through a very complex process of identity reformation and a process with a number of dimensions. This process, evidence suggests, is a very necessary one if the individual is to become a resilient and successful teacher. In that sense such identity reformation must be welcomed and treated as both necessary and 'ordinary'; that is, all teachers go through it and can compare their experience of it, yet for each individual the process is altogether 'extraordinary'. As Hamlet ripostes to his mother in a celebrated exchange about the authenticity of individual experience:

QUEEN GERTRUDE: Good Hamlet, cast thy nighted colour off,
    And let thine eye look like a friend on Denmark.
    Do not for ever with thy vailed lids
    Seek for thy noble father in the dust:
    Thou know'st 'tis common; all that lives must die,
    Passing through nature to eternity.
HAMLET: Ay, madam, it is common.
QUEEN GERTRUDE: If it be,
    Why seems it so particular with thee?
HAMLET: Seems, madam! nay it is; I know not 'seems.'
    'Tis not alone my inky cloak, good mother,
    Nor customary suits of solemn black,
    Nor windy suspiration of forced breath,
    No, nor the fruitful river in the eye,
    Nor the dejected 'havior of the visage,
    Together with all forms, moods, shapes of grief,
    That can denote me truly: these indeed seem,
    For they are actions that a man might play:
    But I have that within which passeth show;
    These but the trappings and the suits of woe.
                        (*Hamlet*, Act 1, Scene 2)

At once we have entered the very special world of English as a subject. This quotation is about identity and experience, about what is real and what is merely 'seeming so'. It is also from an iconic text, from the literary canon and, even more significantly, from the author frequently claimed to be the greatest 'of all time' and the greatest ever English writer. Immediately such claims are made, or contested, we enter the controversial domains of nationalism, politics and, in educational terms, curriculum control. Shakespeare is still the only author who is a subject of compulsory study for all young people in school. Becoming an English teacher means complying with this decision whether it is agreeable to the individual or not. It also means accepting what is a legal requirement to teach Shakespeare, undertaking what some might see as an imposition on young people of a very particular form of national identity.

Becoming an English teacher is to become a teacher who works with the subjectivities of students themselves; is this what makes English teaching such a dynamic and exciting context or is this a remarkably arrogant assumption to make about working 'on' young people? Is teaching *Hamlet* about helping young people to appreciate the literary canon or is it about enabling young people to see that the existential angst of living in the twenty-first century and trying to define 'who we are' can be refracted through a very powerful Elizabethan text? Is it about developing an appreciation of a great English writer, part of a powerful cultural heritage? It is, of course, potentially about all of these things and about much more.

The formative nature of the subject

POLONIUS: What do you read my lord?
HAMLET: Words, words, words.
                    (*Hamlet*, Act 2, Scene 2)

I still remember studying *Hamlet* at A level – it made a deep impression on me. I studied it at university and it stood out as a remarkably powerful text. Some years later I began teaching it at A level and found it exciting and challenging to teach. Since then I have seen many productions and film versions and taken students to see both. The 'I' is someone who moved from studying English to teaching it. To some extent this is the formative experience of any teacher, although especially of secondary subject specialists. This move to becoming a teacher involves the generation of new knowledge, from knowing the subject, whether science or history, to knowing how the subject is taught and learned; this is subject pedagogical knowledge (SPK) (Shulman, 1987) and will be discussed below. The research evidence is clear that this knowledge is what makes a teacher effective and not, despite the very frequent claims of certain politicians, just knowledge of and passion for the subject. The best teachers do bring both knowledge of the subject and passion for it to their teaching, but it is the pedagogical know-how that transforms this knowledge into good practice.

Therefore, a 'passion for the subject' is a commonality across secondary teaching; it is also identified in many studies as one defining element of outstanding teachers (for example, see Hattie, 2003, or Kyriacou, 1997). For the purposes of this chapter there is no point in trying to distinguish between the effects of studying science as compared with the effects of studying art. The question is, what are the effects of having been a student of English as the individual grapples with becoming a teacher and then, having become one, how is that individual's identity affected and shaped over the long term?

Drawing on much research evidence (for example, Goodwyn, 2010; Ellis, 2007, 2003; Turvey, 2005; Marshall, 2000; Grossman, 1990) it is clear that for the great majority of English teachers literature has been the most formative element in both their experience of the subject and the rationale for choosing to become a teacher. Although the subject might be construed as containing a mixture of contributory elements as well as literature, not least the study of language, of drama and of media. Equally it can be conceptualised as focused on the four language modes – reading, writing, speaking and listening – with 'viewing' possibly included (as it has been for some time in New Zealand, Canada and Australia). Research is also clear (Goodwyn, 2010; Blake and Shortis, 2010; Ellis, 2007) that student teachers of English have experienced a wide diversity of A levels and degrees, including, for example, linguistics, media studies, drama and psychology, although these are very much in a minority. Rather more fundamental is the simple fact that English degrees themselves are remarkably varied and that within a degree individuals can have followed very different routes through choosing options and projects or dissertations. It is partly because of this known variety that external bodies such as Ofsted (Office for Standards in Education) express the expectation that a future English teacher should have at least 50 per cent of their degree in English and it is clear that this is meant to be literature. It is also partly because of that diversity that so many teacher training courses expect trainees to undertake 'an audit of subject knowledge'. At worst this is a tick-box exercise inducing in participants a deep sense of deficit; at best it is a thoughtful self-evaluation allowing trainees to see where their previous studies will help them with the current version of the school English curriculum and where they might want to focus any additional short-term study over the next few months, recognising that subject knowledge goes on developing throughout a career (Goodwyn, 2010; Shulman, 2004, 1987).

What is striking about student teachers of English is that they tend to link their identities very strongly to reading, because that is how they see themselves and/ or because that is how they see becoming a teacher of English; it seems very likely that it is a combination of both. Hence a common expression is 'I have always loved reading' and a very uncommon expression would be 'I have always loved writing', even if it turns out that as an individual he or she excelled at creative writing. This 'love of reading', it can be argued, is a powerful factor in choosing to join the profession and in its history and its current conceptualisation (Goodwyn, 2008; Goodwyn and Fuller 2003b, 2003c; Ellis, 2007). Although English is a relatively new subject compared with science or maths (Protherough, 1989), the subject it essentially replaced – 'Classics' – was defined and dominated by texts. So English since its inception in universities in the mid to late nineteenth century was focused on which texts to read from the vernacular tradition. As English grew it also displaced philology from a powerful place in the university curriculum. In the late nineteenth century there were claims that English texts would have to replace the weakening moral and spiritual forces of religion (see Arnold, 1979). After the ravages of the Great War, the 1920's Newbolt Report (BoE, 1921) was elevating the study of literature in English to saving national life and becoming the ultimate social glue. In the 1930s, Frank Leavis and his followers put the study of English literature on the pedestal as the only university subject worthy of serious study (see Leavis and Thompson, 1933, and also Eagleton's account of Leavis' influence (Eagleton, 1975)). If this seems like ancient history then the controversies and struggles around defining which texts should be contained within the National Curriculum for English since its inception in 1988 would illustrate how much the reading of literature dominates the subject's identity and that of its teachers (Goodwyn, 2010, 2008; Goodwyn and Fuller, 2003c; Marshall, 2000; Barnes *et al.*, 1984; Dixon, 1967).

As Hamlet remarks, 'there is nothing either good or bad but thinking makes it so' (*Hamlet*, Act 2, Scene 2). A love of reading is a great strength for any English teacher, especially if it survives the rigours of many years of teaching. If that reading identity is already broad then such teachers are open to the interests of young people themselves, including all kinds of novels, media texts, even computer games. Equally, such an enthusiasm for reading is even more effective if accompanied by an understanding of how readers develop. Each English teacher needs to review their own 'reading autobiography' (Goodwyn, 2003c) and to recognise that they themselves spent much time reading what they might call 'trash' or 'merely popular' texts; thus, they were normal. They often read very particular, repetitive series of texts, still best exemplified by Enid Blyton's many series. This form of 'serial reading' seems likely to be a very necessary stage for many readers and therefore something, perhaps counter-intuitively, to encourage.

In exploring this formative identity Appleyard's simple model (Appleyard, 1985) is very generative. In his book *Becoming a Reader* he outlines five stages which he considers typical of reading development, at least in relation to reading fiction: reader as player, hero and heroine, thinker, critic and, finally, as pragmatist.

He argues that the first three stages are typical of all readers who reach a good level of literacy and a capacity for independent reading of a text; such readers eventually go on to stage five, the pragmatic stage. He is also arguing that the stages do not replace each other; rather, they are both incremental and residual, so the capacity to adopt, for example, stage two and to enjoy texts in this mode remains an affordance. Although Appleyard does not discuss film texts, I would recognise a good deal of my enjoyment of thriller-style films as in this mode. However, it is stage four, the reader as critic, that distinguishes the future English teacher from most others. Some future teachers have decided to choose English teaching before university and consciously choose English as their degree in order to become a teacher. There is no reliable empirical evidence on this but I would estimate it at a sizeable minority, but not a majority. Career changers often say that they were put off becoming a teacher by their degree studies and so have 'come back' to English after considerable life experience. However, many students' decision to become an English teacher is crystallised during their undergraduate degree studies. The nature of this decision is complex and not a straightforward outcome of the degree itself. Some recent research with serving teachers (Goodwyn, 2008) revealed these factors as key:

◻   Love of /enthusiasm for/passion for the subject
◻   Working with young people
◻   Love of literature/reading
◻   Being good at the subject

These four are in order of importance and it is interesting to note that 1. and 3. are very similar but that 'love of reading' is given a distinct status. Respondents did not put, for example, 'love of language'. The three factors below are also significant:

◻   Teaching is creative/full of variety/not an office job
◻   The influence of an inspirational English teacher
◻   Good career/money/holidays

When asked to rate the personal importance of Literature to them then, 75% said 'Very', 20% just 'Important' and 5% 'Fairly', suggesting that, from the teachers' perspective Literature remains central.

(Goodwyn, 2008: 5)

The decision would seem, therefore, to operate within a matrix of factors, some aspirational, some vocational and some pragmatic. Discussion with future English teachers at interview is always intriguing because most candidates conceptualise the subject of English as essentially a creative one; this is understandably often an ill-defined concept. The English teacher's emerging professional identity is often marked by a tension between this faith in the creative and the residual internal pressure of a training in the critical. It is also interesting that whereas English teachers in the majority have embraced the affordances of the digital age (Adams and Brindley, 2007; Goodwyn, 2009a; Goodwyn and Fuller, 2000a, 2000b) it seems to have had no diminishing effect on their faith in 'traditional' reading (Goodwyn, 2010, 2009b).

On being a novice

HAMLET: there's a special providence in
    the fall of a sparrow. If it be now, 'tis not to come; if it be
    not to come, it will be now; if it be not now, yet it will come:
    the readiness is all.

(*Hamlet*, Act 5, Scene 2)

The term 'novice' is used here descriptively in relation to the concept of the 'novice to expert' continuum (see Dreyfus and Dreyfus, 1986; Benner, 1984). It is a well-researched phenomenon that many beginning teachers, under the considerable duress of learning to teach, revert to styles of teaching that they encountered as a school student (Grossman, 1990). Even though they may espouse the pedagogical approaches offered to them as part of their teacher education programme, they often cannot escape the subliminal influences of their own schooling. After considerable research into the issue specifically with English teachers, Ball remarks, 'It would appear that the most profound influences upon the English teacher, in terms of his or her conception of English as a school subject and its concomitant pedagogy – is likely to be the teacher's own experience as pupil' (Ball, 1985: 81). This may be seen as an inevitable element of identity reformation. The knowledge of the individual rests in the memory; without new experiences these memories are unchallenged; without reflection they cannot be questioned (Schon, 1983, 1987). Equally many student teachers were themselves highly successful students, so the teaching that they had may well have left a strong aura of success. It can be argued that this form of identity conflict is more problematic in subject areas other than English. In English the student teacher may be drawing on memories of highly student-centred and 'progressive' pedagogies, not just some old buffer lecturing from the front.

The key point is that the stress of becoming a teacher confronts the novice with the first big question to face, 'what do I know about my subject?' Almost all secondary teachers have very strong subject identities rather than, say, learning-style identities and so the subject's formative influence is extremely powerful (see above) as is, therefore, the question, what is my subject knowledge? Therefore, it is not in the area of 'reading' that novice English teachers particularly suffer any kind of identity 'crisis'. The most generally expressed anxiety is of a lack of understanding about language and that bête noire 'grammar'. If the history of the subject (see above) has been much concerned with the role and status of English literature then there has never been anything but a consensus that it is important. Equally, there has always been a view that students of English should be engaging with the English language and learning about 'it'. However, debates about whether language should be taught as Latin used to be – that is, as a set of well-defined and regular rules, best understood in the abstract and then applied correctly – have been fierce and highly politicised and recur regularly (Goodwyn, 2010, 1997; Goodwyn and Findlay, 2003a; Protherough, 1989).

When the National Curriculum in English was first formulated in the late 1980s it was within the context of the Kingman Committee's inquiry into the teaching of the English language. This inquiry itself stemmed from two somewhat controversial pamphlets produce by Her Majesty's Inspectors in 1984 and 1986 (DES, 1984, 1986), in which they argued that there had been some loss of attention to language over a number of years and recommended the need for more knowledge about language (KAL) – hence the Kingman inquiry, its report and its recommendations (DES, 1988). The KAL project can be read about in detail elsewhere (see Goodwyn, 2010, 1992b) but the main point is that neither the inspectors nor the committee recommended a return to 'old-fashioned' grammar-style teaching.

Hence, the three-year (1989–92) KAL project focused on producing materials for initial teacher training and school English departments. Just as they were ready for publication the government simply 'pulled the plug' and banned them from being made available. This was a purely ideological and political decision; KAL was welcomed by both student and serving teachers but it was seen as tainted by a sociolinguistic approach – that is, based on how language actually works, rather than a prescriptive approach (that is, how certain powerful groups would prefer language to work and so wished it to be taught). The debates of the time were much influenced by the prescriptive forces which always try to connect correctness in language with moral and social order and its opposite. One memorable quotation from Norman Tebbit in 1985, when on the BBC radio, was, 'If you allow standards to slip to the point where good English is no better than bad English, where people turn up filthy at school – all those things tend to cause people to have no standards at all – and once you lose those standards, there's no imperative to stay out of crime.'

So, beginning English teachers are right to see that this is an ongoing 'minefield' and an area fraught with popular views usually expressed by papers such as the *Daily Mail* or the *Daily Telegraph* and strongly influencing many parents. Such teachers, therefore, do find themselves 'falling back on' vocabulary and spelling tests and getting their students to undertake fail-safe exercises that keep them busy filling pages with 'right/wrong' answers about language.

A combination of experience and reflection generally leads teachers to establish a much more grounded identity where the 'strength' of their reading self and the 'weakness' of their grammar self become combined in a much more balanced way. There are many factors that enable beginning teachers to achieve a more relaxed and secured level of confidence but a crucial one is the development of pedagogical knowledge. The work of Shulman (2004) and others has been very developmental in allowing us to both understand how teachers become effective and how it could be that excellent subject knowledge does not automatically translate to good subject teaching; allowing the profession to say with great certainty that, however much an individual has an aptitude for teaching, teachers are definitely made and not born. Shulman (1986, 1987) identifies several dimensions to SPK which I summarise (and somewhat simplify) as: content knowledge, general pedagogical knowledge (e.g. classroom management), curriculum knowledge, pedagogical content knowledge (e.g. a subject) and also knowledge of learners, educational contexts and the purposes and values of education.

One interesting and very resonant element for English teachers as their SPK increases is the way that their reading identity is reconfigured. There is no evidence that years of teaching diminish teachers' personal 'love' of reading but plenty of evidence that they suffer with some role conflict as they find the incredible pressure of the extended professionals' busy life means they can rarely practise what they preach. That is, they cannot find time for much truly personal reading as professional reading has to dominate. This identity conflict is often exemplified by that growing pile of books 'waiting to be read', with the famous 'holidays' the only time that the pile 'goes down'. More profoundly they read differently, reading 'pedagogically' as well as, or even rather than, personally. This pedagogic reading has two elements. The first is that the pedagogue subsumes the critic; that is, the undergraduate training they had to be a close reader or a theoretically informed reader remains but a more powerful lens is a professionally evolving focus on 'would this be good to teach', or, with a set book, 'how will I teach this?' Beginning English teachers frequently recall deep role conflict through their A-level study and even more so at university between the personal reading self and the critic (Goodwyn, 2008, 1995: Goodwyn and Fuller, 2003c). The personal self reads for pleasure, stimulation and absorption; this was a combination of Appleyard's first three modes (see above). The fourth mode, 'the reader as critic', is in real tension with the first three. Beginning teachers frequently claim that they could not bear to read a poem or novel for some time after completing their degree because they were sick of the criticality they brought to all texts. However, more commonly they reflect on the destructiveness and negativity of much critical engagement. It is worth noting that many cite an inspirational teacher of English from their own school days as an influence on their choice of degree and then career but rarely mention any university figures of influence.

The pedagogic reader is critical and makes judgements about texts but will choose texts that are 'useful' for teaching rather than always asserting an aesthetic judgement.

The other element to the pedagogical reader is about the teacher as enthusiast. There is what might be construed as an informal school canon in schools – that is, those texts which many teachers feel 'work' with their students. A long-standing example is a novel like *Of Mice and Men*, a more recent one is *Holes*. Both texts are short as novels go, have strong plots, involve a series of incidents, have a strong focus on social justice and deal with several issues. Much more could be said about their 'teacherliness' but the point is well made that it is because they consistently 'work' with young readers that the teachers find them 'good to teach'. The teacher's SPK is thus refined by returning to the text over a number of teaching cycles. Equally the pedagogic reader does need stimulus, so while accepting the reliability of some key texts the reader is also looking for new and novel texts that will maintain their own enthusiasm in the classroom. Such texts are often recommended in professional journals or by other teachers and so an effort is made to read them in case they provide some freshness. The pedagogic reader is thus always reading professionally but with an eye on the novel and the refreshing.

'Very like a whale': conflicting models of teaching

POLONIUS: And thus do we of wisdom and of reach,
   With windlaces, and with assays of bias,
   By indirections find directions out.

   (*Hamlet*, Act 2, Scene 1)

It is now recognised that teaching is a very complex activity and that very good teachers become extraordinarily adept at handling the complexities of both the classroom and the professional situation demanded of an extended professional. Learning to teach is now also recognised as a highly complex and confusing situation, something that puts a high strain on the individual's identity and self-esteem. For all teachers there is an initial struggle about what is the purpose of teaching as the novice moves from unconscious incompetence to the much more confusing conscious incompetence; in other words, it looked easy but now the experience of being a teacher reveals the difficulty. This 'move' is complicated by the various views of teaching in the culture and in the novice's mind as an attempt is made to try to resolve conflicting models of teaching.

Squires' 1999 analysis is a very helpful starting point. He describes teaching as an activity as typically conceptualised in one of six dominant ways: as 'a common-sense activity', 'an art', 'a craft', 'an applied science', 'a system', 'a reflective practice' and 'a competence' (Squires, 1999). All of these conceptualisations have a very definite real-world presence and influence and are useful not only for helping us think critically about identity formation in teaching but also for understanding how others view it. For example, the common-sense view may well be that of many parents, whereas the system view may be much favoured by politicians and is evidenced in the politically influential McKinsey Report's (Barber and Mourshed, 2007) preference for high- and low-performing descriptions of teaching. Turner-Bissett offers a clear analysis and application of Squires to effective teaching (Turner-Bissett, 2001, ch. 1).

For our purposes it is worth recognising that these paradigms are present in most discussions about teaching quality and may well influence judgements about what is good teaching. The novice is often deeply uncertain as to what kind of teacher they are becoming as they feel the powerful pressure to 'act like a teacher'. Considering the paradigms from that perspective then the common-sense model is a pragmatically grounded approach to doing 'what works' and to 'getting on with things' without too much reflection. It is antipathetic to any recognition of real expertise. Whereas the art model immediately offers a rich perspective as it treats teaching as not only complex and highly skilled but also as an aesthetic and emotional activity. For example, Eisner in 1985 characterised good teaching: '[I]t is sometimes performed with such skill and grace that it can be described as an aesthetic experience; it involves qualitative judgements based on an unfolding course of action; it is contingent and unpredictable rather than routine; and that its outcomes are often created in the process' (Eisner, 1985: 175–6). One interesting dimension to this paradigm is that it positions the performance of good teachers in a comparative relationship to musicians and other 'performers'. This is valuable because it suggests that such performances can truly be outstanding not least because they are affective as well as effective. Perhaps most importantly this paradigm suggests that, as with music, the individual artist is the interpreter and so in a very creative relationship with the notes/script and so forth. Undoubtedly a weakness in this paradigm is that it implies that, as with great performers, there will only be a very few such individuals. Beginning English teachers are often overwhelmed with self-doubt (Goodwyn, 1997) when they begin to appreciate the excellent teaching of their more experienced colleagues: 'I will never be able to be like that!'

In opposition to the artistic mode, much work has been done to establish teaching as based more on scientific principles – the applied science model. This would imply that the 'rules' of teaching can be discovered and then applied rationalistically. There is plenty of evidence that teaching requires rationalist and systematic approaches, especially at the planning level; however, psychology has demonstrated that professions like teaching are very concrete and situational – strict adherence to rules is a problem and not a solution.

The craft (or apprentice) model continues to feature strongly in many education systems as it does in many vocational training models. The essential notion that teaching is learned partly by 'doing it' and partly by copying others who can already 'do it' is very close to the common-sense approach. However, it is fundamentally faulted by the fact that merely reproducing practice is not the way forward and by an absolute reliance on whoever the 'demonstrator' may be.

The system model has had an influence on teaching, sufficient to be credited with a strong influence because it focuses on processes and how they might be improved. This rightly treats teaching as a complex activity that cannot be simplistically understood. However, it does tend to simplify teaching overall as part of the 'school' and 'education' systems. In this respect it is possible to see why a government would create a top-down reform such as the National Literacy Strategy (see Stannard and Huxford, 2007; Goodwyn and Fuller, 2011) believing that 'informed prescription' would actually force all teachers to teach in a certain way that was considered to be best practice; this led to huge training manuals and highly scripted lessons. The research evidence about teachers' views demonstrated how absurd they found these prescriptions and how it both undermined their performance and eroded their self-esteem (see Goodwyn, 2004a, 2004b; Beverton, 2000, 2003; English, 2003).

The most influential paradigm among many educators has been that of the reflective practitioner (Schon, 1983, 1987); the most powerful among government agencies and politicians has been that of competence (see the standards for teaching on various government websites). These two models remain in some conflict and the English teacher can face a duality of identity in trying to fit with certain externally powerful generic standards and with the much more intuitive knowledge developing through genuine reflection. There is a need to develop an appropriate 'centre of self' in order to cope (see the concluding section).

Developing an identity: 'custom and practice', apprenticeship or participation?

HORATIO: Is it a custom?
HAMLET: Ay, marry, is't;

> But to my mind, – though I am native here,
> And to the manner born, – it is a custom
> More honour'd in the breach than the observance.
> (*Hamlet*, Act 1, Scene 4)

Perhaps the most valuable concept for the developing teacher is 'community of practice'. Lave and Wenger's seminal work (*Situated Learning: Legitimate Peripheral Participation*, 1991) provides a very valuable means to understanding how particular sets of practitioners work and insights into how individuals can understand what is happening 'to them' as they become part of such a community and, therefore, identify with it. Lave and Wenger's model can be applied to many groups of specialist practitioners; their original study examined midwives, tailors, quartermasters, butchers and non-drinking alcoholics. Essentially Lave and Wenger explored notions of 'apprenticeship', not as ritualised training models but as a conceptual period for an individual coming to terms with entering a practitioner community. Such a community with have some definition, 'a set of relations among persons, activity, and the world, over time and in relation with other tangential and overlapping communities of practice' (ibid.: 24). The notion of overlapping communities is valuable as it might extend to distinct but comparable professions like nursing or social work but, more importantly, it helps with considering teaching expertise in, say, primary and secondary teachers. 'Expert' secondary teachers and their primary equivalents should be able to acknowledge both their overlap and their distinctiveness. This is an especially important point for beginning teachers, for example, if they spend any time moving between phase settings or are involved with schools trying to improve transition.

Lave and Wenger's argument is that specialist knowledge and practice are inextricably linked: '[A] community of practice is an intrinsic condition for the existence of knowledge' (ibid.: 24). That knowledge, then, exists in the community of practice; it is not somehow acquired from somewhere else. This is a powerful message for initial teacher training and for professional development. However, it does not at all imply that the community of practice is merely in existence when the bell goes; the practitioners might well be sitting together, seminar-style, in any place – it is their shared sense of activity that makes them a community (see below on professional associations).

A key concept for Lave and Wenger is 'legitimate peripheral participation' (ibid.: 34) 'far more than just a process of learning on the part of newcomers. It is a reciprocal relation between persons and practice. This means that the move of learners toward full participation in a community of practice does not take place in a static context. The practice itself is in motion.' They describe newcomers as caught in a dilemma, because they must engage with practice as it exists, 'as they find it', and they are very keen to belong to this established community and to understand it. At the same time they are creating their own identity within the community and, as a unique individual, they immediately bring something distinctive and so enter into an active and change-oriented relationship with the community and its practice. That community offers them this 'peripheral' role while they form their initial identity. Lave and Wenger call this 'the continuity-displacement contradiction'. Therefore, a community of practice is one where knowledge already exists but is in a dynamic condition, practice is moving and newcomers immediately are producers of new knowledge, not just passive recipients.

Whether these are the exact ways that all communities of practice operate is not 'proven'; some experienced teachers might feel that, after the prescriptions and inspections of the last 20 years, this model seems innocent of external interference and control. However, my research over that period (for example, Goodwyn, 1992a, 1992b, 2003b, 2004a) certainly attests to teachers' continual efforts to work in the positive way that Lave and Wenger describe. Experienced teachers in particular have been adamant that their best practice has survived and evolved not just as a coping strategy but also particularly in areas such as the new technologies and media where innovation has been more at teacher level.

The implications for the English teacher, especially the novice, are clear: one must join the community, be not just part of its activity but actively part of its development. We will consider some of the wider implications, for example membership of professional associations and bodies, in the next section.

As Lave and Wenger indicated through their research, communities of practice come in many forms – quartermasters and butchers, for example. However, English teachers have two other fundamental and interlinked commonalities that relate to their professional identities. The first is their formative identity (see above) as students of English who then become its teachers; the second is the subject of 'English' itself as they become 'legitimate participants' in its development. A comprehensive overview of English is beyond the scope of this or any single chapter available elsewhere (for a short introduction see Goodwyn, 2004a; for more in-depth discussions see Goodwyn, 1992b; Goodwyn and Fuller, 1998; Protherough, 1989; Ellis, 2007). Overall this model of peripheral participation places the English teacher in a dynamic, developmental space where identity is a resource from the beginning of training but also is itself in a dynamic situation and will change.

Professional identity?

HAMLET: there's the respect
>   That makes calamity of so long life;
>   For who would bear the whips and scorns of time,
>   The oppressor's wrong, the proud man's contumely,
>   The pangs of despis'd love, the law's delay,
>   The insolence of office and the spurns
>   That patient merit of the unworthy takes.

(*Hamlet*, Act 3, Scene 1)

In the twentieth century the notion of the professional has become absolutely established as a normative role within a highly structured economy and within defined characteristics (Eraut, 1994; Squires, 1999). However, these defining features (see below) must be seen as contested and contestable. For example, with the idea of professional status may come accountability, but how much is a true professional autonomous, and how much accountable and, if so, to whom? This latter point has been a particular issue for teachers, especially new ones in the twenty-first century.

Therefore, although particular professions will set out lists of skills, as does teaching, these can fragment into microscopic items that become almost pedantry. All professions then are skilled, and they debate, principally internally, exactly what the 'skill set' is at any one time. The professions are best understood, as Michael Eraut sums it up, 'as an occupational ideology' (Eraut, 1994: 227). In his excellent discussion of *Developing a Knowledge Base within a Client-Centred Orientation*, he argues that the debate about professional characteristics has become sterile and that 'professionalization can then be viewed as a strategy for gaining status and privileges in accordance with that ideology – the three central features of the ideology of professionalism are a specialist knowledge base, autonomy and service' (ibid.: 227). But, Eraut points out, teaching struggles to be a full profession, especially as politics exerts increasing influence down to classroom level and because of the ever-increasing number of stakeholders who demand influence. Teachers are perhaps confused because, as Eraut puts it, 'Are they meant to be serving the pupils, the parents, the local community, the school district, or the whole nation?' (ibid.: 228). This role and identity conflict was touched on above as that sense 'of duty'.

Although Eraut defines the professions as principally having in common an ideological stance, it is reasonable just to note what are relatively common features associated with professional status. For the beginning teacher these demands exert enormous pressure on the personality and on behaviour as the struggle to prove adequate to professional norms is felt externally but also internally; the question is whether this individual is going to be adequate to these daily demands.

For example, the knowledge base usually comes from an initial period of graduate-level study in the key subject or a related one. In top professions there is then a period of further study, possibly vocational, very often postgraduate. At some point the novice actually enters the profession; they are, as it were, *through the gate*. As the individual professional becomes established this tends to be through developing a specialism which demands further study and ongoing upskilling (continuing professional development (CPD)). Such specialists then have students and novices of their own who they induct into the profession. Most such professions also have a strong, sometimes direct, relationship to a discipline studied in higher education; this academic subject (say, mathematics) may have a very long history. Education as a discipline still struggles to hold its own in the academy, not least because populist views cluster around it but also because teachers themselves frequently undermine it as a subject and its 'theories'. Much of this view comes from the experience of the academic study of education during initial teacher training (ITT) – other professions insist on much more post–initial training studies.

Professions are marked also by their very particular language and technical vocabulary. They have a regulatory body of some kind and the capacity to 'practise' is dependent on belonging to that body. As well as having codes of practice set down in great detail, they tend to have ways of behaving that are much less defined but are the 'culture' of that group. 'Never smile until Christmas', is not a technical term, it is more of a folklore phrase, but it carries meaning within the professional group that are teachers. Teachers do not wear uniforms (compare nurses) or particular gowns (compare barristers) but each setting tends to have a strong dress code although it may not be written down.

Teaching has most of the markers of a top profession; it has, for example, the appropriate level of esteemed qualification (it is almost entirely a graduate-level group), an appropriate initial training period with a strong gatekeeping function and certification of practice that can be revoked. It does now require teachers to maintain their own professional development (see the standards section of the Ministry of Education website) although the lack of any real system persists – teacher in-service development is haphazard at best. There is a well-defined, although constantly changing, career structure. Perceptions of teaching as a career change over time and international comparisons are very interesting. The McKinsey Report (Barber and Mourshed, 2007) discusses how vital the status of the teaching profession has become to attracting the best graduates; this is linked to history and culture but they stress how influential teachers themselves can be and how, in synergy with positive government policy, status can quickly (over five years) be raised. These professional demands affect all beginning teachers and, indeed, all beginning professionals.

For the English teacher, working with what is often considered the most important subject in schooling and one always under public scrutiny by politicians and the media, these pressures on identity are even more intense than in other subjects. However, the community of practice has its 'veterans' who have developed identities that have been made stronger and more resilient as they have learned to accommodate such pressure but without compromising their principles (Goodwyn, 2010, 2009a, 2001).

English representative bodies

HAMLET: Rightly to be great
    Is not to stir without great argument,
    But greatly to find quarrel in a straw
    When honour's at the stake.
            (*Hamlet*, Act 4, Scene 5)

English teaching is best viewed as a 'broad church'. Margaret Mathieson in her classic 1975 study of English teachers called them 'The Preachers of Culture'

(Mathieson, 1975). Since then others have offered (see Marshall, 2000, for a summary) a range of interesting terms such as 'liberal humanists' and 'cultural theorists'; Marshall herself offers 'critical dissenters', 'old grammarians', 'liberals', 'technicians' and 'pragmatists'. Equally what in Schons' terms might be called the 'espoused theories of English' of its teachers have had many terms, for example Ball's 1987 orientations, 'Skills, vocational, *utilitarian*', 'Literature, morals and values, *liberal humanist*', 'creativity, progressive, *cultural alternatives*' and 'Critical literacy, oppositional, *radical*' (Ball, 1987, emphasis added). He suggests that teachers adopt all these approaches but are more oriented towards one. In my own research I have found that English teachers all recognise the five 'Cox models' (see Cox, 1991, 1992): Personal Growth, Cultural Analysis, Cultural Heritage, Adult needs and Cross-curricular, and in general they are very engaged by the first four but see Cross-curricular as a model for all teachers. The great majority always put Personal Growth first (see Goodwyn, 1992a; Goodwyn and Findlay, 1999, 2001).

Can English teachers, therefore, be represented? Do they have a sufficient collective identity to ever speak with one voice? The answer is 'no' – but sometimes 'yes'. As Goodson and Ball (1984) observes a subject community is in itself 'an arena of conflict'. As Lave and Wenger pointed out, even the latest recruit entering the community provides new knowledge; knowledge is by its nature sometimes incremental – that is, building on what is known – but, equally, if it is new knowledge then it will conflict with the old and possibly displace it. Raymond Williams' (1977) view is that in any culture there is what is residual, what is currently dominant and what is emergent. English teaching has strong traditions such as its literary loyalties discussed above, but it is most definitely an arena of conflict. To continue the metaphor, arenas are enclosed and there are those within and those without the walls. However, when the walls themselves are challenged, the conflict in the arena is paused while the arena is defended.

It would be very appropriate to describe the identity of English teachers as frequently embattled. Certainly over the last 40 years the profession has come under constant scrutiny from 'outsiders', typically political forces but sometimes cultural; this is a long story and can be read about elsewhere (Goodwyn, 2010, 1998, 1992).

Two examples of immediate relevance will suffice at present. Although the profession broadly welcomed the first English National Curriculum in 1989, by 1995 it was set against both the revised curriculum and, much more powerfully, against the imposed model of assessment, so much so that English teachers defied the government and boycotted the SAT (Standard Assessment Task) tests at Key Stage 3 for a number of years between 1992 and 1995. English teachers, therefore, are sometimes characterised as militant and 'of the left'.

The second example is very directly about identity. It is very striking that in Australia (also a country with a feisty set of English teachers), its teachers now refer to themselves as 'teachers of English and Literacy'; this is also a trend in the US and New Zealand. The last survey that asked teachers of English in England whether they wished the subject, and therefore their designation, to include 'Literacy', 95 per cent said 'strongly disagree' (Goodwyn, 2009a). At first common sense would suggest this was completely paradoxical: how can you teach English without teaching literacy? It is emphatically the case that English teachers in England will not associate the term 'literacy' with their professional identity. This, again, might seem paradoxical given that the United Kingdom Reading Association (UKRA) relatively recently renamed itself the United Kingdom Literacy Association (UKLA). This organisation is chiefly related to primary education and so there is, perhaps, a simple logic to the name change. However, I would argue that this was a politically motivated change. The introduction of the National Literacy Strategy (NLS) in 1997 and its secondary-focused follow-on, The Framework for English, gave the term 'literacy' a much higher political profile than ever before in the UK. The NLS has its own story (see Stannard and Huxford, 1997) and the Framework has also received critical attention (for example, see Goodwyn and Fuller, 2011). The relevant point here is that teachers of English in the UK associate the term 'literacy' with a top-down, highly prescriptive model of pedagogy and with a utilitarian and functionalist approach to language: hence their emphatic rejection of literacy as a label. In other countries there is no such association. In Australia, 'literacy' is associated with the term 'critical', a model of pedagogy that sits well with progressive models of English and is seen as 'owned' by the profession, not by government departments.

So the UKRA became the UKLA but the National Association for the Teaching of English (NATE) is resolute that it will neither replace the term 'English' nor add the term 'literacy'. NATE chiefly represents secondary teachers. There is another, smaller association, the English Association, which represents chiefly independent schools with most of its focus on A-level teaching.

Can NATE claim to represent English teachers and, therefore, contribute to the identity formation of English teachers? I would argue that NATE has been very influential in the evolution of the subject over the last 50 years and many of the most prominent figures in English in education have been significant members of NATE. NATE provides professional and research publications, runs localised professional development events and courses and has an annual conference. However, as an association it has suffered a decline in membership during the period of the NLS and Framework. Research demonstrates that this is because they have become disaffected chiefly because of the amount of in-service training they had to endure from 'The Strategies' (Goodwyn and Fuller, 2003; Goodwyn and Findlay, 2003a; Beard, 2003, 2000a, 2000b; Beverton, 2000). Subject associations in general all suffered in a similar way during this period.

So an organisation like NATE can certainly provide a degree of representation, a voice and even a lobbying presence on behalf of English. For many teachers in the profession it continues to be an aspect of their professional identity and for a minority (Protherough and Atkinson, 1991; Goodwyn, 2010) a very significant element.

Endnote

This point about NATE leads to a final comment about an English teacher's identity. This chapter has concentrated on the way the English teacher's identity is formed from the past and the present experience of learning to teach English the school subject. It has not explored in any detail the well-understood phases of longer-term development (see Huberman, 1993, and, more recently, Day *et al.*, 2007) but it is important to stress that professional identity not only will but also should continue to evolve, and that this is desirable; this is evidence that the teacher is still aspirational and dynamic. In the long term, successful English teachers develop a strong, resilient professional identity, harmonious with personal identity and this fusion sustains a passionate commitment to the subject and its students.

Chapter 2

Promoting a dialogic pedagogy in English teaching

Frank Hardman

Introduction

The focus of this chapter is on effective classroom talk in English teaching where students are able to actively participate in their own learning and communicate their evolving understanding in spoken forms in group-based, whole-class and one-to-one interactions. It will discuss the centrality of talk in the learning process and consider the extent to which teachers can enhance student learning through questioning and feedback which asks students to expand on their thinking, justify or clarify their opinions or make connections to their own experiences. It will also address how the professional development needs of teachers can be met so as to enhance the quality of spoken interaction in the classroom.

The chapter draws on research dating back over 30 years into the power of talk to shape student thinking and to secure their engagement, learning and understanding in classroom study. Numerous studies using both quantitative and qualitative approaches to study classroom interaction and discourse at a macro and micro level yielded somewhat depressing findings about the character of classroom talk in English lessons covering all phases of schooling (Alexander *et al.*, 1996; Galton *et al.*, 1999; Hardman *et al.*, 2005). When teachers interact with students in whole-class, group-based and one-to-one situations one kind of talk was found to predominate: the so-called 'recitation script' of closed teacher questions, brief student answers and minimal feedback which requires students to report someone else's thinking rather than to think for themselves, and to be evaluated on their compliance in doing so.

From this research has developed the concept of a dialogic pedagogy where teachers are helped to break out of the limitations of the recitation script through higher-order questioning and feedback strategies which promote a range of alternative discourse strategies. Alexander (2008) has described the essential features of 'dialogic talk' as being collective (teachers and students address the learning task together), reciprocal (teachers and students listen to each other to share ideas and consider alternative viewpoints), supportive (students articulate their ideas freely without fear of embarrassment over 'wrong' answers and support each other to reach common understandings), cumulative (teachers and students build on their own and each others' ideas to chain them into coherent lines of thinking and enquiry) and purposeful (teachers plan and facilitate dialogic teaching with educational goals in mind). Most importantly, it can take place in whole-class, group-based and individual interactions between teacher and students.

Talk in learning

The use of a dialogic pedagogy in which teachers talk with students in whole-class, group and individual settings to guide their thinking and co-construct knowledge is seen as being central to the educational process (Hardman, 2008). Vygotsky (1962) was one of the first educational theorists to acknowledge the centrality of talk in the learning process. In his book *Thought and Language*, first published in Russia in the 1930s and translated into English in 1962, he suggested that using language to communicate helps in the development of new ways of thinking: what students learn from their 'inter-mental' experience (communication between minds through social interaction) shapes their 'intra-mental' activity (the way they think as individuals). More importantly, Vygotsky argued that the greatest influence on the development of thinking would come from the interaction between a learner and a more knowledgeable, supportive member of a community, such as a parent or teacher. In what became known as the 'zone of proximal development', the zone between what a learner can do unaided and can manage with expert assistance, social interaction was seen as being central to instruction. A similar emphasis on the social origins of the individual's language repertoire can be found in the work of the Russian philosopher Bakhtin. Bakhtin's work, like Vygotsky's, was published in the 1920s and 1930s (Holquist, 1990). Bakhtin argued that dialogue pervades all spoken and written discourse and is essential where meanings are not fixed or absolute. It is, therefore, central to educational discourse and learning because of the need to consider alternative frames of reference.

Out of the work of these early theorists developed the socio-cultural view of learning which posits that classroom talk is not effective unless students play an active part in their learning through exploratory forms of talk (Mercer and Littleton, 2007). This theory of learning suggests that cognitive development does not take place through the addition of discrete facts to an existing store of knowledge, but when new information, experiences and ways of understanding are related to our existing understanding. Exploratory talk is seen as providing students with the opportunity to assume greater control over their own learning by initiating ideas and responses. In this way, they can contribute to the shaping of the verbal agenda and introduce alternative viewpoints which are open to negotiation and where the criteria of relevance are not imposed only by the teacher. Such a view of learning, therefore, questions the value of traditional whole-class, teacher-led recitation where knowledge is often presented by the teacher as closed, authoritative and immutable rather than as a reciprocal process in which ideas are discussed between student and teacher and student and student so as to take thinking forward and open it up to discussion and interpretation.

The patterning of teacher–student interaction

Work on the linguistic patterning of teacher–student interaction in primary English lessons by Sinclair and Coulthard (1975) first revealed the initiation-response-feedback (IRF) exchange as being central to teacher–student interaction. They identified that a teaching exchange consists of three moves: an *initiation*, usually in the form of a teacher question; a *response*, in which a student attempts to answer the question; and a *follow-up* move, in which the teacher provides some form of feedback. While they found teacher follow-up was very often in the form of an evaluation to a student's response, teachers sometimes used comments which exemplified, expanded, justified or added additional information to student responses, or probed student answers by asking follow-up questions.

The ubiquity of the three-part exchange structure was very evident in studies of the impact of the National Literacy Strategy in primary classrooms in England (Mroz *et al.*, 2000; Hardman *et al.*, 2003; Hardman *et al.*, 2005; Smith *et al.*, 2006; Smith *et al.*, 2007). The following extract, taken from a Year 6 literacy lesson, is typical of the discourse style used by teachers in the studies when interacting with students (Hardman *et al.*, 2003). Here the teacher is exploring the genre of non-fiction:[1]

Exchanges			Moves	Acts
Teaching	T	ok now we've been doing a lot of work on non-fiction texts in our shared reading	I	s
		non-fiction is made up of what Paul		n/el
2	P	facts	R	rep
3	T	it's full of facts that's right	F	e
4	T	I wonder who can remember what the piece of non-fiction text we looked at last week was about	I	s
		Katy what was our piece of non-fiction text about		n/el
5	P	it was about smoking	R	rep
6	T	yes it was about smoking well done	F	e
7	T	and what did the article tell us about smoking John	I	el n
8	P	how dangerous it was	R	rep
9	T	right well done	F	e

The extract illustrates clearly the teacher's pervasive use of the three-part exchange and the elaborate nature of many of her sequences of questions which are chained together to form a lengthy transaction. It also illustrates how the teacher often uses *starter* acts (Turns 1, 4) as a matter of routine in opening moves. These are used to signal that the teacher is about to ask a question and also to give some clue as to how to answer it. The extract reveals the rapid pace of the teacher's questioning and the predictable sequence of the recitation sequence. In contrast to the teacher's contribution, only brief responses recalling information are expected from the students and the answers are evaluated and commented on by the teacher according to their relevance to her pedagogic agenda.

In the above extract the teacher questions were all closed in that there was only one 'right' answer for all the class; however, she did go on to use a more open-ended question to which she was prepared to accept more than one answer:

Exchanges			Moves	Acts
Teaching	T	ok so we read and talked about all the dangers from smoking	I	s
		why then do you think young people start smoking if they know the dangers		el
2	P	because it looks grown-up to smoke	R	rep
3	P	yeah they think it looks good	R	rep
4	P	and they want to show off in front of mates	R	rep
5	T	right so young people can be influenced by friends	F	e
		and we know that once you start smoking it is very addictive as it is a drug and very hard to give up		com

In contrast to the first extract, in a later sequence the teacher is prepared to accept more than one answer (Turns 2, 3, 4) to her question and the student responses show greater elaboration. She also probes a student answer (Turn 3) so as to invite elaboration and uses the answer to shape her subsequent question (Turn 5) which leads to:

Exchanges			Moves	Acts
Teaching	T	so we know that once you start smoking it's hard to stop because it's very addictive	I	s
		what can be done to help people stop smoking once they start		el

(*continued*)

Exchanges			Moves	Acts
2	P	erm you can get those things from a doctor miss	R	rep
3	T	things from a doctor what kinds of things	I	el
4	P	you wear them like plasters on your arm miss my mum used them	R	rep
5	T	does any one know what John's referring to	I	el
6	P	they're called cigarette patches	R	rep
7	P	that's it my mum used cigarette patches	R	rep
8	P	so did my dad miss	R	rep

However, studies of the primary National Literacy Strategy found such dialogic encounters between teachers and students were not common. Overall, it was found that, far from encouraging and extending student contributions to promote higher levels of interaction and cognitive engagement, most of the questions asked by teachers were of a low cognitive level designed to funnel student responses towards a required answer. It was found that open questions (designed to elicit more than one answer) made up 10 per cent of the questioning exchanges and 15 per cent of teachers did not ask any such questions. Probing by the teacher, where the teacher stayed with the same pupil to ask further questions so as to encourage a sustained and extended dialogue, occurred in just over 11 per cent of the questioning exchanges. Uptake questions (building a pupil's answer into a subsequent question) occurred in only 4 per cent of the teaching exchanges and 43 per cent of the teachers did not use any such moves. Only rarely were teachers' questions used to assist pupils to more complete or elaborated ideas. Most of the pupils' exchanges were very short, lasting on average five seconds, and were limited to three words or fewer for 80 per cent of the time. It was also very rare for students to initiate the questioning, making up less than 5 per cent of the questions asked in the class, and most were of a procedural nature seeking information from the teacher. In studies of teacher–student dialogue in the small-group 'guided' sessions in the Literacy Hour, it was also found that teachers exercised tight control over the parameters of relevance and were reluctant to allow student initiation or modification of the topic (Skidmore *et al.*, 2003, Hardman *et al.*, 2005).

A review of research into English teaching at Key Stage 3 in England also suggested teachers were using a narrow range of interactive approaches in whole-class, group and one-to-one teaching (Harrison, 2002). The findings are similar to an extensive analysis of more than 200 eighth- and ninth-grade English and social studies classes in a variety of high schools in the Midwest of America (Nystrand *et al.*, 2003). Nystrand and his colleagues found that whole-class discussion in which there is an open exchange of ideas averaged less than 50 seconds in the eighth grade and less than 15 seconds in the ninth grade. Using markers of a dialogic pedagogy such as open-ended questions, uptake questions, student questions, cognitive level and level of evaluation, it was found that shifts from recitational to dialogic discourse patterns were rare: in 1,151 instructional episodes (i.e. when a teacher moves on to a new topic) that Nystrand and his colleagues observed only 66 episodes (6.69 per cent) could be described as dialogic in nature. There was, therefore, a persistence of closed, factual questioning and low-level evaluation of student responses.

Post-16 English teaching

Research into post-16 English teaching also revealed that the teaching of students about to embark on university study is also dominated by teacher explanation and recitation (Hardman and Leat, 1998; Hardman and Williamson, 1998; Hardman and Mroz, 1999). There was an overwhelming predominance of teacher-directed question and answer and presentation accounting for 63 per cent of the total teaching exchanges in post-16 English lessons and student questions made up 5 per cent of the total number of questions asked. The findings challenge the general assumption about the nature of classroom interaction in the post-16 English classroom where teaching is often conceived as being a seminar in which the teacher is no more than a leading participant and mediating influence in a process of discovery. Such a notion assumes students have the right to challenge and question as they acquire some of the working practices of the subject and participate in the subject discourse in preparation for university study. However, student questions accounted for just 4 per cent of the teaching exchanges, suggesting that exploration of a topic through student initiations so as to allow an interchange of ideas was rarely practised. As in the compulsory sector of education, teacher-led recitation was the most common form of teacher–student interaction. This is illustrated in the following example taken from the early stages of a language lesson where the teacher is looking for invented words in an extract from *A Clockwork Orange*:

Exchanges			Moves	Acts
Teaching	T	right	I	m
		let's see if we can err agree here upon words and even better if we can identify the parts of speech here i.e. nouns verbs adjectives adverbs and let's see if some words are now more frequently substituted than others		ms
2	T	Paula you start us off	I	n
		which is the first word you say is invented		el

(*continued*)

Exchanges			Moves	Acts
3	S	auto it's not really invented it's putting it a different way	R	rep
4	T	yeah	F	e
5	T	auto is	I	s
		are we going to count that invented word or substitute		el
6	S	substitute	R	rep
7	T	yeah short form of automobile	F	e
		actually at one time almost a slang word for a car an auto ok so question mark over that		com

The sequence is typical of the teaching exchanges found in the analysis of the earlier analysis of the primary English lessons. It shows the predictable teacher–student sequence and brief, fast exchanges that characterise teacher-led recitation, with the students being called on to display their knowledge through responding to teacher-initiated dialogue and questions. Student responses to these elicitations are then either positively or negatively evaluated by the teacher for accuracy, form and appropriateness against some predetermined answer. It is the teacher who asserts the 'right' as 'expert' to control the frame of reference and there is little scope for student initiatives leading to a lessening of interactional control by the teacher. The teacher's continued use of questions for initiating, extending and controlling the discourse and his use of the feedback move to evaluate the student's contribution means that the students' contributions are not being extended so as to draw out their significance, make wider connections and encourage a greater equality of student participation. As a result, discussion, in which there is the exploration of a topic and interchange of ideas to enable higher-order thinking, seems to be rarely practised. Clearly this has implications for the range of roles students can play in the classroom discourse and for their linguistic and cognitive development.

Recent studies of higher education (De Klerk, 1995; Boyle, 2010) show that discourse patterns in lecturer–student interaction are similar to those found in schools and post-16 English teaching. Tutors asked more questions than students and student turns were significantly shorter. However, there was a marked difference between the compulsory and tertiary sector in the use of open questions and the use of probes in following up a student answer by lectures: 35 per cent of questions asked by lecturers were open in nature compared with 24 per cent closed questions designed to test student knowledge, and 18 per cent of lecturer questions were probing in nature, requesting confirmation or clarification on what had been said by a student. Student questions were also significantly more common than in the school sector, making up over 30 per cent of the questions asked compared with 6 per cent in schools.

Opening up classroom talk

Findings from the research reviewed above suggest it is easy for teachers to fall into the trap of making question–answer sequences too rigid by asking too many recall-based questions and not giving students time to reflect or pose their own questions. In terms of the feedback they give to a student answer, it is easy for them to fall into the trap of simply evaluating the response as being right or wrong, not probing or commenting on the qualities of the answer and not asking other pupils to comment on the response. However, research suggests these patterns of interaction are not inevitable and may be changed over time through powerful professional development courses. For example, Alexander (2001) found significant cultural differences in the way teachers ask questions and provide feedback. It was revealed that French and Russian teachers are far more likely to stay with and interact with an individual student in front of the whole class than was the case in English and American classrooms. This in turn led to Russian and French teachers making greater use of teacher probes, resulting in more sustained student contributions compared with American and English classrooms.

The research findings discussed above have led to the search for alternative discourse strategies to extend the interactional teacher–student repertoire beyond the recitation script. From his research into teacher questions, Dillon (1994) advocated that teachers made greater use of statements to follow up student responses to their questions. These included the use of referral statements (referring one speaker to another), statements of their reactions to what a student has said, speculative statements and statements drawing on their own experiences. He also advocated that teachers maintain a deliberate silence until the original speaker resumes or another speaker enters the silence, teachers signal their reception to what is being said without taking the floor (e.g. verbal encouragers, quiet exclamations, passing the turn by gesture or word), inviting students to ask questions about classmates' contributions and probing student answers.

Similarly, Nystrand *et al.* (2003) found in their research that when teachers paid more attention to the way in which they evaluate student responses there was more 'high-level evaluation', whereby teachers incorporated student answers into subsequent questions. In this process, which they termed *uptake*, teachers' questions were shaped by what immediately preceded them so that they were genuine questions. When such high-level evaluation occurred, the teacher ratified the importance of a student's response and allowed it to modify or affect the course of the discussion in some way, weaving it into the fabric of an unfolding exchange, thereby encouraging more student-initiated ideas and responses and consequently promoting more of a dialogic pedagogy and higher-order thinking on the part of the students.

Overall, Nystrand *et al.* (2003) found that, when dialogic episodes did occur, teachers often opened up space in the classroom discourse by explicitly encouraging students to review one another's contributions. The teachers also encouraged more symmetric interaction by demonstrating reciprocal engagement with student responses through exclamations of interest often combined with statements relating the student's response to their own personal experience or opinion. Some of the teachers also demonstrated a more flexible approach to unpredicted student responses by turning the feedback move into another question by asking for clarification. Such questions were authentic in the sense that they were asking about something genuinely unknown to the teacher, thereby ratifying the importance of the student's original response, while also creating an opportunity for the student to expand upon their original response. Other teachers explored student contributions by incorporating them into the immediate discussion or using them to frame a new topic or exchange. Nassaji and Wells (2000) also found that teacher feedback could extend and draw out the significance of the answer. From their research they advocated that teachers use comments and probing questions to open up the feedback move so as to invite further student elaboration and create a more equal mode of participation.

If the domination of the teacher-led recitation pattern is to be broken it seems from the research reviewed that English teachers need to broaden their questioning repertoire by:

- asking questions which have more than one possible answer;
- giving students time to answer a question;
- sharing questions at the start of a lesson (e.g. 'These are the questions we will be trying to answer in this lesson');
- encouraging students to ask their own questions;
- beginning a lesson by giving pairs of students a question to answer from the last lesson;
- asking pairs to discuss a question for a minute before they answer it;
- asking a pair or group of students to set questions for another pair or group.

In terms of following up a student response, English teachers need to broaden their repertoire by:

- treating answers with respect and giving students credit for trying;
- following up answers with words and phrases like 'Explain', 'Why?', 'What makes you think that?' and 'Tell me more' to provide greater challenge, encourage speaking at greater length and get students to think around the question in greater depth;
- commenting on a response to exemplify, expand, justify or add additional information;
- building student responses into subsequent questions in order to acknowledge their importance to the unfolding classroom discussion.

Enhancing professional practice

It seems clear from the research that major challenges have to be overcome if classroom talk in English lessons is to be transformed from recitation into dialogue so as to promote the guided construction of knowledge between teachers and students (Hardman, 2008). The persistence of teacher-led recitation found in the studies reviewed in this chapter suggests the need for the exploration and researching of alternative teaching and learning strategies and the introduction of powerful school-based in-service programmes in order to change habitual classroom behaviours and traditional discourse patterns.

In order to enhance classroom practice and promote dialogic forms of talk in the classroom, research into professional learning has started to explore the link between discourse patterns and teachers' theories of learning, arguing that the use of particular discourse strategies reflects certain pedagogical epistemologies (Wells, 1999; Cazden, 2001; Moyles *et al.*, 2003; Alexander, 2008). It is suggested that the choices teachers make about the kind of discourse patterns and pedagogical strategies they use in their classrooms are linked to their pedagogical beliefs, and that the most effective teachers are those who can theorise their teaching so as to make confident and professionally informed pedagogic decisions.

If a dialogic pedagogy is to be embedded in the teaching of English at all phases of the education system leading to different levels of student participation and engagement, teachers will need to pay close attention to their use of questions and feedback strategies so as promote the use of alternative discourse strategies (e.g. probing, student questions, uptake questions and teacher statements). Helping teachers to transform classroom talk from the familiar IRF sequence into purposeful and productive dialogue is, therefore, fundamental to what Tharp and Dalton (2007) see as an alternative 'universalistic' pedagogy. Such an approach to pre- and in-service training would emphasise joint teacher–student activity and higher-order thinking through a dialogic pedagogy and curriculum which is relevant to the lives and linguistic profile of the communities from which the students come. The research also, as Alexander (2008) argues, suggests the need for dialogic principles to inform professional learning and school improvement.

Research into the professional development of teachers suggests monitoring and self-evaluation will need to become a regular part of initial and in-service education and training so as to give teachers a degree of ownership of the process of school improvement. Reflection on teachers' intentions and beliefs about their practice is seen as a way of enhancing expert thinking and problem-solving so as to bridge the gap between theories and actual classroom practice. Teachers also need opportunities to theorise their teaching so as to make confident and professionally informed decisions about the way they interact with students so as to encourage greater participation and higher levels of cognitive engagement.

Studies looking at dimensions of teacher development (e.g. Costa and Garmston, 1994; Showers and Joyce, 1996) suggest that because instructional behaviours of teachers cannot be influenced until the internal thought processes have been altered it is essential, if the recitation script is to be changed, that teachers have supportive interactions with peers through modelling and feedback. Dillon (1994) suggests that coaching and talk-analysis feedback are useful tools for professional development whereby sympathetic discussion by groups of teachers of data derived from their own classrooms could be an effective starting point. Similarly Moyles *et al.* (2003) found using video recordings to identify critical moments in primary English lessons selected by the teacher to be a powerful means of promoting critical reflection on professional practice. Video-stimulated reflective dialogue encouraged teachers to articulate and demonstrate their own understanding of their interactive styles and provided opportunities for monitoring and self-evaluation.

A study of post-16 English teaching also found that approaches to staff development using dialogic processes promoted significant changes in the way teachers interacted with their students (Hardman and Mroz, 1999). It was found that through observation and coaching teachers were making greater use of the recitation-breaking strategies which allowed for greater student participation in the classroom discourse. The authority of the teacher as 'expert' was often relinquished to allow for the interplay of alternative frames of reference, thereby giving the students a greater opportunity to assume control over their own learning by initiating ideas, asking questions and evaluating responses along with the teacher. This allowed them to contribute to and shape the verbal agenda so that alternative viewpoints were open to negotiation and the criteria of relevance was not solely imposed by the teacher. Students could also draw on their own experience and knowledge, giving them more responsibility for and control over the learning process, thereby preparing them for higher education where there is a greater emphasis on knowledge interrogation rather than transmission (Boyle, 2010).

In addition to the provision of more powerful professional development programmes based on dialogic principles to extend the interactive repertoire of teachers in whole-class, group-based and one-to-one discourse, there is the need for more research to provide a comprehensive evidence base, for both teachers and policy makers, that such dialogic approaches encourage more active student involvement in the guided co-construction of knowledge leading to significant gains in cognitive learning, as well as social and emotional benefits. Only then will a dialogic pedagogy take centre stage in English teaching and be at the core of the curriculum and the teacher's professional repertoire.

Further reading

A useful follow-up to this chapter is Robin Alexander's (2008) *Towards Dialogic Teaching: Rethinking Classroom Talk*. Now in its fourth edition and consisting of just over 40 pages, this pamphlet provides a very clear overview of how the power of talk can be used to stimulate and extend students' thinking, and to advance their learning and understanding. It also provides English teachers with good practical advice on how they can try to make their teaching more reciprocal and cumulative.

Exploring Talk in Schools, edited by Neil Mercer and Steve Hodgkinson, also provides good practical advice on how English teachers can develop effective classroom interaction. It brings together many of the leading international researchers reviewed in this chapter and provides teachers with an accessible blend of theory, research and practice.

For a more theoretical look at classroom talk which draws extensively on socio-cultural theory, *Dialogic Inquiry* by Gordon Wells (1999) and *Dialogue and the Development of Children's Thinking* by Neil Mercer and Karen Littleton (2007) are strongly recommended. Both books present the case for a dialogic pedagogy drawing on decades of research on language, thinking, learning and teaching which goes back to the theoretical writings of Vygotsky and Bakhtin.

Note

1 In the Sinclair and Coulthard (1975) system of discourse analysis *moves*, initiation, response and feedback make up the three-part teaching exchange and are, in turn, made up of *acts*: com = comment, e = evaluation, el = elicitation, i = inform, n = nominate, rep = reply, s = starter. Also, T = teacher, B = boy, G = girl. Boundaries between teaching exchanges are indicated by a marker (m) and/or metastatement (ms) showing a change in lesson topic.

Chapter 3

A new theory and model of writing development

Richard Andrews

Introduction

Why do we need a theory and model of writing development? If, as others before us have argued (and a view that is not incompatible with that expressed in this chapter), everyone *learns to write by writing* (e.g. Smith, 1994), there would appear to be no need for theory. We would simply pick up the practical skill and craft of writing by being part of a community or communities that correspond; we might learn by imitation and the needs of response; and no one would need to talk or think *about* what we do – we would simply do it. However, the shortcomings of such an approach are many. One is that the act of writing is a cognitive/conceptual, emotional and/or political act as well as a physical one. It is part of social networking and has specific social functions. Another is that the choice to *write* rather than draw, speak or use some other mode of communication is a deliberate choice from a repertoire of modal possibilities. For example, in a community, a person has died. Friends rally around the members of the family who has suffered the loss. They may call by telephone, write a card or letter of condolence and perhaps cook a meal that can be easily reheated by the grieving family as they will be preoccupied with arrangements for the funeral. It is unlikely that the gesture of sympathy would be a text or a drawing. Writing in this case is a deliberate choice that the writer thinks is appropriate for the occasion.

A theory and model are needed, therefore, to position the act of writing in its social and political contexts and also to justify why writing (and particular genres or hybrid forms of writing) is used on a particular occasion. Theories allow coherence in a field but also a repertoire of choice. Pedagogically, we need as teachers of writing to know why we are writing, know the range of forms we are teaching and know how these can be applied in particular situations.

Furthermore, we need as teachers of writing a *theory of the development of writing* (see Beard *et al.*, 2009; Andrews and Smith, 2011) so that we can intervene, as appropriate, to help young writers develop into better writers.

A theory and model

Theories tend to be the overarching and unifying rationale for a field on practice and enquiry; models tend to be schematic representations of those theories, simplified for practical application and for ease of recall. It so happens in the field of writing practice and research that a theory is likely to take verbal form (an account in words, like this chapter) and a model is likely to take diagrammatic form, as a distillation of the theory. There are a large number of models of writing and writing development, but there are fewer theories of writing development. A surfeit of models can be confusing, as each seems to have its own perspective and justification. The aim of this chapter is to create a new theory and model that will be fit for purpose in the contemporary world. The theory, and its model, should be able to 'explain' a range of different writing practices.

Figure 3.1 could be re-drawn with the writing practices at the top and the model and theory below, suggesting that the theory *supports* the model, and the model in turn *supports* the range of writing practices. The conventional depiction in Figure 3.1 merely uses the metaphor of the theory and model being 'higher' and more abstract than practice, thus informing practice.

The theory and model expressed in this chapter assume a range of writing practices. These vary in function and form (including whether they form part of a multimodal array) according to social situations and needs. There is a vast number of writing practices, and they change and develop in time according to social and political situation, and need. The reason we need a new theory and model in the contemporary age is that the current theories and models do not only not account for the range of writing practices that are extant but also they do not account for writing development in the current environment.

A new theory of writing development: the constituent elements

Like any theory, this theory of writing development is made from a number of key elements or concepts. These are *the rhetorical context, framing, multimodal choice, composition* and *development*.

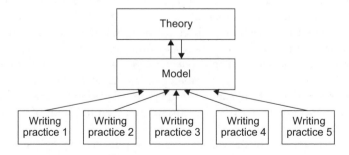

Figure 3.1 The position of a theory and model in relation to writing practices.

The rhetorical context

Any act of communication is a question of who is communicating with whom, why, what is the substance of the communication, when is it taking place, where and how? These seemingly simple questions cover the range of what *rhetoric* is interested in. Whereas classical rhetoric was designed for the particular functions of persuasion, largely within public forums in pre-Athenian and Athenian democracies, contemporary rhetoric covers the full range of functions and forms of communication. Whether writing is being used to set down a formal constitution for a nation, for correspondence with a newspaper, for more informal reasons like a personal letter, email or text, or merely for a message on a Post-it note, left for someone who will act upon it and then throw it away, writing has rhetorical function.

The first consideration in a rhetorical view of writing or any kind of composition is *who is communicating with whom?* The 'who' could be a single person or a group of people (for example, a group composing a manifesto or a memo of agreement between themselves or with others). Similarly, the 'whom' (the 'addressee') could be a single person (even the composer him- or herself, as in the writing of a private diary) or a group of people or a very large audience (for example, a speech written for a large public gathering). Whatever the dynamic of the addresser and addressee – and these technical terms will be used sparingly as the theory must be accessible and close to functional everyday use – there is always a power relation between the sender and the receiver of the message. The power factor changes the nature of the language used in the exchange, and the outcome (if any) of the exchange. It fundamentally affects the choices made by the writer, especially if the writer is in the less powerful position. He or she has to choose a language that will persuade the powerful to read/listen and to move towards the less powerful person. At the same time, the discourses and diction of the exchange are probably determined by the powerful. For example, a lecturer bidding for a grant from a research foundation will need to follow the rubric and use the language that is appropriate for that particular foundation. If he or she fails to use the appropriate language it is likely that the bid will be seen in an unfavourable light from the start. To use a more everyday example, asking a scaffolder for a quotation for the erection of scaffolding outside a house in order to paint a window requires not only politeness in the approach but also precision: how high is the window, and what width of scaffolding is required?

As the second consideration, it is clear, then, that the 'why' of a rhetorical approach takes into account the *function* of the communication, whether that function is mundane and brief and ephemeral or – at the other end of the spectrum – whether it concerns the creation of a major artwork. The function partly determines the choice of language. If writing is to be used in the communication, the circumstances determine the decision to use it and the kinds of written language that will be employed.

Third, the *substance* of the message is important, not only for itself but also because it is affected by and affects the way in which the message is conveyed. This seeming truism is not the same as the notion that 'the medium is the message'. In rhetoric, it is essential to think of the function and substance, along with who is addressing whom, in the first instance, so that the 'social is prior'. Rhetoric therefore reflects the creation and development of language, rather than being seen as a self-justifying communication system in its own right. It seems to us that the mistake made by rhetoric in the past has been when it reifies itself into a system that is self-perpetuating, as in manuals and guides to communication, rather than letting itself be driven by the social requirements of communication. Rhetoric gains its strength as a discipline through the driving momentum of need and substance.

The 'when' and 'where' of writing place it in time and space. To approach these aspects of rhetorical propriety through negative examples: it is inappropriate to send a letter to someone who has just had a delightful or devastating personal experience with a request for money (at least in most cultures). The request for money, if it is an invoice, for example, could follow later. Lest it seem, however, that a rhetorical approach is too concerned with 'propriety', it is important to say that rhetoric does not only deal with the 'appropriate': humour, resistance, political activism and other kinds of communication that require a subversion of the norm or some kind of contrapuntal statement do not tread a careful line of compliance. They intervene when it is inappropriate, if necessary. Decisions about when and where to communicate can be as much about upsetting received assumptions and conventions as they are about using 'appropriate' forms of communication.

Finally, the 'how' of a rhetorical approach to communication concerns exactly the questions that we will address in the following sub-sections: how to frame communication, when to use writing as opposed to other modes, how to use writing in a multimodal context and how to shape and compose it.

Framing

Andrews (2010) sets out the advantages of rethinking approaches to literacy in terms of *framing* rather than frames. Without repeating the argument here, the essential points are that frames, which derive from genre theory that sees genres as text-types rather than as social action, tend to become fossilised. These in turn are taught as scaffolds for writing, often constraining the act of composition and reverting to a box-filling exercise. The commodification of writing in this way puts emphasis on the *product* rather the process of writing. This commodification leads to imitation of models of text-types themselves, or of an assumed 'structure' to the text-type. In other words, students are forced into the same position as those in the Renaissance in Europe who learned the various text-types from *progymnasmata* or exercises in which a model was provided which they had to imitate. This is a clear example of the *form* of the communication gaining dominance in pedagogical terms over the function and substance. Ultimately it leads to enervation on the part of the communicators.

Framing, on the other hand, retains the power of shaping the communicative act in the hands of the composer or rhetor. He or she chooses the genre (as social act rather than as text-type) or hybrid genre in which to couch the message that is to be sent. The act of framing is a creative and critical act in that it draws a line around the parameters of the communication, it creates an 'inside' and 'outside' to the communicative act, it invites transgression of the boundaries or frame and yet at the same time it gives meaning to the transaction through the very creation of the frame. The point is that the frame must be created by the person making the communication, and must be understood by the person receiving the message. If the frame is not clear, the message that is being conveyed may well not be understood. Receivers of messages bring framing to the understanding of communication, just as composers create frames (or use existing ones). If the two sets of frames do not match up – at least roughly speaking – there will be non-communication or miscommunication.

Multimodal choice

Kress (2010) sets out perhaps the clearest statement yet for the case for a multimodal perspective on contemporary communication. The essence of such an approach is that communication cannot be conceived of merely in terms of writing or, for that matter, any other mode. It is always multimodal in that more than one mode – speech, writing, still or moving images, physical presence, spatial considerations and so on – is present in an act of communication. This is a different matter from multimedia, which describe the vehicles via which communication is carried: computer screen, television screen, mobile phone, paper and pen, in sound waves through the air and so on. Here the point is that within an emergent theory and model of writing development we need to ask and answer the question: what role does multimodality have within our theory and model?

The answer is partly economic, partly communicational and partly aesthetic. From an economic point of view, the person who wishes to communicate something must ask themselves: what resources do I have to make such communication? Is it a question of inscribing something on a piece of paper and sending it to the addressee somehow, or do I have wireless connectivity and a laptop or third generation mobile phone at hand? These questions of resource are questions of the *media* that are available, but they play an important part in determining which modes of communication are possible or desirable for the act of communication. The communicational dimension asks the question: what are the affordances of the particular modes that I could use, and what will work best for the situation I find myself in and the message I want to convey? Do I use a single or (seemingly) monomodal form of communication, or do I deliberately go for a multimodal combination? From an aesthetic point of view, the question that will be raised is: what is the most elegant means of representation I can use in this particular circumstance?

A key issue with regard to writing and the development of writing within a multimodal framework is whether the writing is foregrounded or backgrounded, or whether it assumes equal status with other modes in the act of communication. The issue is not necessarily always one of which comes first in the composing process. It is possible to design a page in which the ultimate intention is for writing to be foregrounded, but to start with issues of design: what font will I use? where will the writing appear? what images shall I place and where in order to complement the writing? Once the design and composing process is complete, however, and the message is ready and attains the status of a product, it is usually clear which mode is foregrounded and which mode(s) is or are backgrounded. In the eye of the reader, where the attention is first attracted will most often be the area of fore-grounding. But one of the most interesting aspects of multimodality is the dynamic interrelationship between the various modes that make up the message.

Lastly, *affordance* is a key factor. The affordances of writing include its capacity to capture abstract concepts, its close relationship with speech, its capacity to contain conceptual and narrative sequences and its regularity (in relation to speech). But disadvantages include its embodiment in a particular language (English, Mandarin, Spanish and so on); and its second-order symbolic system (based on the first-order system of speech) which requires learning and apprenticeship.

Writing benefits from a position within multimodality because we become more aware of its affordances and can deploy it more effectively when we know its strengths and weaknesses as a mode of communication.

Composition

Much of what has been said above about writing has implied that learning to write is learning to compose; that rather than 'write' something that is an act of 'writing' and, in due course, becomes the product 'writing' itself it is better to see writing as an act of *composition* that produces a composition. The advantage of the term 'composition' is that is literally means 'putting in place'. In other words, composition is an act of putting elements with other elements – a collage-like act. In writing, we put parts of words together to make up words; words together to make up clauses, phrases and sentences; sentences together to make up paragraphs and other sub-textual units of meaning and all these parts together to make up whole texts operating in particular contexts. The process is not just bottom-up, as described. It is also top-down, so that the contexts and environments for writing determine the texts we create (see the section on rhetoric above), and these texts in turn determine their parts, and so on.

Another advantage of seeing writing as composing is that we can align it more readily with acts of composition in other fields, like music, architecture, engineer-ing, art and sculpture. In all these fields, and in others, makers put together works that are compositions. The creative act is the act of composing.

By changing the emphasis to composing rather than writing the pressure is taken off writing as a medium of instruction and as a system to be learned. There is no doubt that it still has to be learned. But when writing is seen as composition the wider aperture brings meaning and colour to the act of writing. Images, sounds and other forms of communication can help the interpretation as well as the composition of writing, by providing cues, supporting information and other means by which the writing – and writing development – is highlighted.

Development

What place, then, does *development* have among the constituent elements of writing that include rhetorical context, framing, multimodality and composition? As the concern of this chapter is with the emerging writer of whatever age who is trying to improve his or her grasp of the written language (in whichever language), the principal form of development that is the focus of interest is individual development that combines cognitive, emotional, experiential, formal and (to sum up the four constituents described so far) communicational elements. We cannot separate these developmental concerns from social or, indeed, political and economic factors: the person who is learning to write is part of a society and of a global community where resources are unequally distributed; where learning is an effect of the community and communities (including electronic communities) in which he or she operates and where power relations obtain.

Development, then, is a matter of progression for the individual within these parameters. *Writing development* traces the progression in command of the writing system in any particular language, taking into account the elements described immediately above and the dimension of writing in the digital age. It should be noted here that development is seen as neither lagging behind teaching and learning (which, to put it crudely, is a Vygotskian position) nor as preceding them (the more Piagetian position). Rather, development can be seen as a matter for the individual in his or her social and political *milieu*, measurable in terms of progression and intimately linked to learning in the sense of transformation from one state of knowledge and being to another.

In the next section the lineaments of the theory of writing development itself are set out, followed by a model of writing development which distils the main elements of the theory.

A theory of writing development

So far in the present chapter the ground for a new theory of writing development has been laid. Now that foundation is used to help us design and develop a theory.

In essence, every writing act is an act of communication, even if the communication is with oneself as writer (as in, for instance, writing that is personal and private, like a diary that is not for public consumption or notes to help record and/or clarify thinking). As such, the rhetorical context for writing is an important first consideration. As stated above, such consideration includes deciding the what, why, where, who, to whom, when, where and how of the communication. In many cases it will be decided that writing is *not* the preferred or appropriate means of communication, and others will be used. But when and where writing *is* chosen as a principal or secondary mode of communication the next stage in the theory will be triggered.

This is the stage of framing, in which the parameters of the communicative situation will be judged and set; without such framing there can be no communicable meaning as both parties need to be able to locate the utterance in some kind of interpretative frame. If the frames do not coincide there could be miscommunication. The act of framing may choose preset frames (text-types) to convey the message, or it may adapt existing frames into new hybrids. It may define its own new frames by using a metalanguage to alert us to those frames. Whichever approach is taken, an act of framing has taken place. Mostly, frames are invisible in the world of writing in that they surround a written text with space; it is a way of separating the writing from its immediate physical context. Such creation of a space around writing is most obviously seen around poems, which 'do not go up to the right-hand edge of the page' and which often finish with white space below them. (There are other ways in which poems distinguish themselves from other forms, but that is not the main focus of the present chapter.) But these spaces are there also in less formal or less consciously rhythmical text-types, like novels, reports, manuals, letters and so on.

Once the rhetorical setting and its agent, framing, have determined the nature of the written communication (driven by the writer) issues of composition come into play. Composition is not simply a matter of 'putting things together' in words; it is also usually a matter of choosing whether to use only written words, or whether to use other modes of communication too. In a sense, other modes are always there, as words have a visual identity defined by the spaces around and between them. But there is a more complicated arrangement when words interact with other specific modes like still images, moving images and sound. The full range of these other modes is depicted in the model which follows the explication of the theory, as are the specific aspects of each mode (e.g. the integration of whole text, sub-sections of text, sentences, phrases, clauses, words, parts of words and spelling in writing). Composition, then, is the act of making; it includes, within each of the modes that are possible, further refinement through 'shaping' (e.g. drafting and editing words, digitally changing images and so on).

Development in writing adds a temporal dimension to the above. Such development can take place within an individual over a period of time, within each element in the theory and within each sub-element (e.g. the specific sub-elements of the written code). Thus, to make a complex issue more simple: if a parent asks of a teacher, 'How has my child developed as a writer since we last met a year ago?' the answer must be much more detailed than the general observation that 'he or she has improved'. The answer must also certainly move well beyond the notion that his or her grades have improved, as these are abstractions that are calibrated each school term or year for reasons other than to indicate progress in writing. Rather, the answer – to really reflect the development that has taken place – must be something like, 'She has strengthened her command of sentence structure and widened her vocabulary, and has also become more aware of how writing changes when it sits alongside other modes', or, 'He has achieved a better sense of relating text to audience'. Such detail has implications for forms of assessment at the micro and macro levels in writing development.

Essentially, this emergent theory locates writing in the real world, embracing through a rhetorical perspective both fiction and 'non-fiction'. It brings meaning to writing, acknowledging that writing is one of the modes that seeks to communicate. And it posits a way of understanding development in writing, from the micro level of the development of individual elements of writing to the macro-level of personal development of the writing repertoire over a period of time.

A model for writing development

In this section the proposed theory of writing is transformed into a model, by distilling its constituent parts. The model is then explicated further. Once the design is complete, the theory and model are interrogated in the rest of the present chapter, subjecting them to criticism in order to strengthen them.

The theory can be depicted in a series of frames leading to the central aspect of writing: making and composition.

Framing theory will help us explicate the model. The definition of the communication and rhetorical context at the outer limits of the model indicate that this is the frame within which acts of writing take place. Beyond that outer frame are other worlds, not mediated by rhetoric. These would be worlds in which there is no signification, no semiotics, no ostensible communication (there are plenty of these worlds, like landscapes, the sea, animal life itself – these operate with signs and semiotic systems, but they also have a life of their own beyond the world of signs and rhetoric). Some believe that philosophy, logic and thought operate beyond the world of signification, but clearly they do not, as the first two at least would not be possible within some form of communication.

Within the frame of the rhetorical context is the act of framing itself. This level has been well documented above and in *Re-framing Literacy* (Andrews, 2010). Suffice it to say at this point that framing is the creative and critical act that determines the extent, scope and broad shape of the message to be conveyed, drawing a frame that acts as 'common ground' on which the writer and his or her audience can meet.

Within the boundaries created by framing, the writer-as-composer chooses to make writing the primary and sole mode of communication; or combines it with other modes, still in the primary position (e.g. with illustrations in a reading book that operates largely through words); or puts writing in the secondary position in relation to other modes that carry the main burden of communication (as in a reading book that operates largely through images). Writing itself operates according to the combination of language units that have already been described: whole texts, sentences, phrases, clauses and so on. But it also operates in relation to the other modes. These modes can be variously placed in relation to the written verbal

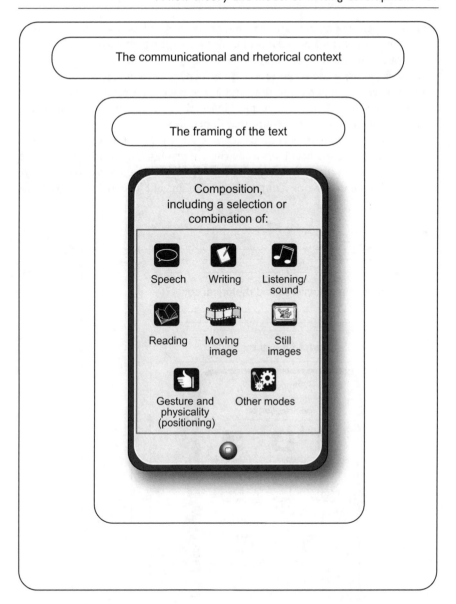

Figure 3.2 A model for writing.

code. Figure 3.2 is intended to suggest that writing can be placed next to any mode, although it does have a strong connection with speech and with reading. So, rather like an Apple iPhone screen, the individual applications' icons can be moved around into different configurations according to purpose. What the icon of writing appears next to suggests particularly close reciprocities and relationships – like the reciprocity between reading and writing, or the close relationship between word and image, or the dynamic relationship between speech and writing. But other modes of communication can also operate in close proximity to writing.

Rhetoric, framing and composition can be depicted in a single plane. But development, because it operates in time and at the micro and macro levels, needs a second dimension in order to depict it. Hence, the emerging model to date needs to be extended to take into account that dimension.

This model begins to look like a Battenberg cake, a stick of rock or roll of sushi. As in sushi, to take the healthier of the three metaphors, the dried seaweed and packed rice contain the different ingredients that make up compositions; so, too, in our writing model, rhetoric and framing 'contain' and 'enclose' the ingredients

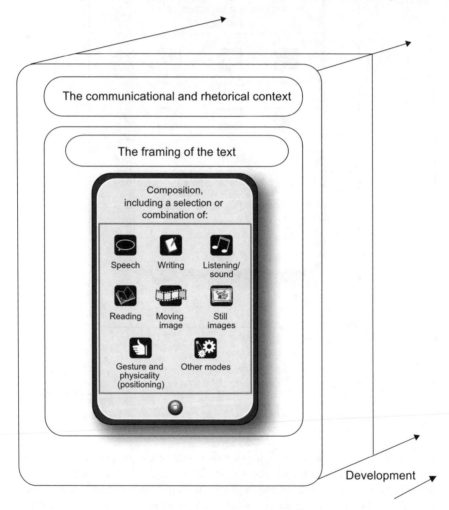

Figure 3.3 A model for writing development.

of communication. Development will happen maturationally, cognitively, emotionally, morally along that developmental axis; but it will also happen in relation to writing. The development in writing will not be steady; it is partly dependent on how the elements within writing develop, and how the other communicational elements outside and near to writing develop too. Along the developmental plane, there is also the phenomenon of a widening range of genres and hybrid texts that are possible as command of the field increases. Such widening of the scope of communication is sometimes accompanied by specialisation within each of the modes; at the same time, it can still be accompanied by multimodal choices and combinations that enrich the acts of communication.

Objections to the theory and model

It is important to subject both theory and model to critique in order to test its strengths and weaknesses.

The theory and model are too simple

Objections could be made that the theory and model are too simple; that they oversimplify what is, in fact, a highly complex set of relationships and practices that cannot easily be unravelled, let alone depicted, in distilled form. Furthermore, such oversimplification masks the huge variety of writing practices that exist in the world and the differences in approaches to writing that exist between individuals. Responses could be made in a number of ways to this objection. At the most general level it has to be reiterated that theories and models are useful in that they provide generalised patterns that describe how phenomena operate and interact. Their very aim is to simplify, and many theories (like good designs) are quite simple. They are the identification of pattern which is then realised in words and in the diagrammatic form of the model. At a more specific level, it could be said that the art of theorising and modelling is to find the right balance between complexity and simplicity: to be able to express the complex in a relatively simple set of terms and their relations. Yet further, it could be pointed out other theories and models are too complex; their complexity defeats the purpose of a theory/model in that they cannot be applied in the learning or teaching of writing.

The theory and model do not sufficiently distinguish between process and product

This objection can less easily be rebuffed. Whereas models in the past have tended to either describe products or processes, the proposed theory and model do not distinguish particularly between the two. This emphasis can be seen as a weakness, as it is not always clear whether discussion is about the process of composition or the actual compositions that are created. A rejoinder is that through choosing the term 'composition' to sit at the heart of our theory and model of writing development, a term has been chosen that embraces both product and process. Like the term 'writing', 'composition' is a term that denotes both. But whereas 'writing' as a term has the imprint of the physical act of putting pen to paper, or keyboard strokes to screen, 'composition' is more to do with the act of 'putting things together' – not just words but words and images, words and sounds and so on. Composition, then, is the element of the present theory and model that captures the essence of the act of making, but at the same time describes the products that are made.

'Development' is insufficiently theorised

There is still a static feel to the proposed theory and model. It does not seem to have the dynamism that might be depicted in a medium more fluid than the printed page. Such dynamism would reflect the human characteristics of development which are tied in closely with physical, emotional, moral, imaginative and other types of 'naturally occuring' maturation. It might also be objected that the theory and model do not fit every individual. That would be a difficult challenge, as individual developmental characteristics cannot always be predicted. What is proposed here is a broad framework for understanding writing development; one that is sufficiently applicable to be useful, at the very least in providing a model *against which* as well as by which individual development could be charted. It is also possible to say that the theory and mode do not resolve the relationship between the learning situation, in all its social and political characters, and the individual's position in relation to that situation. One answer to that objection is that rhetoric has been posited as the point of reference and *primum mobile*. Because the nature of rhetoric is to embody the social and political in its deliberations about the function and form of the communicative act, consideration of the social and political context in each act of writing is implicit.

We don't need another theory and model of writing

Objections might be forthcoming that there are already too many theories and models of writing, and that what is needed is good practice or best practice disseminated more widely. Few could argue with the dissemination of good and best practice (once it is identified). What is useful about a theory and model of writing development is that it provides a framework against which good and best practice can be evaluated, and a starting point for the generation of new practices. In time the theory and model will be superseded by more appropriate identifications of patterns in writing development; that is because the nature and also the environments of writing will change, just as they have changed over the last 50 years. In addition, a theory and model of writing development provides a foundation on which pedagogies and assessment systems can be built. Without such a foundation, fashions will dictate what is taught and how. There is no evidence to date that research or even systematic research reviews and experimental studies can determine what works in the teaching and learning of writing, even though it is hoped that better relationships among research, policy and practice might be developed. Rather, writing practices have developed according to underlying paradigms and theories that have not always been articulated. Where they have been articulated, such theories and models have helped teachers and curriculum and assessment designers to build better and thus longer-lasting structures upon them – structures which can be justified because there is an underlying or overarching theory.

Summary

This chapter has proposed a new theory and model of writing development. Its constituent parts are contemporary rhetoric, framing, composition, multimodality and a notion of development that constitutes progression from one state of writing capability to another. Such a new prototypical theory needs to be tested in practice, with curriculum design and assessment being conceived, applied and evaluated; and with pedagogical approaches being created to teach writing more effectively and with more concern for the rhetorical context that is currently the case. If found to be useful, this theory and model can apply equally to writing in digital formats as well as with a pen a paper, because its focus is not on the media in which writing takes place but on the modes that surround it in the contemporary world. Seeing writing as one (very powerful and flexible) mode among others is a way of liberating the teaching of writing from too narrow a focus on the mechanics of writing as a system. Rather, the new emphasis is on the rhetorical functions of communication, writing's affordances and the relation of writing to other modes that can be used to ensure that communication is effective, appropriate to intention and engaging. Once the teaching of writing is matched to its real-world and fictional practices it is likely that developing writers of any age will find the mode of writing more relevant and powerful and closer to their own communicational needs.

Further reading

Andrews, R. (2010) *Re-framing Literacy: Teaching and Learning English and the Language Arts*, New York: Routledge.

This book sets out the argument, with copious illustrations, for drawing on the visual and performing arts, as well as sociological theories, for moving the debate about the teaching of writing and reading from a concern with frames to one that has *framing* and *re-framing* at its heart. It therefore suggests a more dynamic, creative approach to literacy teaching and learning.

Andrews, R and Smith, A. (2011) *Writing Development: Teaching and Learning in the Digital Age*, Maidenhead: McGraw-Hill/Open University Press.

This text sets out the problem with the teaching of writing and writing performance in schools. It then reviews existing theories and models of writing, comparing process- and product-based models. The book as a whole represents an expansion of the argument in the present chapter, including a much more thorough look at writing in the digital and multimodal age and at implications for practice, assessment, research and policy.

Beard, R., Myhill, D., Riley, J. and Nystrand, M. (eds) (2009) *The Sage Handbook of Writing Development*, London: Sage.

This handbook critically examines research and theoretical issues that impact on writing development from the early years through to adulthood. The wide range of chapters provides a comprehensive account of the field. The international range of contributors makes for a kaleidoscopic review of the state of the art of writing development and its teaching.

Kress, G. (2010) *Multimodality: A Social Semiotic Theory of Contemporary Communication*, Abingdon: Routledge.

One of the more recent and comprehensive critical accounts of multimodality in contemporary communication, this book draws on rhetoric, communication theory and particularly social semiotics to make its case for an awareness and application of multimodal approaches. It includes consideration of composition via digital media.

Chapter 4

Living language, live debate
Grammar and Standard English

Debra Myhill

Introduction

Language is so fundamental to what it means to be human, so central to the forging of relationships, to the construction of national identity and to the communication of cultural identities that it is perhaps not surprising that language, specifically grammar and Standard English, remains a perennial source of heated debate. Language allows us to express the most sophisticated of intellectual ideas and the most deeply felt personal emotions; language allows us to share the past and to speculate about the future; language allows us to create new ideas and generate new possibilities. And in every generation, there have been 'language mavens' (Pinker 1994: 373) who have deemed it their responsibility to rail against the pervading social influences which lead to the perceived degradation of language, from Thomas Wilson's (1553) cry against 'outlandish English' to the Queen's English Society (QES), established in 1972 by Oxford graduate Joe Clifton, who deplored 'the current decline in standards of English' (www.queens-english-society.com/about.html). Language matters. It was, therefore, no accident and no surprise that in 1988 when the first National Curriculum for English was being shaped arguments about language were at the forefront of the debate. Marenbon (1987) argued that teachers who allowed 'casual speech and non-standard dialects to predominate in their classrooms' (1987: 36) threatened the very fabric of nationhood, because, as he claimed, 'in the future of its language, there lies the future of a nation!' (1987: 40).

This chapter will map the landscape of the grammar and language debate and offer a critical perspective on grammar and language teaching in a twenty-first-century literacy curriculum. First, the chapter presents an overview of the historical debates, illustrating how current debates mirror those of earlier eras. An outline of definitions of the contested concepts of Standard English and grammar is offered to clarify subsequent discussion. The chapter will then consider the more contemporary debates, first about Standard English and then about grammar, looking at both pedagogical and ideological thinking. Finally, the chapter will suggest ways of conceptualising language and grammar in the curriculum which may go some way towards a resolution.

A historical perspective

One of the earliest examples of the language debate is the 'inkhorn controversy' (Crystal 1995: 61) of the late sixteenth/early seventeenth century. This coincided with the flourishing of the arts and sciences in the Renaissance and led some writers to question whether English as a language was sufficiently sophisticated to engage with new ideas and scientific concepts. An inkhorn term was a loan word, borrowed from another language, and in this period vocabulary in the English language had expanded rapidly through the use of loan words from Latin, Greek, French and Italian. Thomas Elyot (1531) argued that this influx of new words was necessary to compensate for 'the insufficiency of our own language' (1531: 2). But others felt that the use of loan words threatened the purity of the English language: Thomas Wilson (1553) called for English speakers never to 'affect any straunge ynkehorne termes, but to speake as it is commonly received' and condemned those who spoke such 'outlandish English, that they forget altogether their mothers' language'. Although, on the one hand, the inkhorn controversy represents a linguistic debate about vocabulary and language, it is also a sociological debate about national and social identity. In general, it was the educated elite who used the expanded lexicon and, as such, this version of English was prestigious and powerful, and those who aspired to the respect and status this conferred might try to appropriate this discourse themselves. Shakespeare, in his portrayal of Don Armado in *Love's Labour's Lost*, mocks the affected speech of the courtier whose self-importance is mirrored by his affected use of language:

ARMADO: [*To Moth*] Chirrah!
HOLOFERNES: *Quare* chirrah, not sirrah?
ARMADO: Men of peace, well encount'red.
HOLOFERNES: Most military sir, salutation.
MOTH: [*Aside to Costard*] They have been at a great feast of languages, and stol'n the scraps.
COSTARD: O, they have liv'd long on the alms-basket of words.

(*Love's Labour's Lost*, Act 5, Scene 1, 32–39)

Here Holofernes, the schoolmaster, and Don Armado use Latin (*quare*) and Latinate (*salutation*) words, while Moth, the page, and Costard, the clown, sarcastically observe, with the wisdom of fools, that they have stolen their language from the leftovers of others, like charitable alms.

The desire to protect the English language from degradation underpins many of the historical complaints about language, although the issues of class, status, power and privilege are never far from the surface. Locke (1690) observes that 'the Errors and Obscurity, the Mistakes and Confusion, that is spread in the world by an ill use of Words' raise doubts about whether language 'has contributed more to the improvement or hindrance of Knowledge amongst Mankind' (1690: 448). By 1635, both France and Italy had established academies (Accademia della Crusca,

1582; L'Académie française, 1635) to maintain the 'purity' of the language and to guard against inappropriate usage or linguistic introductions. By 1712 Swift was calling for a similar academy in England to monitor and regulate the use of English to remediate what he saw as a decline in the quality of language used: '[O]ur Language is extremely imperfect; that its daily Improvements are by no means in proportion to its daily Corruptions; that the Pretenders to polish and refine it, have chiefly multiplied Abuses and Absurdities; and, that in many Instances, it offends against every Part of Grammar'.

In the twentieth century the language debate begins for the first time to look to formal education as the solution to the perceived problem of language degeneration. The imagery of the debate over preceding centuries had been almost evangelical in its zeal to promote language purity, cleanliness and perfection in the face of corruption, abuse and offence. This imagery is sustained in the twentieth-century debate. The Newbolt Report (BoE 1921) was one of the earliest reviews of English teaching and, in many ways, was forward-looking: the report argued for the subject of English to have its own identity and focus and to abandon its dependence on classical models. Written in the post-war period, it reflects a time of national anxiety and argues for subject English as a way of maintaining national identity. In this context, Newbolt called for speech training in Standard English from an early age for those children who spoke a dialect or whose speech was 'disfigured with vulgarisms' (BoE 1921: 59). He maintained that teachers in primary schools faced the challenge of fighting against 'the powerful influence of evil habits of speech contracted in home and street' (BoE 1921: 59). Newbolt's view that English teachers had a responsibility to combat the negative influences of home was echoed by Sampson, who laid upon English teachers the duty 'to purify and disinfect' (1924: 28) the language of the lower classes, and reiterated in the later Norwood Report (Norwood 1943), which called for a systematic campaign against lip-laziness, vulgarisms and street idioms. Reflecting on these attitudes, Cameron (1995: 96) notes that 'the teaching of correct English is persistently and quite melodramatically depicted as part of a more general "struggle" against dark social forces, and specifically as a means to counter the anarchy of the (working class) home and street'. In more recent times, such metaphors of education as a remedy to cure language ills and the quasi-religious discourses of purity and evil remain, and increasingly it is English teachers who are the focus of criticism, as the statement below, taken from the Queen's English Society website, vividly illustrates:

Linguistic criminals

Defacing public property is an offence for which the perpetrator can be arrested, charged, tried and sentenced. The English language is public property and those who deface it are equally guilty of an offence but the Law does not provide for the punishment of such 'criminals'. Indeed if imprisonment were the lot of criminals defacing the language, our streets would be empty because most of the population would be behind bars. But among all these unpunished criminals, the arch-criminals are teachers. Nowadays, those who teach English (and other subjects, too) are the products of educational systems that have in Britain been eroded by petty bureaucracy and in the USA by intrusive psychology gone mad. The term 'school teacher' no longer applies; our children are today being educated (?) by 'professional educators(!)' totally obsessed by their latest methods, none of which methods produces the results and quality of education that was achieved by the good old school teacher 50 years or more ago. This is a downward spiral for as each generation of teachers is trained, firstly in school and later at university, to a lower standard than the preceding generation, so they pass on their degraded level of mastery of the language to the next generation . . . and so forth . . . All teachers should be required to prove that they have attained a certain (not a minimum) level of command of the English language before they are let loose on classes of school-children. Even if these teachers are experts in their subjects – mathematics, science or history – they should be required to put the subject across eloquently in order to set their pupils a good example. English language teachers, in particular, must be required to demonstrate an exemplary level of articulate English delivered in an acceptably educated (albeit regional) accent.

(www.queens-english-society.com/errors.html)

Defining terms

At this point, however, it may be helpful to explore in a little more depth the multiple interpretations of the two key terms for this chapter – 'grammar' and 'Standard English'. Given the passion with which the debate for and against the teaching of Standard English is fought, it may be surprising to find that defining Standard English is not an easy task, as Table 4.1 reveals.

Looking at these definitions, the dominant understandings of Standard English seem to be that it is a dialect and that it is widely used. As a definition this is neither precise nor helpful, particularly if you wished to teach students how to use it – there are many dialects and many of them are widely used. Crystal elaborates on his definition to provide a more comprehensive explanation of Standard English:

- ☐ Standard English is a variety of English:
  — A dialect, but not a regional dialect.
- ☐ Linguistic features of Standard English are chiefly matters of vocabulary, grammar and orthography.
- ☐ Standard English is not a matter of pronunciation: it can be spoken in a wide variety of accents.
- ☐ Standard English is the variety of English which carries most prestige in a country.
  — It is the variety used by the powerful.

— It is the variety used by leading institutions, e.g. government, law, education.

◻   It is widely understood, but not widely produced.

— Only a minority use Standard English to talk.

— Most people speak a mix of Standard English and regional/social Englishes.

— Standard English is only required in certain types of writing.

— Standard English is most commonly found in print.

(summarised from Crystal 1995: 110)

Table 4.1 A range of definitions of Standard English

DES 1989: para. 4.9	Linguists generally define Standard English as a dialect which has historical, geographical and social origins although with some variations, it now has worldwide uses
Macarthur 1992: 982	[A] widely used term that resists easy definition but is used as if most educated people nonetheless know precisely what it refers to
Crystal 1995: 110	A minority variety (identified chiefly by its vocabulary, grammar, and orthography) which carries most prestige and is widely understood
Trudgill 2001: 165	If Standard English is not therefore a language, an accent, a style or a register, then of course we are obliged to say what it actually is. The answer is, as at least most British sociolinguists are agreed, that Standard English is a dialect. . . . Standard English is simply one variety of English among many. It is a sub-variety of English
Greenbaum and Nelson 2002: 3	In countries where the majority speak English as their first language one dialect is used nationally for official purposes. It is called *Standard English*. Standard English is the national dialect that generally appears in print. It is taught in schools, and students are expected to use it in their essays. It is the norm for dictionaries and grammars. We expect to find it in official typed communications, such as letters from government officials, solicitors, and accountants
Wright 2000: 6	A consensus dialect
Ofsted 2009: 28	The term 'Standard English' refers to English which is used widely in public and professional contexts. It is not associated with geography or social groupings and should not be confused with aspects of pronunciation. Standard English can be spoken with any accent since it is defined not by its sound but by its grammar and vocabulary, although it is usually associated with what is known as 'received pronunciation'

Standard English is simply one dialect of many and no better or worse than any other; however, it is a prestige dialect, and tends to confer social privilege on those who speak it. Of course, these definitions are principally from linguists and reflect their interests in describing language; many would define Standard English much more prescriptively as an accepted norm, the 'correct' and historically legitimated version of English. It is frequently regarded as 'proper English' and the use of other varieties viewed as 'a deviation from the norm, the deviation being due to laziness, ignorance or lack of intelligence' (Trudgill 1995: 8). When linguists use the word 'standard' they are referring to the process of language standardisation, where variations in language use become increasingly unvaried and standardised. It is the tendency of all languages to standardise, probably as a consequence of the efforts to communicate with others. But the word 'standard' also has other overtones – notably the link to quality (for example, a gold standard; a decline in standards). This connotation of the word 'standard' leads to a view of Standard English as the model against which other versions of English are measured, the quality mark for English language. To an extent, this difference in interpreting the word 'standard' is at the core of the debate about Standard English.

Standard English and grammar are, of course, connected in that there is a grammar of Standard English; and one way of drawing learners' attention to the difference between Standard English and other varieties of English is to analyse the grammatical differences. There is a reasonable consensus around a definition of grammar, largely founded on the idea that grammar is about how the units of language combine to create meaning. Carter and McCarthy (2006: 2) argue that grammar is 'concerned with how sentences and utterances are formed', while Greenbaum and Nelson (2002: 1) claim that it is 'the set of rules that allow us to combine words in our language into larger units'. Most agree that grammar has two branches of study: morphology – the study of words and their structures – and syntax – the study of how words build into bigger units. But there the harmony ends. Modern linguists all operate with a conceptualisation of grammar as *descriptive*: a way of describing how language works. They analyse and examine language in order to describe language structures and patterns of language use. Descriptive linguists do not attempt to determine what is 'correct' usage or to make judgements of language use. In contrast, many non-linguists hold a *prescriptive* view of grammar: that there a set of rules for how language should be used which are outlined and set down for common reference. A prescriptive grammar establishes a norm and sets a value on that norm, and critiques as inherently inferior usages which do not conform to that norm. Just as different understandings of the word 'standard' are at the heart of the Standard English debate so, too, is the difference between descriptive and prescriptive perspectives at the heart of the grammar debate. One way to look at the language debate about Standard English and grammar is to see it as a fundamental difference in understanding between academic linguistic discourses and political and public discourses.

Exploring the debate: Standard English

Central to the debate about Standard English is the principle of standardisation, which, as noted above, is a natural tendency in all languages and, as Wright (2000: 6) observes, it is 'a continuing and changing process'. Even lexicographers, who in effect are trying to pin down a standard meaning of a word, understand that the process of standardisation is unstoppable. Samuel Johnson mocked any dictionary compiler who suffered under the misapprehension that 'his dictionary can embalm his language, and secure it from corruption and decay, that it is in his power to change sublunary nature, or clear the world at once from folly, vanity, and affectation' (Johnson 1755: para. 85). One tendency in the process of standardisation is to remove gradually the inflections of the language. English now has far fewer inflections than its Old English counterpart and currently the possessive apostrophe is almost certainly an example of an inflection which is tending towards absence. The apostrophe is the only marker of the genitive case, or possession, in English, and is itself a variation on the former fuller form of the genitive which was 'es'. So in Middle English 'God's son' would have been 'Goddes son'. Many upper-case signs already omit the possessive apostrophe and many first-language users of English make errors with the apostrophe. This is language in the process of change.

And language change, of course, is frequently the point of tension in debates about Standard English. Linguists understand that language will always change and that 'it is in no sense wrong for human language to change, any more than it is wrong for humpback whales to change their song every year' (Aitchison 1991: 210). Johnson's American counterpart, Noah Webster, likened the inevitable force of language to 'the course of the Mississippi, the motion of which at times is scarcely perceptible yet even then it possesses a momentum quite irresistible. Words and expressions will be forced into use in spite of all the exertions of all the writers in the world.' (www.ourcivilisation.com/smartboard/shop/gowerse/complete/chap4.htm). But, in contrast, conservative views of Standard English are inclined towards 'the gold standard' perspective of the word 'standard' and resist change, at the level of both vocabulary and grammar.

In terms of vocabulary, English is constantly developing new words, through borrowing from other languages (*al fresco, panache, sauna, coulis*), through devising new words to describe new inventions or ideas (*iPod, dyson, viscose*) or through creating new words from old. Shakespeare introduced thousands of new words into the English language (Bryson 1990: 57) through the process of back-formation, whereby new words are formed from existing words, or through exploiting word class mobility in English and using an existing word in a different grammatical position. Common words such as *monumental, excellent, submerged, lonely, summit* and *castigate* are all examples of words introduced by Shakespeare from pre-existing variations (Bryson 1990: 70). The shifting of a noun into a verb role is evident in 'Season your admiration for a while' and 'The hearts that spaniel'd me' (Crystal 2002: 214). This process is one of the most typical ways that Standard English changes and it is easy to think of many current examples of new words coined from old words:

◻   the verb *to text* from the noun *text*
◻   the verb *to google* from the noun *Google*
◻   the noun *typo* from the noun *typing error*
◻   the noun *globalisation* from the adjective *global*.

A valuable classroom activity is to collect modern examples of new words being created from old words, or even to invent a new back-formation and attempt to make it an accepted word within the school vocabulary. But it is these very words that language-preservers rail against as impure and inappropriate use of English: Swift (1712) complained about the use of the new words 'mob' and 'banter' just as the Queen's English Society denounces the use of 'proactive' (http://www.queens-english-society.com/errors.html).

Many complaints about Standard English relate to grammatical constructions. The 'standards' view of Standard English is inclined to classify such usages as grammatical errors, whereas the linguists will often highlight that the non-standard usage is not an error but frequently a dialect usage. So 'I was waiting for a parcel' is recognisable as Standard English, whereas 'I were waiting for a parcel' is non-standard: the latter is a common grammatical construction in many rural dialects, such as Devonshire. The double negative ('I don't want no trouble') is another oft-cited non-standard construction which is typical in many dialects. But here, too, language change is evident as some non-standard forms do not originate in a dialect but develop as a variation on the standard form. In a study investigating children's use of spoken Standard English, Hudson and Holmes (1995) found that the six most frequent non-standard usages were:

◻   there is (plus plural)
◻   this guy
◻   she come
◻   out the window
◻   have fell
◻   them books.

Some might argue that 'out the window' is an example of changing preferences, rather than dialect influence. Another very current example is the 'I was sat/I was sitting' alternative. 'I was sitting' would probably be deemed the Standard English version, as it uses the past tense of the verb 'be' plus the past participle of 'sit', whereas 'I was sat' uses the past tense version of 'sit' as a participle. However, this is now so common that many find the distinction a fine one and it may well be that in the future 'I was sat' will become perfectly acceptable. In written English, another example of common usage which may become accepted as Standard English is the use of 'like' as a subordinator, rather than 'as though', as in the following examples:

▢ I could smell the sweet smell of lavender, like I was standing in a herb garden.

▢ It seemed like he had stopped trying to get him and gone away.

(Myhill 2009: 408)

Hudson and Holmes (1995: 4) found that 32 per cent of the children in their study did not use any non-standard forms, and of those who did many switched between standard and non-standard usage, even in the same utterance:

> The man *come* out of his house and he said to him, 'You've got my parrot,' and he says 'What parrot?' and he says 'You've got my parrot – you pinched it,' and the man *ran* off so the young boy waited for him to come back and he sneaked back in through . . . the back [inaudible] and he *came* out the front . . . and the boy *ran* . . .

(1995: 16)

Here the speaker opens the narrative with a non-standard present-tense usage of 'come', but uses standard past-tense forms in the rest of the account. It is possible that the non-standard construction is not 'error' but a choice, for narrative effect or for social engagement. In writing, the inappropriate use of non-standard English is not a major problem and tends to be confined to weaker writers, awarded grade F at GCSE (General Certificate of Secondary Education) (QCA 1999). However, Massey *et al.*'s (2005) study comparing examination scripts over time indicated a trend towards increased use of non-standard English and an 'increasing use of colloquial or other informal language' (2005: 64). They suggest that writing has become more inclined to use forms which in earlier times would have been restricted to speech and they note that 'sometimes this seems appropriate, but often it looks more like poor judgement or simply failure to appreciate the distinction' (2005: 64).

Although linguists and many teachers argue that Standard English is about appropriacy and code-switching, about knowing when to use Standard English and when not to, it remains true that in many countries Standard English is prescribed by school curricula and this mandated endorsement of Standard English provokes intense controversy. In England, the Kingman Report (DES 1988) and the Cox Report (DES 1989), which preceded the first version of the National Curriculum, both argued for the importance of Standard English. The Cox Report did not argue for the linguistic superiority of Standard English, but maintained that the social advantage it conferred made it necessary to ensure that all children could speak it:

> If pupils do not have access to Standard English then many important opportunities are closed to them, in cultural activities, in further and higher education, and in industry, commerce and the professions. Those educationalists who deny children these opportunities are confining them to the ghetto, to a restricted discourse which will close to them access not only to the professions but also

to leadership in national politics. In our democracy Standard English confers power on its users to explain political issues and to persuade on a national and international stage. This right should not be denied to any child.

(Cox 1991: 29)

In line with the notion of an entitlement curriculum, which underpinned the first version of the National Curriculum, learning how to speak Standard English was framed as a 'right'. Thus, the first iteration of the National Curriculum for English (DES 1990) had a section on Knowledge about Language which, broadly speaking, adopted a sociolinguistic approach and encouraged the teaching not simply of Standard English but also the understanding of accent and dialect and the history of the English language. In many ways, this represented a liberal attitude to Standard English and one which was, in general, supported by the English teaching profession. Nevertheless, this version of the National Curriculum was critiqued for its lack of clarity in distinguishing between written and spoken Standard English and for the confused thinking it conveyed around formal and informal English (for a detailed discussion of this see Crowley 2003). Stronger dissent emerged from right-wing politicians and thinkers who felt the curriculum had not gone far enough in 'asserting the supremacy of Standard English' (Pound 1996: 239) and in promoting a firm sense of national identity and respect for the English cultural heritage. By 1995 the English curriculum had been re-written, with a new section, Standard English and Language Study, giving greater prominence to a requirement that all children should write and speak in Standard English. The emphasis on Standard English and on a literary canon was at the heart of the clash between English teachers and politicians which led to the boycott of the national tests in 1994; the heated debate is articulated in many articles written in this period (Stubbs 1989; Pound 1996; Cheshire and Edwards 1993). Anderson (1995), for example, contrasted the hegemonic treatment of Standard English in the English National Curriculum with the greater tolerance and respect for diversity expressed in the Norwegian curriculum.

Hegemonic discourses which advocate the imposition of Standard English over local dialects or Englishes always raise difficult questions about class and ethnicity, power and national identity. In the US, this is best exemplified in what is now known as the Ebonics debate. In 1996, a Californian school board passed a resolution which acknowledged the legitimacy of African American Vernacular English (AAVE) or Ebonics, as it was popularly known. This sparked a heated national media debate which, in effect, set linguists and educationalists against right-wing conservative views of language and identity. Wolfram (1998) noted the quasi-religious zeal which accompanied this debate and how 'everyone seems to have an opinion about Ebonics, and these opinions are typically quite dogmatic' (1998: 111). More recently, in Singapore, a similar debate has revolved around a local version of Singaporean English, known as Singlish. Standard British or American English is preferred by policy makers and, in 2000, the Singapore government instigated 'The Speak Good English campaign' which, according to Farrel and

Tan Kiat (2007), had the aim of eliminating Singlish altogether. The Ministry of Education in Singapore emphasised that Standard English, the 'internationally acceptable English that is grammatical, fluent and appropriate for purpose, audience, context and culture' (Ministry of Education 2001: 3, cited in Farrel and Tan Kiat 2007: 383) was the only acceptable version. Wee (2005) argued that this policy was discriminatory and ignores people's linguistic human rights.

Wolfram argued that the Ebonics controversy has highlighted three things about public understanding about language:

1. the intensity of people's beliefs and opinions about language and language diversity,
2. the persistent and widespread level of public misinformation about issues of language variation and education, and
3. the need for informed knowledge about language diversity and its role in education and in public life.

(Wolfram 1998: 109)

But it also highlighted the relationship between language and power, and, in particular, the powerful role that language can play in shaping classrooms and student outcomes. On the one hand, English teachers have been positioned as failed guardians of language propriety. In Singapore it was argued that teachers 'should play a more active role in halting the alleged deterioration of the standard of English' (Farrel and Tan Kiat 2007: 382). In England, the Queen's English Society attributes the 'abysmal state of the language' to 'the way English is taught – from primary school to university' (www.queens-english-society.com/qesapproach. html). But conversely, elsewhere, the debate has focused more on how children's spoken characteristics influence how teachers see them and how this affects educational outcomes. Blake and Cutler (2003: 165) noted that research has shown 'a correlation between negative teacher attitudes toward the AAE [African American English] dialect and lowered expectations and evaluations of its speakers' and Park and King (2003) noted the damaging impact of a discrepancy between the discourses valued in the home and those valued in the school. They suggest that 'children who bring culturally different practices to school are misunderstood, academically underestimated, and devalued'.

Exploring the debate: grammar

The fundamental philosophical and political discourses which underpin the grammar debate are fully consonant with those which sustain the Standard English debate, and much of the thinking outlined in the previous section permeates the grammar debate. In particular, prescriptivist versus descriptivist perspectives on grammar divide those who view grammar as an visible testimony of linguistic correctness and those who see variations in grammar as witness of language in change, both diachronic (over time) and synchronic (across contexts, groups or geographical spaces). The notion of 'error' is a strong theme in discourses about grammar. Keith (1990: 69) noted that the topic of grammar suffered 'the misfortune of being associated with the negative, the corrective, the inevitable remedial half of English teaching', a view which is not restricted to the UK: Hancock (2009: 195) in the US similarly observes that '[g]rammar is error and error is grammar in much of the public mind.' Public or political discussions about grammar tend to be driven by ideas about error or correctness, and especially the application or breaking of rules, many of which derive from Latinate understandings of grammar which modern linguists would reject.

The 'grammar as error' stance is exemplified by the Queen's English Society (QES) (www.queens-english-society.com), an organization for those with 'an interest in preserving the English language and in halting the decline in standards of its use'. They acknowledge that discussion about language is a subjective matter, and they recognise that their position is very much on one side of a polarised debate. They articulate reasoned arguments about why prescriptivism is the appropriate line to follow. As a society they are committed to promoting the Queen's English, which they describe as 'a form of cultured English' – as such the QES 'defends The Queen's English and therefore prescribes that style of usage'. In arguing in favour of the importance of grammar, they make the link between grammar and error which typifies this discourse, maintaining that grammar 'is particularly valuable for the diagnosis of faults or problems in one's own writing and in that of others'. They also insist that everyone needs to abide by the rules of grammar in order to secure comprehension. Linguists, of course, would disagree. First, it is evident that very few grammatical 'errors' obscure comprehension, and, indeed, compliance with the rules of grammar do not guarantee comprehension, as the grammatically correct sentence below indicates:

> I was eating washing machines horticulturally when the grasshopper united underwear with spectacles to create the last dreaming clarinet.

Descriptive views of grammar use the tools of linguistic analysis to present descriptions of grammar in usage, including in different social or functional contexts, and over time. As noted earlier, descriptive linguists do not attempt to define what grammatical structures should be used; they simply describe how they are used. Prescriptive grammar, however, is normative, pushing towards adherence to a common set of rules and linguistic practices.

However, alongside this emphasis on grammar as being quintessentially concerned with grammatical errors is a deeper discourse which links precision and accuracy in grammar usage with moral and social standards. Cameron (1995) records British politician Norman Tebbit's direct linkage of allowing 'bad English' with a decline in moral standards, where there is 'no imperative to stay out of crime' (BBC Radio 4, 1985, quoted in Cameron 1995: 94). In an article in *The Guardian*, author Philip Pullman sardonically reiterates the political subtext of the social impact of 'good grammar':

Teaching children about syntax and the parts of speech will result in better writing, as well as making them politer, more patriotic and less likely to become pregnant.

(Pullman 2005)

Just as with the Standard English debate, a socio-cultural analysis of the grammar debate reveals that the prescriptive emphasis on correct grammar is often about social class and hegemonic pressures which sustain social privilege and social capital. Correct grammar is, of course, the grammar of Standard English, which is the grammar of the upper and middle classes and the grammar of power and access to power. A sense of how more descriptivist perspectives on languages are seen as threatening to dominant discourses is evident in MacDonald's (1995) polemical attack on the writing process movement in the US which abandoned rule-bound grammar teaching in favour of a more critical and exploratory approach to language. She argues that 'rather than studying possessive pronouns, students are learning how language silences women and blacks', implying that the latter is of less value than the former.

It is one small step from a prescriptivist view of grammar and a belief that language is in decline to a view that English teachers are not fulfilling their duties adequately in this respect. Marenbon claimed that 'grammatical and literacy failings among young people are evidence that, in most schools today, English is badly taught' (1987: 16) and such views fuelled both the introduction of the first statutory National Curriculum and the subsequent National Strategies. MacDonald's (1995: 3) scathing critique of abandoning grammar teaching in favour of 'an indigestible stew of 1960s liberationist zeal, 1970s deconstructivist nihilism, and 1980s multicultural proselytizing' suggests that this has led to a position where 'the only thing that composition teachers are not talking and writing about these days is how to teach students to compose clear, logical prose'. Yet within the profession of English teaching there is no consensus on the role of grammar in the curriculum (see, for example, *English Teaching Practice and Critique*, December 2005 and May 2006, and the *English Journal*, 1996, 85: 7). In essence, the professional debate divides those who see no place for grammar, because of no demonstrable impact on students' learning, from those who believe that knowledge about language in its own right has a role in a language curriculum.

Towards a resolution

Summarising the thinking outlined in this chapter, it is probably already evident that some of the discourses in the grammar and language debate appear certainly irreconcilable: prescriptivist and descriptivist views of language are positioned as binary opposites, and linguists and politicians may never agree because their goals and purposes are different. But in practice, rather than being at opposite ends of a language spectrum, prescriptivist and descriptivist views of language are better thought of as a Venn diagram, with two overlapping circles. There are many instances where everyone, including linguists, would agree that there are rules governing the language, particularly in terms of word order and syntax. In many ways language *is* normative, otherwise we'd find it hard to understand each other. Equally, there are many aspects of language use in which a descriptive approach is more appropriate – the evolving patterns of texting and tweeting, for example. It is in the intersection of the two circles where the debate is contentious, where a prescriptivist will argue for a normative rule and a descriptivist will argue that language use is changing ('I was sitting/I was sat', for example).

Many English teachers and educationalists advocate a pluralist approach to teaching, one which values dialectal diversity but also acknowledges that giving learners access to Standard English may help them in gaining access to powerful discourses and powerful positions. It is important not to romanticise the emancipatory potential of teaching Standard English, just as it is equally important not to romanticise local dialects: speaking Standard English may be necessary in a global world but it is not sufficient to ensure access to power. That is a far more complex issue, influenced by many societal factors, of which dialect is only one. In the English classroom, this pluralist approach would involve comparing linguistic differences between regional and social dialects and examining social attitudes to them. It would embrace the richness of dialectal variations and the language potential this offers but also support students in code-switching to Standard English, where appropriate. The teaching of both Standard English and dialects would be embedded in critical analysis of language in use and explicit discussion of issues of language and power.

The role of grammar in the English curriculum is perhaps more ambivalent than Standard English. Linguists with a strong understanding of the English curriculum, such as Ronald Carter, have argued for the study of grammar as an end in itself, part of a broad and balanced language curriculum. Certainly, access to a metalanguage enables much more precise discussion and analysis of language; for example, analysing how talk varies in informal conversation between friends and in an interview situation or analysing how transitive and intransitive verbs differently position men and women in romantic novels. In such contexts, grammar is a tool in the English classroom for critical analysis of spoken and written text.

The more contentious issue is whether teaching grammar can support students in developing their own talk and writing. There is very little evidence that teaching grammar has a positive impact on writing development, though there is good evidence that linguistic analysis can provide valuable insights for teachers into developmental trajectories and patterns (Perera 1984; Myhill 2008) which might inform teaching decisions. However, a study currently being undertaken at the University of Exeter is showing a significant positive impact (effect size 1.52) of contextualised grammar teaching on writing attainment. Unlike previous studies, this study adopted a meaning-centred approach to grammar and writing in which meaningful aspects of grammar where taught, relevant to the genre of writing under study. The focus in this study is not on addressing grammatical errors, but at opening up alternative grammatical possibilities for meaning-making and developing a repertoire based on choice and understanding.

No doubt the language debate will continue, but Crystal neatly summarises a resolution of the debate as one in which there is recognition that grammar, language and meaning are inextricably intertwined, and that understanding these inter-relationships is empowering:

> Grammar is the structural foundation of our ability to express ourselves. The more we are aware of how it works, the more we can monitor the meaning and effectiveness of the way we and others use language. It can help foster precision, detect ambiguity, and exploit the richness of expression available in English. And it can help everyone – not only teachers of English, but teachers of anything, for all teaching is ultimately a matter of getting to grips with meaning.
>
> (Crystal 2004: 24)

Further reading

English Teaching Practice and Critique, December 2005 and May 2006 issues.
  This double issue of this journal provides an international perspective on the debates about language and grammar. It reviews both the historical and the current debate and considers what is meant by knowledge about language and policy issues related to grammar language teaching.
CyberGrammar website (www.cybergrammar.co.uk).
  This is an electronic resource which supports the development of grammar subject knowledge for teaching English. It provides interactive tests to check developing understanding and, most importantly, it offers teaching implications for the various grammar terms, making a link between the metalanguage and the teaching of writing.
Crystal, D. (1995) *The Cambridge Encyclopedia of the English Language*, Cambridge: Cambridge University Press.
  This is a classic coffee-table book but it is also a fabulous resource for teaching knowledge about language and grammar, with authentic examples and an easy reading style.

Chapter 5

The politics of early literacy

Kathy Goouch

The vein of dichotomous discourse runs deep.
—Robin Alexander, *Children, Their World, Their Education*

In England we seem still to be struggling to understand how children learn and how they should be taught. In addition, political interventions have apparently served only to polarise the debates. Public concern about literacy levels is easily rallied and everyone claims to be an expert in how young children should be taught to read and to write. In this chapter only brief attention will initially be given to the political–academic divide, the history of early literacy education and the impact of the Rose Review (DfES 2006a). The ways in which babies and very young children encounter literacy at home and in communities seem to be fundamentally influencing factors in children's later success and this will be considered, as well as children's literacy experience before statutory school age.

In a world of fast media transmission and immediacy in response time, everybody claims expertise, particularly in relation to the education of young children which Rose has declared is not rocket science (DfES 2006a). Tabloid headlines proliferate and are exploited by politicians as the nation is told what is going wrong so that putting it right validates political action. In 2008 the *Daily Mail*'s headlines such as 'Thousands of five-year-olds can't write their own name after a year at school . . . despite £12bn spent on nursery education' were testimony to the way that public concern is drawn into debates about education, through the use of everyday language, and without depth of analysis or indication of the complexities surrounding the issue. At the most basic of levels, this headline and its article fail to comment on the fact that, across Europe and other parts of the world, children at 5 are not at school, not expected to be able to read and write formally, not tested, not constructed as failing, nor defined as a drain on the public purse. It is in England, not in the rest of the UK, that enormous pressure is placed on the results of young children's performance in academic subjects and where the stakes are set high for very young children as they learn to read and write. In England the high levels of accountability for teachers and schools to perform at preordained levels result in the exertion of considerable pressure on the youngest children to also demonstrate skill attainment, or at least momentary performance. It seems that this kind of pressure is not without cost. The Effective Provision of Pre-School Education (EPPE) study and the associated study, Researching Effective Pedagogy in the Early Years (REPEY), were both commissioned by the DfES and included reports of research indicating high levels of stress among young children in formal settings whose education was aimed at achieving short-term high-level goals. These studies' findings indicated that academic achievement in these cases is often short-lived and carries additional concerns:

> Highly structured, didactic teaching has also been found to result in young children showing significantly increased stress/anxiety behaviour (Burts *et al.* 1990). A longitudinal and rigorous study conducted by Schweinhart and Weikart (1997) showed very little difference in the academic performance of young children provided exclusively with direct instruction, but they did find significantly more emotional impairment and disturbance leading to greater need for special educational provision.
>
> (Siraj-Blatchford and Sylva 2004: 5)

More recently, government statistics have shown that there are a worrying number of children in state-maintained, mainstream educational provision with diagnosed mental health problems and, in 2007, £60 million was being invested to support schools to work with mental health practitioners and others to improve the emotional well-being of pupils (Balls 2007). Pressure to achieve high levels of attainment begins with the very youngest children as the incentives to intervene in early years education are reported as having high social and economic rewards (Siraj-Blatchford and Sylva 2004).

Although successive national governments in the UK consistently claim to provide schools with the freedom to teach, constraints exist in arrangements for national testing with the subsequent publication of tables of results, combined with stringent statutory curriculum requirements and inspection regimes. The resulting narrowing of school education provision impacts very heavily on young children's learning. While other countries' emphases reported by the Organisation for Economic Co-operation and Development (OECD) consist of a focus on values and learning processes, the UK government focus remains on skills attainment, narrowly defined in literacy as predominantly skills related to reading and writing, described in their own materials as 'a relentless focus on the basics' (DfEE 2001). The style of early years provision in England, in common with some other English-speaking countries, has been described as 'schoolification', which consists 'frequently [of] a prescribed ministerial curriculum, with detailing of goals and outcomes . . . [with an] assumption that the curriculum can be "delivered" by the individual teacher in a standardised way whatever the group or setting' (OECD 2006:141). This is compared with the 'Nordic tradition' where a broad national curriculum is informed by 'a culture of research about what children want to learn and how they learn' (OECD 2006:141). By the time that children in England reach the statutory school age, in the term after their fifth birthday, they are required to have achieved 19 goals in relation to Communication, Language and Literacy, five of which relate to knowledge of sounds in words and an additional five of which relate to knowledge of and use of print (DCSF 2008a). For some children this kind of early educational literacy beginning will result in a permanent state of 'catch-up'. Their peers in other European countries remain at kindergarten or in other play establishments and will undertake their formal educational experiences much later – at 7 in Finland, Sweden and Denmark and at 6 elsewhere in Europe. Beginnings matter and how young children are formally introduced to literacy in educational contexts such as nurseries or schools will affect children's self-esteem, their perceptions of literacy and their understandings of what literacy can do for them – its worth in their lives. It will also ultimately affect their performance. Significantly, in Finland, where children experience much less time in school than children in the UK, children far outperform their English counterparts in relation to reading competence as well as reading attitudes (Mullis *et al.* 2006, Alexander 2010).

One of the most contentious aspects of early literacy education, after decades of research, relates still to the teaching of phonics. Debates range over how much of children's time should be spent on phonics activities, what kind of phonics approach should be used – synthetic or analytic – and whether phonics instruction should be provided at all to young children. The government review of phonics teaching in school (Rose 2006) led to the now statutory requirement in the Early Years Foundation Stage for all children to be taken through a prescribed, systematic instructional process (DCSF 2008a). Those challenging this approach point out that the English language is too complex to be understood simply through a phonics-based approach and that it defies 'teachability' unless children are taught 'a highly simplified version of phonics, a gross caricature of the actual system' (Strauss and Altwerger 2007:300). Strauss and Altwerger further point to research evidence demonstrating that intensive phonics programmes do not lead to increased use of phonics cues during reading but do lead to increased miscues and loss of meaning (p. 315). As part of a study into the reading behaviours of boys in an inner-city secondary school, a group of teachers complained of the ways in which children were coming from schools which had recently adopted the new structured and intensive approach to phonics instruction. Their particular concern was that the children arrived 'blinded by phonics' to any sense of what they were reading (Goouch and Lambirth 2010). Although there is a very significant weight of research evidence against this kind of instruction and towards a more balanced, individual and needs-driven approach to phonics teaching and learning, governments in the UK seem reluctant to learn from research, instead favouring evidence from their own personal school experiences or from vocal pressure groups. It is interesting to note that commercial schemes to support phonics programmes have benefitted greatly from decisions in the UK and in the USA to advocate a 'phonics first and only' approach to the early teaching of reading in schools (Shannon 2007).

Babies and literacy learning

One of the very many problems that governments have overlooked in their rush to thrust phonics to the fore of early literacy education is that of early pre-school experience in families and communities. Young children arrive in nurseries and schools already with experience of language and literacy and frequently with knowledge and understanding of how to engage in literacy events. Literacy learning begins in babyhood as infants watch, listen and learn in the company of others. Evidence from the research work of psychologists and neuroscientists is throwing new light on children's learning from birth to school age, and also the significance of learning that occurs prenatally. It is now known that babies are born already attuned to the sounds and patterns of their mother's voice and that their attention is drawn towards these familiar sounds in the first days of their life (Karmiloff and Karmiloff-Smith 2001). This kind of research is important as it indicates that babies are born ready to learn from others, curious, and as listeners and watchers in the families, cultures and communities in which they find themselves. Although it has long been known that 'babies need books' (Butler 1995), modern research is forging new understandings for educators about how complex and fast-growing infant brains are and the kind of experiences that support rapid growth and development (Blakemore and Frith 2005). This is not about 'hothousing' babies and young children but instead about ensuring that they have the right environment, the right resources and the right support to ensure that development and learning takes place. It does require that we see babies and young children not as 'defective adults' but instead as constructors of their own world of understanding through the use of powerfully developing brains, the architecture of which takes shape before birth and continues through infancy – a time when many previously thought that babies were inert (Gopnik 2009, Gopnik *et al.* 1999, Greenfield 2000). Knowledge of research relating to babies' developing brains and forms of consciousness is highly relevant to our understanding of how children become literate. Babies learn about learning and about the world in the company of those occupying the cultural space into which they are born. It is at home, in social contexts, that babies and infants are developing a state of consciousness that incorporates their learning from others. The physical shape of their brain is being constructed to fit this new cultural learning – Greenfield tells us that, among the 'tangle of invisible cells, electrical impulses and molecules . . . a unique, subjective experience is generated in each of us – an experience of consciousness' and that it is with 100 billion neurons in place at birth that life begins; '[M]emories pile up and this accumulation of past scenarios, all stored within your brain, gives you a unique perspective from which to interpret the flood of sensations that bombard you every waking moment. Memories and mind are, therefore, inextricably linked' (Greenfield 2000:61).

Rather than the popular image of a baby's brain as a 'sponge', babies are self-constructing the complex web of connections that will help their sense of their worlds. Indeed, the essence of Paolo Freire's extensive and passionate work in relation to literacy learning is that 'reading the world always precedes reading the word' (Freire and Macedo 1987:35). The literacy world that children in the twenty-first century encounter to read has changed from previous generations. There is an increasing recognition now that multimodal texts are prominent in children's early lives and that image forms a large part of children's early cultural experience of reading (Marsh 2005, Bearne 2003, Kress 1997, Pahl 1999). Nevertheless, print remains a consistent feature in all children's early world experience. While books and stories may not dominate all children's early family experience, print of varying kinds surrounds us, particularly in the Western world. However, the ways that adults induct children into print worlds differs across Europe. In England it is common to see very young children's attention being frequently directed towards meaningful print at home and outside, for example in packaging, advertisements, shop signs – all manner of environmental print. In other countries this kind of adult–child incidental teachable moment in relation to print knowledge would not be seen as so important with young children, and the print interventions that we take for granted would not be considered to be of great significance or to take priority in their learning (David *et al.* 2000, Goouch 2007a).

As babies and infants are born into social environments, literacy encounters with significant family members are inevitable. The affective relationships created at this early stage have a lasting impact on later achievements and on the kinds of learners that children become (David *et al.* 2003). And so, those infants and young children experiencing conversation and everyday talk, as well as stories told and read, quickly learn the power of language and the impact it has on others. Language learning at home occurs in meaningful contexts; we learn from each other and children develop their 'voice' (Goouch 2010). However, children do not grow and learn in a neutral space; as Bakhtin claims, words are always half ours and half someone else's: '[T]he word does not exist in a neutral and impersonal language (it is not, after all, out of a dictionary that the speaker gets his words!)' (Bakhtin 1981:294). As children build vocabularies and collect language experience so their knowledge of story comes from the same culturally bound source, and the ways in which young children develop to translate their experiences into spoken and 'played' texts are part of a sophisticated process of evaluating and making meaning from everyday experiences of the world. Young children's early narratives, made explicit through talk, gesture, their use of the cultural litter of their homes (Pahl 1999) and play are the subject of rich research and help to explain the importance of children's developing cultural knowing. Rosen emphasises the importance of narrative in everyone's lives and makes the case for stories and meanings:

> We might be disposed to take stories much more seriously if we perceived them first and foremost as a product of the predisposition of the human mind to narratise experience and to transform it into findings which as social beings we may share and compare with those of others.
>
> (Rosen 1988:12)

In these early days, before any institutional or formal teaching, children are encountering a rich range of talk and print experiences and learning important literacy lessons, informally and in the company of significant people in their lives. The seminal texts of Wells (1986) and Brice Heath (1983) and the work of Bissex (1980) and Campbell (1999) all tell of the ways in which this informal learning contributes to the building blocks of literacy; they are the steps children take towards becoming literate in the familiar terms and tones of home. However, for some children in England (approximately 20 per cent), much of their waking lives is spent in day care settings with a different number, range and varying quality of literacy experiences offered to them (Powell 2010).

First tastes of literacy 'lessons'

In England children from birth to 3 can be cared for by private child minders, playgroups or at day nurseries and this translates into the highest amount of private day care in Europe (OECD 2006). Unlike other countries in Europe and elsewhere, practitioners working with young children in day care settings are not required to have a university education or training and in fact at least 30 per cent of those working with children in settings before school have no qualifications at all. In this sector it is reported that not only are there too few appropriately trained staff working with children but also there is an approximate rate of 40 per cent annual turnover of staff which has a resulting impact on the quality of care and education offered (OECD 2006), particularly as we know the importance of attachment to children's development. Research findings also indicate that staff working with young children in nurseries and day care have very limited opportunities for professional development of any kind, although training related to health and safety and food hygiene is routinely offered (Goouch and Powell 2010). Findings from this research (limited to those working with infants under 18 months) also report the limited understanding that some practitioners had of the need for talk between adult and child, or of stories to be read and told. This information about *who* is looking after children, their qualifications, professional knowledge and understanding and their practice is important in relation to very young children's early access to literacy events as well as support for language development, and it reflects the lack of status given to professional educational services for the youngest children in this country. It also conflicts with advice from research that suggests that language and literacy encounters from birth onwards impact heavily on children's later development and achievements.

In this country there exists a very tight control of curriculum detail, pedagogy and policy relating to the care and education of young children and in the hands of inexperienced and/or poorly trained and unsupported practitioners this invariably results in either the use of a 'scripted pedagogy' (Gibson and Patrick 2008), cascaded, interpreted and filtered down to individual practitioners through a range of sources, or in professionals who are able to 'ventriloquate' the contemporary national discourse in relation to literacy and, as Hall claims, 'to masquerade as

conforming' (Hall 2007:97). Either situation results in children being offered
what is often a very crude and narrow view of literacy, reduced in many instances
to delivery of a national curriculum in England focusing in the early years on
decontextualised phonic training. In nurseries and other day care settings, practitioners have few, if any, opportunities for professional dialogue or for policy to
be mediated in support of their practice unlike in, for example, Reggio Emilia
pre-school settings in northern Italy where pedagogic support and documentation are embedded in the institutional and local requirements (see, for example,
Edwards *et al.* 1998, Clark *et al.* 2005). Consequently, as outlined above, some
practitioners without qualifications, training or support and as individuals with their
own contexts of influence (Bryan 2003), including the popular media versions
of appropriate practice and their own lived experiences of school literacy, are left
to translate central and local government policy in the best way that they can. In
her discussion about literacy practices in school contexts, Hall asks for 'accounts
of how the teacher, as complex self, negotiates new meanings around the many
uniform representations of phonics practices in current official documents' (Hall
2007:98). This question raises challenges about professional identity and individual
teachers' abilities to manage the discourse and maintain professional integrity in
school contexts. In those educational institutions, nurseries and other day care settings, where practitioners themselves seem unaware of their professional status and
responsibilities, where they feel little sense of autonomy, power or ownership of
their daily activities, it seems unlikely that they will do anything other than deliver
the official 'science'. The introduction of the Literacy Strategy in England (DfEE
1998) had an enormous top-down effect on the literacy practices of those working with 3- and 4-year-old children, causing Whitehead to brand it memorably as
a 'literacy juggernaut' and to call for 24-hour literacy in nurseries rather than the
performance of a Literacy Hour (Whitehead 1999:52). More recent, and arguably
even more prescriptive, policies relating to the teaching of reading and phonics
are embedded in the Early Years Foundation Stage.

Other children, between the ages of birth and 4 are cared for at home or by
extended family members. In either case they will be encountering print and other
forms of literacy as part of their everyday lives, although, as Lambirth claims,
'learning to read occurs in a cultural and political context', and he points to 'differences in economic status and consequently differences in social class and power'
(Lambirth 2007:121). This is a complex argument but for the purpose of this
chapter it is significant as it indicates *difference*: that *differently* situated children
encounter *different* forms of print (and other forms of literacy), with *differing*
levels of pleasure and with *differing* degrees of adult support and intervention.
The emphasis is on 'difference' rather than pejorative judgements. The seminal
work of Brice Heath (1983) has provided salutary lessons about such difference,
identifying contrasts in culture between home and school and demonstrated how
different literacies may predominate, although only one literacy discourse retains
power and status.

Many children receive informal, affective reading lessons with significant adults and other family members long before starting school, in the form of shared texts that are written, told or read. It has been estimated that some fortunate children may have 'received' 6,000 stories before starting school (Barton 1994) and, thankfully, legislation cannot impinge on these reading lessons. These children may, in many ways, have a head start when they begin school literacy lessons, with their rapidly developing vocabulary, their knowledge of how stories work, patterns and tunes in stories, understanding of the relationship between illustration and print as well as some clear information about how print works drawn from reading and re-reading favourite tales – and the close cultural connection between these home literacy practices and school literacy. The children with this kind of early literacy experience (Goouch 2007b), which is sometimes determined by economic circumstances or class divisions, will mostly be able to withstand reductionist or narrowly focused reading tuition in school. It is likely, though, that even some of these children may become disaffected when 'literacy' becomes 'phonics instruction' in new school contexts. In contrast, however, those children who have not had the benefit of mediated early experiences in a range of literacy and reading practices before they start school in England in an era of prescriptive practice will find their first reading lessons to be the recall and chanting of sounds rather than the joy of tuning in to meaning in encounters with high-quality books and stories.

And so to school . . .

Such a very unequal literacy beginning, whether children spend the majority of their time in day care settings or at home with families and other community members, although visible and readily acknowledged by teaching professionals, is not readily acknowledged by policy at the start of children's formal schooling in England. Although, as already stated, statutory school begins for all children in England in the term after their fifth birthday, formal schooling most frequently occurs when children reach the age of 4 as they are then eligible to join a reception class in school. The reception class in school represents the final year of the Early Years Foundation Stage and immediately children are required to participate in a school culture of learning that assumes a 'one-size-fits-all' approach to the teaching of reading or a 'uni-dimensional approach to the teaching of a multi-dimensional process' (Wray 2006:128). Formal approaches to the teaching of reading are not universal. In England, the notion that learning to read is anything other than complex is clearly stated in policy documents proclaiming 'The Simple View of Reading' (Rose 2006). Much of the rhetoric relating to phonics is similar in New Zealand. There, the situation in practice is reported as varying from central policy discourse. It is interesting that, although New Zealand and England have much in common in relation to educational policy, the impact of centrally held views about literacy learning and the place of phonics is very different:

> [I]n contrast to the present situation in England, the position of phonics in New Zealand remains rather marginal [and has] melded with other ongoing

educational, social and political debates. These include debates over the extent to which teachers and schools can be held directly responsible for the academic progress of their students, and the ongoing controversy over the origins, nature and causes of educational inequality.

(Soler and Openshaw 2007:342)

Of course, in New Zealand, the policy relating to early years practice in general is vastly different from England. There, Te Whāriki (New Zealand Ministry of Education 1996), the early childhood curriculum representing the inspirational metaphor of interwoven principles and aims, was born not out of political or economic imperatives but in response to local initiatives and a political will to demonstrate 'shared knowledge and agreed understandings' (New Zealand Ministry of Education 1996:7).

National policy in England which is driving the 'phonics first and fast' approach through early years practice is particularly said to be in response to low-achieving children who, it is claimed, are from low-income families (Solity 2006). Some commentators on national policy are very clear where the focus of phonics instruction should be:

Those from socio-economically disadvantaged backgrounds need good, sharp, upfront teacher-driven interactive phonics right from the minute they start school. Middles-class kids who come with quite a lot of book knowledge do better when they are given self-directed activities at the beginning, and a more sharp, hard input of more complex phonics later.

(Ellis quoted in Scott 2010:2)

There are contrasting messages in the two countries. The message in New Zealand, where there is equal concern over standards of reading and literacy achievement, is that local policy and academic debate in relation to poverty and inequality have prevented wholescale national adoption of a simple phonics approach. In England, legislation and systems of inspection and public accountability measures ensure that policy is translated literally into practice. Also in England, those children known to be from economically disadvantaged backgrounds are assumed to be in need of the most reductionist and least affective drilling of phonic rules.

Any approach that adopts phonics as the core method to teach reading *is* seductive as it appears simple and efficient, with letters and sounds to be ticked off by teachers when they have been memorised and some teachers, particularly those who are less experienced or confident in teaching reading, will be enticed into such a system. However, reading is not simple and cannot be defined by sound knowledge alone. Learning sounds in our language is also a complex business (Goswami 2007, Goswami and Bryant 1990). Some countries' (including England's) preoccupation with efficiency and quick wins in reading contrasts with the efficacy of literacy learning and teaching in other nations and cultures where children at the same age, of 4 and 5, are not at school at all, nor are they receiving reading instruction but, instead, can be found playing at home or in kindergartens. The successful results of this kind of informal and slower start to formal learning are clearly evident in international statistics (as above, see Mullis *et al.* 2006, for PIRLS (Progress in International Reading Literacy Study)).

The contemporary language of politics and policy in relation to early literacy, for example 'quick wins' and 'efficiency', 'systematic approaches' and 'incremental learning' reflect the dominance of short-term goals and easily measurable outcomes. Frequently these are also the basis of popular headlines and sound bites which appear persuasive and seem to reflect popular views of common sense and quality in education. In classrooms, young children themselves unknowingly challenge such notions and make life slightly more complex, as their learning progress is often messy rather than systematically secure and where their learning happens over time rather than as a single event. Children's literacy learning occurs as they make connections with prior learning, often from outside of school contexts, and across subject barriers.

It has been claimed that, when children learn to read, the 'language of written texts is accessed via the eyes rather than the ears' (Rose Review, DfES, 2006a, appendix n. 62) but teachers and parents, rather than laboratory scientists or politicians, know that this over-simplistic explanation is not the case. Children become 'attuned' to texts from a very early age, as infants when they hear the sounds of nursery rhymes, mobile jingles, familiar TV programme music as well as traditional songs and stories; they learn the tunes and language of print and oral texts in affective contexts, which is why multi-sensory approaches are often successful and why the knowledge and experience of those adults around them needs to be secure. This may also explain why it is in other European countries such as Finland children who are in kindergarten or other home and play contexts until the age of 6 or 7 are in later years found to achieve highly in international comparative tables of attainment, as stated earlier (see PIRLS, as above).

Further evidence can be found in the work of neuroscience and now neuroimaging research activities from where it has been learned that the activity of the brain during reading takes place in more than one region of the brain, with connections being made across those regions as readers both decode *and* experience words (Price 2000), which makes the idea of children using only their eyes rather than ears to access print somewhat naïve.

Didactic approaches to teaching literacy to young children, while politically seductive, may not achieve long-term aims or provide affective experiences to intrinsically engage children in literacy activities. In England, where the school starting age is so very young, a rich mix of the kind of play, playfulness, multi-sensory and instructional approaches, combined with opportunities for children to delight in story and storying and frequently led by and managed by the children themselves, will serve to induct children into the pleasure of literacy without introducing them to the potential for failure or anxiety. Such activities will be close to the kind of experiences that other European children have and will connect with the research findings indicating that self-esteem, affective engagement and opportunities for volitional learning all contribute to children's success in learning to be literate and that rich and resourceful environments, conversation and the presence of significant adults are essential ingredients (Whitehead 2009, David *et al.* 2003, Rogoff 1990, Greenfield 2000).

In summary

A literacy curriculum for young children that overlooks or denies the social nature of learning, the pleasure to be gained from rich literacy experiences, the self-esteem of young literacy learners and the volitional nature of learning should be questioned. The adults, sometimes teachers, who work with young children need to be knowledgeable about how children develop and learn, their early literacy experiences, children's existing knowledge and understanding about how language works, the pleasure to be gained from literature and particularly high-quality children's literature – everybody needs to know books and stories. In addition, they need to be confident in their knowledge from research to help them to understand how to prioritise children, their intentions, their talk and their play as they learn the power of language in both school cultures and their own lived lives.

This chapter has ranged across many complex and well-researched areas, including the impact of politics and policy on early literacy, early brain development, the social nature of early literacy, the contrast between the 'schoolification' of early literacy activities in England and some other English-speaking countries and the emphasis placed on children living their childhood in other European contexts. There are essential lessons to learn from the ways that other countries work with children but the most important learning of course emanates from children themselves as they discover that literacy matters in their lives. Finding ways to help young children to uncover both the power and the delight of literature and literacy is everybody's responsibility, but especially the joyful task of knowledgeable adults whose job it is to support them in their journey.

Chapter 6

'Whatever happened to the Literacy Hour?'

Jo Westbrook and Hazel Bryan
with Karen Cooper, Vicky Hawking and
Sean O'Malley

Introduction

Whatever happened to the Literacy Hour?

Can you remember the thrill, when, as a child, you leaned over the castellated ramparts of a ruined castle and peered, butterflies in your stomach, far below? That sense of amazement when you realised that the stones you could touch, the ruins you could wander through, were signifiers of a social and political structure of past times? Or that first, delicious sense of excitement about the genesis of words and language when your teacher introduced you to Viking or Latin words that remain with us today? Built structures from bygone times within the physical landscape and language structures within our oral landscape provide us with a sense of place, a means by which we can locate ourselves today.

We found this a rich metaphor for reflecting upon the Literacy Hour and what has become of it. Just as one can travel around the country and pass castles in greater or lesser states of ruin and road signs that carry the names of towns and villages given by our ancestors, we wondered what *structures* the Literacy Hour introduced and are still to be found in classrooms today. We wondered also about the *words and terminology* that were introduced into teachers' lexicon at the time of the great Literacy Hour invasion and if they are still in use. In other words, what remains of the landscape that was the National Literacy Strategy Framework for Teaching English, Years 1–6 and 7, 8 and 9 (DfEE, 1998, 2001)?

This chapter encompasses an analysis of the vision of New Labour in 1997, the tensions around the development of a corpus of literacy subject knowledge and the implementation of the National Literacy Strategy for primary schools (NLS). The chapter moves to a consideration of the last ten years of literacy teaching and achievement. The third section of this chapter considers literacy teaching today, in terms of political shifts, global influences and multiple forms of show literacy. Throughout the chapter we have woven the reflections and insights of three teachers who have been practising over the last ten years. Their comments contextualise the political and theoretical perspectives explored below.

The contours of the literacy landscape twelve years ago, 1997–8

We first examined the NLS (DfEE, 1998) a year after it had been launched as Secretary of State for Education David Blunkett's highest-profile initiative and was presented as the vehicle through which reform in standards in literacy would be realised, albeit reshaped from primary mathematics pedagogy taught in the Pacific Rim countries. The 'seamless join' (Ball, 1999) between the previous Conservative education policies and New Labour was particularly evident in relation to literacy policy.

The primary perspective

From a primary perspective, the implementation through the training materials and development days was dramatic. In the early days of NLS implementation, primary teachers were regarded as lacking the necessary subject knowledge and pedagogic knowledge to raise standards. Teachers reported feeling very deskilled and tense about their practice, unsure of what was 'allowed'. In this sense, the NLS had at that time a reified epistemology; the nature of knowledge was presented as residing outside of primary teachers and the training materials were designed to 'give' teachers sufficient knowledge to practise. The NLS represented a tightly defined corpus of subject knowledge within the framework of objectives and an assembly of elements of literacy which were compiled to represent the specific subject knowledge that teachers should teach in the classroom.

The notion of boundaries being drawn around literacy is an exercise in power struggles, in terms of those whose agenda finally becomes represented or partly represented in policy and those whose views are silenced or overlooked; as we are reminded, the whole business of the teaching of English is a 'deeply political act' (Raban-Bisby, 1995). The NLS can be seen, retrospectively, to be an attempt to fix in time a particular definition of primary literacy subject knowledge. Fraught with tensions, this was, arguably, a 'realignment of priorities to utilitarianism' (Hogan, 2000: 373). The style of writing of the policy texts was authoritative and 'readerly' (Barthes, 1976), leaving little room for teachers' personal interpretations. Policy texts positioned the primary teacher arguably as the transmitter of literacy policy.

Additionally, policy was driven through by teams of literacy consultants working to the director of training for the NLS. The training materials were conceived as a total approach to literacy, not as an add-on to teachers' current practice. The notion of a palimpsest is useful to us here. A word of Greek origin, a palimpsest is a slate or parchment which can be rubbed clean and written on again. It can usefully be applied metaphorically to teachers during educational reform (Smyth and Shacklock, 1998: 4) and is a particularly helpful way of understanding how primary teachers were treated during the early days of the NLS training programmes. Teachers were regarded as blank slates, to be re-inscribed with an approach to literacy teaching.

Headteacher and literacy coordinator responses to the implementation of the NLS varied:

> I think the whole concept of bringing in the Strategy is what teachers have been crying out for, for years! We've all been groping in the dark! Everyone's been educated by it. Even the teachers. Most of us had never been taught English formally, just bits of it. It's given them a lot of confidence. Those who weren't too sure how to approach literacy actually find it being so prescriptive helps them.
>
> (Bryan, 2003: 204)

This is in contrast to another headteacher who felt that the NLS had 'taken away my professionalism, my creativity, my autonomy. It's far too strait-jacketed. We went to the training days and you could hear the panic in people's voices' (Bryan, 2003: 205). What seems to have emerged from data generated in 2003 is that, rather than falling into the category of the 'listening practitioner' in a 'listening school' (Gunter, 1997), or a 'vocal teacher' in a 'vocal school' (Gunter, 1997), it can been seen that headteachers and literacy coordinators presented degrees of listening and vocalisation, depending on the issue. The 'starting gun' effect of new policy reform (Gorard *et al.*, 2000) was clearly articulated by teachers feeling panicked, deskilled and wondering what they were allowed to do.

However, geographically located and psychologically oriented towards their own schools, headteachers did not present as palimpsests but, rather, emerged as filters through which NLS messages were considered. Literacy reform did not simply wash over teaching staff in cascade training sessions; rather, headteachers filtered NLS messages, and this prismatic effect distributed different hues and density to each school. While there was a concerted effort to control teachers' purposes and practice in literacy, they were not completely re-inscribed; during this period of rapid restructuring of teachers' work, the role of the primary headteacher emerged as ever more complex. The dynamic interplay between policy texts, policy drivers and localised school practice characterises this period in primary literacy reform as critical in changing teachers' perceptions of ownership of the curriculum and teachers' expectations of continuing professional development or 'training'.

The secondary perspective

For a secondary perspective on the NLS, in our chapter of 1999, we put together two composite pictures drawn from research to illustrate what was happening some three years *prior* to the roll-out of the NLS in secondary schools in 2001 (Westbrook *et al.*, 1998). The first reconstruction focused on a fictional struggling reader, Paul, who was put in an ability-set class (levels 3–4), withdrawn on a daily basis to work on SuccessMaker software and included in a literacy project in Year 8. There was little independent reading done in English or elsewhere because of pressure to get through the curriculum. In other subjects Paul was given little to read and write in any meaningful way with worksheets used ubiquitously and little oral work. His teachers considered the English Department to be responsible for teaching him English. There was no whole-school coherent effort to improve literacy skills for SEN (special educational needs) students, no connection made between subjects nor time for Paul to reflect on his learning and he ended up getting a level 4 in the Key Stage 3 SATs (Standard Assessment Tasks), and then statistically destined to achieve Ds and Es at GCSE (General Certificate of Secondary Education).

We also envisaged a more idealistic 'multidimensional view of literacy across the curriculum' in secondary schools, drawing on innovative practice we identified in tandem with less inspiring practice. In the 'William Shakespeare Comprehensive School' the focus was on whole-school approaches to literacy, embracing school, community, family and students with a school-based working party drawing together localised good practice. The timetable was made more flexible, with literacy support assistants assigned to work in one curriculum area for a term and more English timetabled, INSET (in-service education training) days on talking about texts and oral language skills, close tracking of individual pupils matched with observations and student work, more books, regular whole-school slots for silent reading, class libraries and the library filled with books as the hub of the school.

There were, therefore, disparities in teachers' practices, a patchwork of different interventions to support those 30 per cent of students who were unable to access the secondary curriculum. Since then, there has been 12 years of the primary and then secondary NLS in state schools in England designed to create greater parity and higher results. The roll-out of the NLS in secondary schools was carried out in just the same way as at the primary level.

Although the NLS was not statutory, Secretary of State Blunkett stated that the content was 'non-negotiable' (DfEE, 1997: 20). This was the language of confident government and, newly elected on a tide of overwhelming support, the Secretary of State was confident in his vision and his method of achieving that vision. The question we are asking is, was he successful?

The remains of the day: whatever happened to the Literacy Hour?

Sean, one of our teachers in this study, working across Key Stages 3 and 4, reflected:

> In my garage, there are two cheap DIY store shelving units full of yellow and white Literacy Strategy ring binders, plastic packs, shrink wrapped documents, meetings records and failed attempts to apply recommendations. I look at them gathering dust. All those good intentions and all that work from some central engine – even distribution rules changed and were revised quicker than I could keep up. It reminds me of the Lord Of The Rings films where all those orcs are reproduced in that brown, intense, driven furnace.

We tried to keep up. It tried to keep up with itself as it revisited material repeatedly. It has had a profound effect on the 'feel' of English delivery. Eight of eleven staff qualified in its shade. They know skills teaching, objective-led lesson design, writing genres, the role of the model extract, grading which works backwards from assessment objectives and level descriptors.

I've incorporated a lot of this in my teaching, too. There are good things in the documentation. But I don't really look at them. The progression maps were the best for me – now re-worked yet again online. The substrands and Assessment Focuses are worth laying against each other – it does make you think about what students learn and what equals progress. The objective banks from early on (Speaking & Listening, spelling, reading, etc) were much more useful than I gave them credit for and I often think I should disinter them from the garage. Guided reading was good – but there was nothing new in it, as I remember and I struggled to implement it in any major way.

Karen, another teacher in our study, has worked across Key Stages 1 and 2 over the last ten years. She commented:

When the Literacy Strategy was first introduced I was teaching in Reception and I didn't ever experience any of the pressure. But then our Head didn't make us slavishly use the Literacy Hour anyway, so I didn't feel pressure from the NLS even in Year 1 or in my Key Stage 2 teaching. I know the NLS folders are somewhere in the school, but we didn't really follow it to the letter. So now I do Guided Reading with groups where we explore meaning and mood and inference and so on – the children decide the book with me. We do interactive whole-class work – I try to keep it snappy – but the big thing for me is to help the children with their creative writing. They work independently too. So over the course of a week I will spend time on grammar, on spelling and so on, but the most important thing is to enrich their vocabulary.

Listening to Sean and Karen made us realise that much *has* become embedded, but it has been moulded into the localised context – right from the start. Sean saw how many of his teachers were imbued with the language of the NLS through their training but how some of the suggested structures were never used or were later discarded in their polythene-wrapped state, such as guided reading. Karen also talked about 'guided' reading and writing, even though her headteacher and colleagues hadn't embraced the suggested model of the Literacy Hour. She talked about 'whole-class' activity and how it needed to be 'snappy', which again carries echoes of the 'fast pace' of the Literacy Hour, and 'independent' work: 'frequent, fast-paced revision of insecure skills' (DfEE, 2001: 16–17). Significantly, Karen felt no pressure, no gravitational pull, from the work teachers were undertaking at Key Stage 1 or 2, in terms of the work she undertook in Reception.

As reflected in the two teachers' voices above, the literacy landscape in England altered dramatically over recent years, with even some of the 'non-negotiable content' changing, the government responding to shifts in political opinion and schools, headteachers and teachers, accepting some directives while resisting others so that even in 2003 there was 'considerable disparity across teachers in subject knowledge, pedagogical skill and the understanding of NLS and NNS [National Numeracy Strategy]' (Earl *et al.*, 2003: 8). So how successful has the NLS been in raising standards in literacy as measured by the targets set by government itself?

The contours of the literacy landscape ten years on

> There is troubling evidence that, in England (United Kingdom), '1.7 million people (5% of those aged 16 to 65) perform below the level expected of seven-year-olds on the National Curriculum test, and 5.1 million perform below the level expected of eleven-year-olds.
>
> (UNESCO, 2009: 96)

> One in six people in the UK struggle with literacy. This means their literacy is below the level expected of an eleven-year-old.
>
> (Jama and Dugdale, 2010: 2)

By 2008, exactly ten years after the primary Literacy Hour had been introduced, it was obvious that 'despite initial success, overall achievement rose only slightly over subsequent years, and many children failed to progress at all' (Slavin *et al.*, 2009: 3). It is worth looking at the pattern of attainment from *before* the NLS in 1995 to grasp the whole picture. There was a larger increase in the numbers of students gaining levels 4 and 5 from 1995 to 1998 *before* the NLS in primary schools than there was once it started (Earl *et al.*, 2003). In this time period from 1995 to 1998 there was an increase of 16 per cent of students gaining a level 4 or above in English so that by 1999 71 per cent of children were at level 4. From 1999 to 2008 there was certainly a rise in levels of achievement, from 71 per cent to 81 per cent of pupils gaining level 4. This was not as impressive as the 16 per cent leap as prior to the implementation of the NLS.

This pattern was repeated at Key Stage 3 with a big leap of 9 per cent in 1995 to 1999 in the numbers gaining level 5 or above from 55 per cent to 64 per cent prior to the implementation of the NLS in secondary schools. There was a distinct rise of 10 per cent in the numbers who gained level 5 or above from 2001 to 2005 and again in 2007 when it rose to the highest peak of 74 per cent. Results plateaued at 74 per cent but dropped to 73 per cent in 2008, the last year of the Key Stage 3 National Curriculum Test results (Ofsted, 2009: 9). An overall rise, then, of 9 per cent can be directly attributed to the NLS – but not any more than the attainment prior to the NLS. And with the government target of 85 per cent of students gaining level 5 or above from 2006 onwards, the picture looks distinctly mixed.

This begs the question – was there enough good practice at a local level, stemming from the first National Curriculum in English in 1989 ('the Cox Report', DfES, 1989) and increased professionalism of teaching, that resulted in a steady rise in attainment without the millions of pounds spent on the NLS that revising and repackaged strategies – and would this rise have continued it? Or did the political focus on education and literacy in particular create enough of a Hawthorne effect to raise standards without any specific intervention? That is, was it the mere fact that literacy was under the microscope, with attention paid to practice, that caused an increase in standards?

Although results have risen overall from 1997, and gaps between schools from different socio-economic groups have lessened, students from Black and Minority Ethnic groups and white working-class boys continue to under-attain in comparison with White and Asian groups. This is despite strategies aimed directly at these groups such as the Black Pupils' Achievement Programme and Aiming High (DfES, 2004b). Literacy is intertwined with issues around culture, gender, class and race in a more complex relationship than can be reflected in a neatly packaged set of training materials.

The current landscape, 2010

So if actual levels of literacy have not risen, or been sustained to the level government have set, has English teaching improved because of the new structures in place over the last ten years, the guidelines, the training, the materials, even while some were rejected from the outset, and others tried out, accepted? Sean indicated the complexity surrounding the question:

> It's not a simple answer. Generally speaking, before the Strategy, we were complacent, inventive, inspirational, differentiating, obsessed by coursework, gave broad comments in assessment, mixed ability, sat in groups, whole text driven and we had a social theory to back our judgements. The change is enormous, and yet . . . What I feel most bothered about is the independence zone – thinking for oneself, synthesising, setting own goals, knowing how to research and reflect – it's not here now though I know we were complacent about it in the past. The latest strategy has Personal, Learning and Thinking Skills (PLTS) in its rhetoric – but not foregrounded as much as it likes to think. So is it better? No, but in ways KS3 [Key Stage 3] can be. But KS4 and KS5 – ridiculous. Still, I used to think 100% coursework was wonderful – I'm precisely why all the changes came. There are good things about the last ten years – it tried to bring a science to what we do and good practice but I don't look there for inspiration.

The new landscape altered the shape of English teaching for good, as Sean says, bringing a 'science' to teaching through the 'research-based' pedagogic structure and the numerous sets of criteria by which to assess learners. This is in contrast to the looser, more professionally independent and creative approaches pre-NLS that had been seen perhaps as too eclectic to warrant being taken seriously by a government intent on raising standards. One important point made by Sean is his confident assertion that English teaching had been underpinned by a 'social theory' rather than political aspirations, one based on an egalitarian view of English teaching, even its emancipatory possibilities. This view was manifested in the use of mixed ability classes, group work and 100 per cent coursework options at GCSE with the teacher choosing whole texts that reflected their class's cultural backgrounds and interests.

Another teacher in the study, Vicky, a Key Stage 3 coordinator, elaborated on what constitutes the 'science' of English teaching – the Assessment Focuses from Assessing Pupils' Progress in English (APP) (DCSF, 2008a):

> The biggest impact in the last couple of years has been the introduction of APP. This has taken a while to embed, and there are possibly too many Assessment Focuses in both Reading and Writing, but it has given far greater clarity and thought to precisely what to focus on in teaching literacy. The danger is that the 'English' engagement is lost if one is drumming in Writing AF5 and 6, but I think it is hugely empowering for the students.

However, Vicky also pointed out the differences between the last ten years and the current landscape in terms of teachers' workload and conditions – painting a far from inspiring portrait:

> The previous ten years was much more hard going – slogging through far more prescriptive National Curriculum guidelines [than now] in what had to be covered, and the literacy hour expectation.

Despite the prescription, as we have seen, literacy results did not continue to improve. From 2006 onwards re-elected New Labour had to have another push at raising standards to meet their own targets (DfES, 2006b). The result is a cautious step towards giving schools and teachers greater professional freedom, heeding the advice given in the evaluation of the NLS: 'The challenge now is finding ways to embed accountability and capacity building in the culture of schools' (Earl *et al.*, 2003: 6). The superstructures of the Primary and Secondary National Strategies are being dismantled and handed over to Local Authorities to deliver in a localised form. The four-part lesson plan has been quietly rescinded in favour of a range of pedagogies and lesson structures (DCSF, 2008).

The new 2007 curriculum insists that whole texts are read, multimodal literacy is centralised and the very 1980s notion of writing for a real audience in different forms is back in favour. School-wide, cross-curricular planning and teaching has suddenly become the norm – with English taught together with the humanities in Year 7 or science and maths conjoined for a day. This creativity appears to replace basic 'literacy' with teaching children to read and write through a new focus on topic or theme such as the First World War, or the civil rights movement in the US. Literacy demands became a means to an end rather than being an end in themselves. This may raise achievement, as some researchers suggest that direct instruction, of vocabulary, and an overemphasis on form rarely lead to depth of learning and may reduce engagement (Gardner, 2004; Franzak, 2006; Wittner and Renkl, 2008).

From a primary perspective, Karen commented that the cross-curricular approach her school adopts

> is a great learning opportunity. But it's reductive if it's ruled by the clock. It's daft to focus on children's learning and then have your day ruled by the clock. There's so much to get through . . .. I sometimes think 'I know you've done this and I thought you'd got it' but I have to remind myself that there are social and economic factors that surround the children's learning . . . they don't have it enriched at home, there are so many difficult concepts for them to grasp, and in spite of all of that I have to keep to the clock. But I do think topic-based work makes it more alive, more interesting. It makes it more meaningful.

The new Framework (DCSF, 2008b), however, sits awkwardly amidst these more creative approaches to literacy, interrupting what seems a sensible relationship between the curriculum and the Assessment Focuses.

Literacy across the curriculum sits awkwardly here, also needing recasting. The case studies of leading-edge schools outlined in Barton (2009) are remarkable for their innovative approaches to literacy across the curriculum such as getting students to design and teach literacy starters or having withdrawal groups work through small courses before school. These are localised strategies, small-scale in nature.

The current landscape is, somewhat ironically, beginning to partly resemble that observed in 1999, with home-grown literacy activities taught in cross-curricular teams, a variety of pedagogic approaches and more systematic support for less able students but with some key differences: with the 'slippage' (DfES, 2006b: 15) in meeting government targets, the pressure to get students through two levels rather than the original one level of attainment in each Key Stage is greater than ever. The onus, however, is now on identifying individual students' progression and interventions to improve their grade. This is what has embedded more than any other structure or strategy, as Vicky points out:

> The pressure to move the students I teach on two levels from KS2–3 is immense – from government to county to school level. However, I have been able to look with clarity at each individual I teach, and decide how to help them move forward and progress. There is a greater sense of urgency and responsibility on the teacher to provide evidence of progress in the students' books, rather than leaving it to the SATs exam.

Sean describes a similarly pressured landscape dominated by the need to show evidence of students' progression:

> The moral imperative of it all drives us on and we can't stop to look objectively at things. At KS3 we are awash with APP checklists and trying to moderate without time. Mind you, I'm so opposed to SATs that I'm prepared to take this new machinery on. The pressure on students reaching baselines and making observable steps towards and beyond them has become the dominant discourse. It's all SLT [Senior Team] think about and it just sharpens the pain students, parents and staff feel about transition from Year 6 to 7 where everything slips its moorings – the opposite of what is intended.

There are further differences. The army of teaching assistants has grown but they may be more useful at primary school in group work or one-to-one tutoring context rather than at secondary with its more specialist literacy demands, and their effectiveness as unqualified paraprofessionals in helping the least-able students has been critiqued (Slavin, *et al.*, 2009). Certainly Karen reported that her teaching assistant was intrinsic to how she conceptualised learning and teaching in her classroom: 'We [the teaching assistant and Karen] spend time every day with groups on Guided Reading or Writing'. Libraries are filled with computers and books but are rarely the hub of the school, with few regular visits made apart from being used for withdrawal groups (Westbrook, 2007). And there is a *Back to the Future* feel to the incorporation of Functional English skills for 2010–11, reminding us of Prime Minister John Major's clarion call to teach 'the basics' from 1993.

Will this reconstruction of the literacy landscape be enough to inspire our English teachers, Sean, Vicky and Karen?

Sean categorically stated that he did not find 'inspiration' in the initiatives of the last ten years, looking elsewhere for that, for example in courses run by professional associations of individuals '*delightfully*' independent from government advisors, as Vicky said.

She voiced what all the teachers seemed to feel about the flattening out of the English literacy landscape:

> There is still not enough thought given to fun, joy and love in teaching. Perhaps these qualities cannot be discussed by policy makers – they immediately sound naff perhaps! However I find most English teachers are extremely conscientious and they get worn down trying to cover so many areas asked of them. Students need to create relationships and trust alongside seeing an enthusiasm for a text, and for them, from the teacher. If teachers are too stressed in working towards an ephemeral approval from an Ofsted rating they will lose that sense of life and fun. It has to be explicitly valued somewhere?

A further irony: Ofsted's report from 2009, *English at the Crossroads*, itself reflects a bewilderment about what has become of English, acknowledging the plateau in achievement and continued weaknesses in wider reading and independent learning and thinking (Ofsted, 2009: 5). The report queries quite what shape English will take in the future.

Alternative literacy landscapes

Just literacy is never enough (Cox, 1998). Literacy is far more than a simplistic, linear process measured in a series of calibrated steps. Rather, it is a uniquely human activity that shapes us as powerfully as our DNA.

Social constructivism views the child as mediating with the world and culture through language with the adult or more capable peer supporting that upward development, always just ahead of the child's developmental level (Vygotsky, 1986). As such, speech and literacy is socially situated, taking place through verbal and written interactions in both formal and informal learning contexts (Brice Heath, 1983; Street, 1999; Barton *et al.*, 2000). These 'textual practices' include parent–child, family, community, peer and schooled literacy practices, and the newer virtual communities formed by technology (Andrews, 2003). The literate person reflects and is shaped by social and cultural backgrounds that impact on individual interests, identity and gendered ways of behaving. Literacy is also thereby an intra-personal process (Millard, 1997; Moss, 2007).

Critical literacy places particular demands upon the experienced reader. It requires the reader to position 'texts' in such a way as to enable a multiple reading of a text. F. R. Leavis (1948) located texts in terms of the canon and the reader was thus positioned in relation to the canon. Knowledge existed outside of the reader, and the reader became knowledgeable through demonstrating a sophisticated understanding of received knowledge. In England, this began to alter when James Britton (1970) challenged this perspective and located the reader at the heart of engagement with text and so was more attuned to a social constructivist world view as outlined above. The life experiences of readers became valid in terms of responses to texts, and diverse language use began to be celebrated in contrast to a slavish adherence to Standard English. From a critical literacy perspective, the reader is positioned as knowledgeable, as relevant and as a powerful language user. In this way, the reader is given permission to respond to texts from a politically critical, oppositional perspective. In this way, texts have no one 'meaning' but can be interpreted according to the life experiences of the reader. Freirean critical literacy deconstructs texts from a social justice perspective. It enables the reader to realise that language is never neutral and that texts are constructed in such a way as to coerce, oppress and manipulate certain groups in given societies.

Multimodal literacy can be described as sets of discourses created through a combination of text, image and sound of computer games, the World Wide Web and moving images of film, TV and DVDs (Ong, 1982; Meek, 1988). Reading becomes non-linear, with decoding/deconstruction of text, image, sound and colour to construct meaning. Reading skills are *transferable* across media, so that inference and following a plot through television or listening to stories from a young age enhances the reading of print narratives (Kendeou *et al.*, 2008).

These richer, interrelated interpretations of literacy can be discerned in many of the teachers' comments on these pages but have yet to make real inroads politically although lighter shades of them are discernible in the National Curriculum.

While the UK has been trying to raise standards of literacy according to a given template, developing countries see child and adult literacy levels as impacting on not only the quality of life but also on life itself. In this context the precarious nature of learning to read can be understood most starkly.

The literacy landscape in developing countries

Literacy provides a solid foundation for poverty reduction and sustainable development in pursuit of a democratic and stable society. It provides a basis for the respect for human rights, the universalization of basic education, conflict resolution, nutritional sufficiency, and for an overall improved quality of life . . . Literacy is, indeed, a first major step to most other forms of learning.

(UNESCO, 2006)

There has been much progress since 2000 at the Dakar World Education Forum when the international community pledged to get universal, free primary school education for all children by 2015. In developing countries, many more children are enrolled in school and there is a 10 per cent increase in adult literacy. However, 'literacy remains among the most neglected of all education goals, with about 759 million adults lacking literacy skills today. Two-thirds are women' (UNESCO, 2010: 1). Seventy-two million children never enrol in school, and in sub-Saharan Africa 54 per cent of those not enrolled are girls – some 12 million. There is a strong link between literacy and basic hygiene provided at schools: with many adolescents remaining in primary schools because of delayed enrolment and repetition of grades, girls in particular may only attend school in the regular daily and weekly pattern required to achieve literacy if the latrines are clean, private and there is water available.

Even going to school does not guarantee functional levels of literacy: children who do not attain certain levels of reading fluency in the early grades will lapse into illiteracy if they then drop out of school (Chabbott, 2006). Half of all dropouts do leave after grade 1, having failed to pick up basic reading skills – and four years of education is needed to achieve basic literacy (UNESCO, 2009: 9). Good reading programmes, with sufficient books for children to access and learn to read from, however, cost more than the current level of resource and involve better teacher preparation and one-to-one reading practice with an adult. To compound the issue, 221 million children learn through to read in a language at school that is not their mother tongue, nor is it familiar to them (UNESCO, 2009: 10) – a main cause of drop-out. There are few reading materials in local languages (LL) available, nor is LL visible in the environmental print. Little is understood or taught about how to teach in multilingual, multiliterate classrooms of sometimes up to 150 children in teacher training colleges, with different orthographies requiring different teaching methods (Trudell and Schroeder, 2007; Trudell, 2009). Children are further disadvantaged if they progress past the early years when, for example, in Tanzania English becomes the language of interaction (LOI) from secondary school upwards. The global economic downturn and the rise in food prices are resulting in cuts in overseas aid from developed countries; this will mean that developing countries will find it harder to educate and feed their population.

Despite this reality, UNESCO (United Nations Educational, Scientific and Cultural Organization) continues to advocate for Education for All (EFA) through a recognition of literacy as more than just a set of skills but as a set of activities embedded in a variety of contexts:

> [T]he success towards Literacy for All requires comprehensive yet context-specific and flexible actions rooted in countries and communities, with the involvement of every corner of society – governments, communities, NGOs, schools, the private sector, media – in literacy actions linked to diverse spheres of social, cultural and economic activities.
>
> (UNESCO's (2001: 25) EFA under its 'Major Programme I: Education')

With government-run schools often unable to educate the marginalised such as girls who cannot walk long distances to school, disabled children who need specialist teachers, children who are withdrawn from school to work or move with their cattle, non-governmental organisations (NGOs) or larger donors step in with literacy interventions that help to get children back into formal schooling. There are many of these affecting some 3.5 million children (UNESCO, 2009) such as Pratham in India, BreakThrough to Literacy in Uganda, School for Life in Ghana, Reading Tents in Uganda and Kenya. One interesting example took place in Malindi in Kenya, whereby teachers taught three tightly designed reading lessons three times a week over a year to grade 1 and 2 students, focusing on phonological awareness, phonics, fluency, vocabulary and comprehension in English and Kiswahili in line with the Kenyan curriculum and the US National Reading Panel 5 pillars of reading instruction, an example of Western reading strategies influencing teaching and research in developing countries. Great improvements were noted in both the experimental *and* control schools; both sets of schools had received reports on what needed improving and news of the training sessions had leaked rather helpfully to the control schools – who promptly put them, or a version of them, into action (Crouch *et al.*, 2009). This is an example of schools self-improving in response to external pressure and specific accessible training that meets their needs. Such complementary schooling serves a purpose and shows what can be achieved with the right pedagogy, resources and teacher education.

However, deciding which intervention 'works' effectively enough to invest in scaling up such initiatives across the country is more than challenging for any government, let alone those with scarcer resources than the UK. Uganda launched a child-centred, thematic, integrated primary curriculum in 2005 with the major local language to be the LOI for the first three years and all teachers trained in the new approaches – including a 'Literacy Hour' three times a week with a focus on reading and writing. So that's what happened to the Literacy Hour! Results are mixed. While there is apparent greater student participation and group work (Altinyelken, 2010), the in-service training was too rushed, some schools still do not have copies of the curriculum and the whole approach depended on the will of the headteacher: 'a school looks like its headteacher', as a local language specialist teacher educator pointed out.

Conclusion

This chapter opened by asking what structures and language features have been left by the National Literacy Strategy. From an analysis of New Labour's vision for a tightly defined corpus of subject knowledge, and listening to the three teachers in this study, we find that there has been an attempt to reconstruct the literacy curriculum and, therefore, reconstruct teachers' work. We have found that at the point at which policy and schools meet, headteachers have played a front-line role, not in an oppositional sense but in filtering messages and contextualizing practice – in the UK and in developing countries. Those messages that have filtered through have in turn been adapted by teachers in situ. It is questionable whether models of practice, like fine wine, travel well – they are often superficial layers that surround teachers' deep-seated beliefs and values (Goouch and Bryan, 2006).

So legislating for literacy by scaling up local initiatives doesn't always work and there is no magic formula to achieving literacy. Major global initiatives such as the 2003–12 United Nations Literacy Decade focus the world's attention on literacy issues but remain reliant on a complex relationship of donors, countries, local communities and NGOs working together, with small amounts of funds. The NLS in the UK was backed by vast amounts of money, resources, training implemented in classes of less than 30 – and still there is a 'long tail of underachievement' at Key Stage 3 (Brooks *et al.*, 1996: 10), often the marginalised. In the attempt the government dug up the previous literacy landscape – or rather, got the teachers, the 'workers' in Sean's addendum below, to dig up the landscape by decree, using the allegory of the owners of a country home

> creating vistas to be picturesque at enormous cost – Capability Brown, Repton?? Lots of workers digging to the caprice of owners and their half-understood ideas from abroad.

Such vistas will remain, as successive governments will continue to legislate for literacy, undoing the past and restructuring in perhaps courageous attempts to make all children fully literate. We therefore have to live with the folly of the fast-paced Literacy Hour and the ha-has of extracts while some legislation has rotted down well, such as modelling and formative assessment. Old perennials of just enjoying reading good books and writing powerful poetry, such as clematis and roses, will always bloom each year despite the Very Hungry Caterpillar and occasional Sick Rose of tests and tables. As intellectual labourers (Giroux, 1988) teachers have to both toil and theorise, manage children and idealise, and the teaching of 'literacy' acts as a paradigm for this.

Further reading

Alexander, R., Armstrong, M., Flutter, J., Hargreaves, L. Harrison, D., Harlen, W., Hartley-Brewer, E., Kershner, R., Macbeath, J., Mayall, B., Northen, S., Pugh, G., Richards, C. and Utting, D. (eds) (2010) *Children, Their World, Their Education*, Oxon: Routledge.

This text is the final report of the Cambridge Primary Review. The report explores in detail primary education policy, children's learning, curriculum aims and pedagogy including assessment and standards. As such, a consideration of 'literacy' is located deeply within these broader contextual issues. This text is essential reading for primary practitioners.

Cremin, T., Bearne, E., Goodwin, P. and Mottram, M. (2008) 'Primary teachers as readers', *English in Education*, 42(1): 1–16.

A beautifully crafted journal article that reminds primary teachers of the importance of reading children's books themselves, and having a wide understanding of genre and creative use of texts.

Earl, L., Watson, N., Levin, B., Fullan, M. and Torrance, N. (2003) *Watching and Learning 3: Final Report of the External Evaluation of England's National Literacy and Numeracy Strategies*, Toronto: University of Toronto.

The final report is fascinating for its finely tuned and even-handed analysis of the continued implementation of the NLS (and NNS) in primary schools, with interesting comparisons made with similar large-scale reforms internationally. Many of their comments made in the 'challenging' section of the report will be familiar to teachers.

Trudell, B. (2009) 'Local language literacy and sustainable development in Africa', *International Journal of Educational Development*, 29(1): 73–9.

This paper gives a useful introduction and overview to issues around development and literacy, expanding on the different forms of literacy including critical and situated literacy and the politics involved for governments and communities in deciding which language should be used to teach early reading in, and adult literacy.

Chapter 7

Access, choice and time
A guide to wider reading in schools

Jo Westbrook

Introduction

Reading gives access to other people's thoughts, constructions and experience of the world so that readers can move, even momentarily, away from their own island state to the wider continent of different minds. Conversely, reading also situates individuals within their own culture, recording its history and heritage to re-interpret and add to. At a localised level reading is a form of rapid communication, a sharing of information about events, games, ceremonies, births, deaths. Reading is also a form of play through symbol-making and manipulation, of entertainment, of pleasure, of satisfaction, particularly through story. Narrative is an inherently human activity, a primary act of mind and the way we organise and make sense of our experience (Hardy, 1977). Readers are recipients of new words, learned highly efficiently through reading, which provides a more nuanced, subtle understanding of the world. Reading facilitates the accrual of vast amounts of knowledge, facts, theories and concepts – far more than individuals acting independently could gather from daily interaction with the world and through conversation. In fact, reading makes the reader a great deal smarter (Cunningham and Stanovich, 2001).

This chapter queries why it is, then, that students in England are still not reading a variety of texts in a sustained way at school when all the evidence points to the cumulative benefits of reading. It takes a theoretical view of the reading process and relates this directly to practice, exploring five key questions around reading:

◻   How do children learn to read and read for meaning?
◻   Why do some children fail to learn to read for meaning?
◻   Why do some children succeed in reading?
◻   What kind of reading is good for children?

And taking up most of the chapter:

◻   What more can schools and English classrooms do about increasing children's wider and independent reading skills?

Characterising the reading process

Reading originates from the words, structures and rhythm of oral language, itself a symbolic system with sounds representing things, actions and feelings and inflections at the ends of verbs in English signifying the past, present and future. Unlike speech, which we are hardwired to attain, reading requires direct instruction from a skilled reader. Reading begins with enhancing children's oral skills through phonological awareness, recognising the sounds of vowels and common consonants in spoken words to attune their ear. Children need to hear the difference between the final sounds of 't' in cat and 'r' in car, to hear what is left if you take the 'pit' out of 'sandpit'. At the same time, children learn to recognise familiar objects in pictorial form, another symbolic system, and to link pictures to make a story – supported by hearing stories and following or 'reading' stories from picture books. Then comes learning that individual sounds or phonemes are represented in written form as letters/graphemes, all 26 letters and their combinations as digraphs and blends to make the 46 sounds in English. Children have to make the association between sound and letter and for this to be memorised and then automatically recalled: 'sp' and 'st' perhaps distinguished by the downward 'tail' of the 'p' to discern in 'spot' and the sterner upright 't' in 'stop'. Children begin to add up graphemes to read words, blending digraphs and recognising syllables (synthetic phonics) as well as breaking down words into their phonemes (analytical phonics). At the same time, children build up their sight vocabulary, recognising words as whole entities (Ehri, 2002). This leads to joining words together in phrases and then simple sentences so building up knowledge of the 'rules' of written grammar and syntax. Reading these words and sentences aloud and then silently increases familiarity with words, increasing fluency and reading speed. This allows word and sentence meaning to take precedence over the harder, slower work of sheer decoding. Reading and listening to many stories increases oral comprehension and teaches children to recognise and respond to the cadences of written stories, poems, explanations as well as showing how the familiar world known to the child can be reinterpreted by the writer or even new worlds created. Direct instruction by a teacher or skilled reader is needed for phonological awareness and phonetic application but is also needed in how to read and understand a story; as in, prediction ('what do you think is going to happen next?'), or early inference ('do you think the baby in the story will ever go to bed?') or empathy ('do you sometimes want to stay up late?').

All these rich activities are taught in pre-school and in Reception, Years 1 and 2 and generally in English primary classrooms they unfold simultaneously rather than a step-by-step approach; that is, a balanced or integrated approach which is neither just skills-based with phonics nor 'whole language' with Real Books. The discrete skills in learning to read have a positive effect on the other skills through reciprocal causation or 'bootstrapping' for children who 'get' reading early are pulled up by the interaction of their own early prowess, a 'causal chain of positive reactions' (Stanovich, 1986: 363).

As children learn to read they develop more sophisticated comprehension skills that are characterised as 'an intentional and thoughtful interaction between the reader and the text' (NICHD, 2000: 13). These skills include monitoring their understanding, stopping when the words fail to yield up their meaning and re-reading the sentence or paragraph or even whole last page again, visualising the scene and characters, running the plot through their heads like a film, and, most importantly, learning how to infer or read between the lines of the text. As such, they build up a mental representation or model of the text, at first a basic text-based model constructed through the direct information in the text – plot, character, setting, theme – which gradually develops into a richer interpretive situation model (Kintsch, 1988). These models arise primarily out of inference-making.

'An inference is a reasoned conclusion derived from understated information' (Philpot, 2005: 150) and as such underpins comprehension. There are four main types of inference – bridging and referential (direct and literal in the text); coherent inferences that make links between ideas in the text at clause, sentence, paragraph level and between text sections; and elaborative inferences that draw on or refer to knowledge of the world (Cain *et al.*, 2001). Elaborative inferences can only be made when the reader has enough background knowledge to draw on to fill in the textual gaps or make sense of the topic, especially when it is specialised. Those who have a good knowledge of primates through pouring over well-illustrated non-fiction texts and watching *Monkey World* on TV will make much better inroads on a denser piece of non-fiction text about chimpanzees in the wild and will be able to remember larger parts of the information given in the text – and so not only improve their existing knowledge about primates but also practice reading harder texts with specialist vocabulary, complex syntactical structures and sophisticated discourse markers (Koziminsky and Koziminsky, 2001; Wolfe and Mienko, 2007). Matching readers' interests and expertise to texts is a crucial part of being an English teacher so that it is possible for a child with a reading age of 9.6 but with a fanatical interest in dinosaurs to read a non-fiction text on why the dinosaurs died with a reading age of 15 or more.

Build up of conflict: why some children do not learn to read

Most children do learn to read in the UK. However, children who do not make the initial connection between phoneme and grapheme consciously read slowly at word level, unable to extend their energies to work out what the words *say* so further disadvantaging them. Those causal chain reactions can also act negatively (Stanovich, 1986):

> Thus reading for meaning is hindered; unrewarding reading experiences multiply; and practice is avoided or merely tolerated without real cognitive involvement.

> (Cunningham and Stanovich, 1998: 1)

Such children are less likely to construct a school and home environment in which reading is selected as a daily activity and the adults around them induced to support through giving and sharing books. They change books continually when there is free reading time at school to avoid reading and being seen publicly to struggle and do not know how to select books they are capable of reading fluently and independently. They gain no knowledge of related texts and their vocabulary acquisition remains limited through little incidental reading. Their lack of progress can be compounded in school by being placed with similarly less-skilled and demotivated children and given isolated reading exercises focusing on form rather than meaning in levelled readers. Teachers may ask closed questions focusing on 'what' paradigms in the text rather than 'why' or 'how' open questions. As children move up the school they read short extracts rather than longer ones and experience texts in isolation from one another. They read non-fiction as a relief from longer texts manoeuvering around visuals and short one-line paragraphs but do not read the longer chunks of writing. They can, however, retrieve information at a basic level. Their knowledge of the world and of how texts work is limited and they make fewer inferences, particularly of the elaborative type. They read around 0.5 hours a day at the most. If their teacher does not read a whole text with the child or aloud to the whole class then these children rarely get to finish a whole book (Stanovich, 1986; Stanovich, 2000; Cunningham and Stanovich, 2001; Moss, 2007; Mertzman, 2008).

Parallel plotting: why do some readers succeed?

Good readers develop accurate and rapid phonological awareness and so read more texts willingly at a faster pace. The cognitive elements work together simultaneously so that from the start words and sentences say something to the reader. They read a variety of different stories, many familiar ones repeatedly so building up a wide sight vocabulary and recognition of story structures and the way these are subverted and altered in texts. They can comprehend aural stories of some complexity. They induce adults at home to construct rich reading environments and so practise more reading at home than they do at school. Their incidental vocabulary acquisition increases at a huge rate each year. At school these good readers know how to choose books because they are familiar with so many and know what they like. They are also willing to risk reading books they may not like or are at a higher level than their current reading age. In many schools they are grouped with other good readers who confidently demonstrate how they read as part of the guided reading lesson with the teacher and who can talk knowledgeably about books. The teacher talks about the meaning in the books and asks 'why' questions focusing on causation. These children can sustain reading for some time in class and at home and begin to be serial readers, following up trails, recommendations, reading books from related texts such as films and computer games. Average readers spend about 2 hours a day reading, precocious readers 4.5 hours in Year 9. They create informal reading networks outside of school where they talk about, share and swap books they like. They read non-fiction texts related to their own interests. Their knowledge of the world increases vastly through reading and so they make many rich coherent and elaborative inferences when they read. This leads them to experience local and global coherence of texts drawing on multiple sources and so pleasure and satisfaction in reading is usually addressed, without which they leave the book and move on to another.

Flashback: the how and what of reading

From the discussions around better and poorer readers, we can assume that regular reading in great volumes of a variety of whole texts in a sustained way incrementally accrues improvement in fluency, vocabulary acquisition and comprehension (PIRLS 107). Interestingly, the influential US National Reading Panel in their analysis of hundreds of research studies on independent silent reading did not find such reading a *cause* of such improved skills but simply that a correlation or positive relationship existed between the two (NLP, 2000: 13). What they did find was that independent reading works when supplemented by more direct comprehension reading strategies. However, as with all good research, other international and national studies offer alternative perspectives even while these are again correlations rather than causes – but insisting on causal effects reduces reading to a pure science which it is not, being caught up in language, culture and social relationships as well as cognitive processes. Well-informed English teachers will need to take critical account of both forms of reading research.

The Progress in International Reading Study (PIRLS) found that 'perseverance in reading longer texts was an important facet in reading proficiency' (Twist *et al.*, 2003: 54) while *engagement* in reading is seen to have the largest correlation with reading attainment (ibid.: 124). Getting through a longer newspaper article, poem or novel without giving up and getting caught up in its content therefore improves skill and attainment. Furthermore, acquiring and understanding new words is far more effectively learned during voracious reading than through watching TV or talking, especially when supplemented by direct vocabulary instruction prior to the reading (Stanovich, 2000). For a start, you are more likely to meet unusual words in print than in the spoken language because people's spoken vocabulary is usually less rich in specialised words than written language because it is augmented by non-verbal communication. In addition the reader is more likely to meet that word several times in one text or several when related to the same topic and so will make a visual recollection of it to store in long-term memory (Gardner, 2004).

While there are specific reading skills unique to narrative such as inference and understanding narrative structures such as flashbacks and cliffhangers, the best news is that good readers are not necessarily those who read 'school' fiction: '[T]he gap in reading proficiency between those reading comics and those reading fiction is not huge' (Twist *et al.*, 2003: 106). Higher reading scores, for example, were found in Japan and Finland where students reported reading only newspapers and comics. This goes some way to ameliorating the disappointing findings that while England has a greater diversity of reading cultures, perhaps because of our class system and school structures, students in England still read less for pleasure than other countries (Twist *et al.*, 2006). This was supported by a National Literacy Trust (NLT) report that found that even if a healthy 30 per cent of 5- to 8-year-olds read a book every day, only 17 per cent of 15- to 17-year-olds do so, with children more likely to read websites, social networking sites, email and blogs than books (Jama and Dugdale, 2010).

Despite the gloom, this still looks promising – students do not need to read great big novels to become skilled readers as long as they are reading comics, newspapers and magazines in a sustained way every day. Easy! Even more significant is the finding that engaged reading has the power to transcend any disadvantage connected to the socio-economic status of a reader: 'Fifteen-year-olds whose parents have the lowest occupational status but who are highly engaged in reading achieve better reading scores than students whose parents have high or medium occupational status but who are poorly engaged in reading' (Twist *et al.*, 2003: 106). However, the report also finds that 14 per cent of readers in lower-socio-economic homes report that they rarely read books for pleasure – but this may still mean that such children and young people are reading other texts for pleasure but just not fiction. This suggests that books continue to be perceived as constituting 'real reading', a rarified activity that may be linked to dull learning in English classrooms for the norm of the middle-class school student (Clark *et al.*, 2009).

So why are not schools doing everything possible to get all their students to see reading as integral to their learning?

Cliffhanger: how can schools encourage children to read more?

Primary schools have greater opportunities to develop a reading culture because of the flexibility of the curriculum allowing library visits and free reading in the morning and often more qualified teaching assistants and parent volunteers reading with individuals or groups. At Key Stage 1 it is possible for students to read or to be read three whole picture books a day, amounting to over 100 books a year – just at school.

At secondary school, the relaxed pedagogy of recent legislation, the enriched National Curriculum with a renewed emphasis on whole texts and independent reading and clarion calls for cross-curricular teaching offers great opportunities for English departments to reinvigorate wider reading. Schools do already encourage wider reading through Book Weeks and library visits. None of these are without their problems, however, and, according to Ofsted, wider reading remains a significant weakness in secondary schools (Ofsted, 2009). Let us explore these further to find out why children still are not reading.

Large-scale drives

Schools can take part in the events organised nationally around World Book Day, or Reading Connects through the NLT. They can organise readathons more locally, or Book Weeks where children come dressed as picture book characters or invite writers in to talk to the whole year group or even school, or organise a reading programme with feeder primary schools. They can get children interested in the Reading Challenge, run comic clubs or graphic novel clubs, even book clubs who shadow the Carnegie award. Libraries can have the latest books written for young people – Twilight, Angels, other worlds, Horowitz, laid out on tables ready to be gobbled up, with newspapers distributed around and enticing image-rich non-fiction texts artfully placed near the computers where boys congregate. Class libraries can be stocked with old, unread readers from the back of the English stock cupboard or even heavy with new stock bought through the Parent–Teacher Association with the covers facing the class.

But this does not mean students are reading. You can take a horse to water but you cannot make him drink.

If . . .

there is no time in the school day for students to go up to those books in the library, flick them open, scan the first page, chat to their neighbour to see if they have read it, read quietly and without interruptions and get so far into the story they have to take it home to read that night, but rather students head for the computers or grab *The Guinness Book of Records* so avoiding a sustained read or wander desultory around the shelves chatting about other things and the teacher has not given a structure to the lesson and only lets them in occasionally for 10 minutes on a Friday afternoon . . .

then few will be reading and the books will not be read.

If . . .

the teacher running the Reading Challenge leaves at the end of the Easter term and there is no one else to run it, the books remain unread, the folders half-finished, the bronze, silver and gold certificates left to curl at their edges . . .

then no one will be reading and the books will not be read.

If . . .

the whole school gets involved in Book Week but the rest of the year reading is put on the back shelf . . .

then no one is really reading in the school.

If . . .

the class teacher has to move away from her book-filled classroom for half the timetable, or does not allow students to rummage in tutor time, or does not persist in 10 minutes daily of silent reading in tutor time because five students are unsettled, noisy, disrupt the others or there are bits of administration to do, students to sort out . . .

then no one will be reading and the books will not be read.

If . . .

the class novel takes a term to get through with 7 minutes of the teacher reading aloud followed by some whole-class talk except only four students say anything and then they are taught a particular reading strategy or go into groups for guided reading because the teacher is worried about noise and discipline but the students are not allowed to take home the book to complete that chapter . . .

then the book will not make sense, will not be read properly and the students still will not be reading.

If . . .

the teacher sets reading homework but does not check it or do this regularly or give good recommendations to read or insist everyone reads out their best bit ever from their reading homework . . .

then no one will bother to read at home and reading will not be taken seriously.

Conflict resolution

But imagine if . . .

sustained reading was so embedded in the daily rhythm of the school and the English classroom in particular that it was impossible for any student to avoid becoming a reader.

Imagine if . . .

the library was used on a weekly basis by the English teacher who regularly audited her students' reading interests and so spent the lunch hour before the lesson pulling books out on World War I, fashion from the 1960s, fossils, the history of the World Cup and Nelson Mandela and spread them out on the tables invitingly with current fiction books including the complete set of Twilight, Harry Potter and Mes Roscoff's books all laid out in a row. The students come in, listen as the teacher reminds them they have 15 minutes to browse, 25 minutes to read in silence – strictly enforced, 5 minutes to jot down two lines in their reading diary about what they are reading and what they feel about it, 5 minutes to read a good juicy part out to a friend or to the whole class and talk about it, 10 minutes to take a book out. And that is what they do. The teacher talks to each student briefly about their book, makes a note of it in her record book, sensitively hears six students read aloud, quietly, to her, intervening to support them as appropriate and several more as they read to one another, makes notes about problems, suggestions about the next book to read, and lets them out of the classroom. She checks with the librarian that all have taken a book out and takes further action on which students need to read different or more challenging texts.

Imagine if . . .

there was *good old-fashioned silent reading* every morning for 10 minutes or whenever there was the tutor group and the library provided book boxes for those who forgot to bring a book or who finished theirs, including newspapers, individual articles from science magazines, short stories and comics. Those five or six 'disruptive' students are challenged by the teacher to read something they are interested in and after one week of mutters and sighs they select magazines, non-fiction texts, books and read. The tutor has enough presence of mind to collect what they leave on their desks, stick a Post-it note with their name on and ensure it is on their desk when they return the following day. A teaching assistant is employed to keep those book boxes turned over with new material and current comics. That makes 50 minutes of independent reading a week, adding . . . new words to those students' vocabularies. Precocious readers who are reading a book a day are challenged with getting through a short story or article in 10 minutes – a kind of speed-reading. Struggling readers are given graphic novels and high-quality readers designed for them, as well as cartoons and joke books. Tutors who are not reading specialists are given a 2-hour continuing professional development (CPD) training session in how to encourage wider reading in more- and less-skilled readers.

Imagine if . . .

guided reading – that is, a small group of readers reading with a teacher – could take place regularly, during a tutor period or the library lesson (the second half when all have settled down) or as a part of an English lesson where the rest of the students are reading their own book or doing cross-curricular work with a history teacher and a specialist teaching assistant. Guided reading here involves reading from a shared novel, talking about the text with the teacher tuned into each student's strengths and weaknesses and showing/teaching a particular strategy or just talking in a nuanced way about the text, getting students to generate the questions and describe their own comprehension-monitoring strategies with the goal of making them independent in their reading – 'I drift off, Miss, if I don't get it, and then catch myself thinking about other things apart from the book and have to shake myself back into it and that can be hard'.

If *group reading* took place whereby a group of five students read the same text together grouped according to how they chose from a list of six titles covering different genres – fantasy, romance, science fiction – having been given the chance to browse through each one and read the blurb and first chapter fully. They then had a set time to get through the book – a maximum of three weeks, with each group member given a defined role: Reading Chair, who sets the agenda for each lesson and sets the amount of reading for the next week or day; Reading Specialist (the most able reader), who offers advice on how to read; Illustrator, the best artist who can sketch out how the group see characters, setting, even storyboard the plot, so keeping an alternative record of the group's discussions; Riddler, who plays devil's advocate and asks difficult questions of the text and the group and, finally, Reader, who reads aloud particular chunks to the group. The teacher will have a four-page guide to the text with particular activities they have to do and some they can opt for including creating a web page or poster of the book and where to find further information on the text through internet addresses. A group effort, if one fails to read up to the required amount the whole group has to get the miscreant up to speed by re-reading, retelling and dish out an appropriate punishment – clearing up the classroom, or extra reading homework.

One key outcome from this is for each member to write a short story or comic or piece of non-fiction writing on the same theme as the group text and for the group to edit these into a bound collection, organised by the Reading Chair and illustrated by the Illustrator to add to the class library.

Imagine if . . .

the same text was read by a whole year group at the same time so that students in Year 8 could talk about the text in corridors and the playing field in an informal manner without the teachers having to do anything in particular as happened in one school:

> It meant that the children were all then talking about *Holes*, and it became *Eastenders*, it really did . . . there is something real going on, it is tangible. (Mark, an advanced skills teacher)
>
> (Westbrook, 2009)

Imagine if . . .

a class got used to reading a shared reader in under three weeks, reading large chunks in class, especially the first few chapters to support all the students in 'getting' the initial text-based model, the opening scenario, setting, characters and problem. The teacher reads aloud and volunteer students, with silent reading, listening to a CD and, to vary it, watch sections of the film-of-the-book. The teacher recaps what has happened at the beginning of each lesson to jog students' short-term memory. Students are then practising sustained, uninterrupted reading under the tutelage of their teacher and without any bits being missed out:

> I probably wanted to have like read it all because there might be a tiny detail that you missed. I would rather either not read a book or read all of it. (Tina, Year 8 student)
>
> (Westbrook, 2009)

The created world of the book takes shape in each student's head, supported by direct instruction from the teacher or peers at the complex parts and by constantly referencing up and down the text to support students in making those larger connections between parts of the text. Group talk around the text, brief notes, pictures or plot charts support a long-term memory of the book. The end of any book, of course, needs to be savoured, treasured, students left with a few minutes to react in quiet or laughter and for it to be discussed – 'what do you think of the ending?' Analysis and evaluation becomes the dominant classroom discourse once the reading is completed so that the students can discuss, argue and write about an understood whole text rather than little misunderstood bits of it.

If a class got through a reader in three weeks they could read a novel together every term. That would be six novels a year with plenty of time for everything else on the curriculum.

Imagine if . . .

wider reading was conceptualised as including those texts thematically linked to the shared reader so that students increased their background knowledge of the text by reading related non-fiction texts, web pages and newspaper articles. For example, with *Holes* these could be myths around the Wild West, segregation in the Southern states of America and the emergence of the civil rights movement and the viewing of *Blazing Saddles* as daily accompaniments to the ongoing reading. Reading the two kinds of texts together strengthens the reading skills in the other and increases the chances that unfamiliar vocabulary will be met several times in a variety of contexts and so meaningfully acquired (Camp, 2000; Greenleaf *et al.*, 2001; Gardner, 2004). The reader would accumulate sophisticated background knowledge to support an enhanced level of inference and comprehension of *Holes* and would be motivated to read more complex related texts. This is more likely to occur, too, if students are encouraged to read these linked texts relatively rapidly to get the overall meaning rather than a slower analytical read.

That could be 30 minutes of concentrated reading, made more meaningful by purposeful paired (or group) talk about the texts for a total of 15 minutes with 10 minutes of teacher talk/whole-class talk.

There would still be time to cover the rest of the curriculum, for non-fiction and multimodal texts – because much of it would have already have been covered.

Imagine if ...

students independently read a whole novel or other major text related to the shared reader after the class reading. If there was a real choice of text and proper time given to read the novel in class, supported by the teacher as needed and with specific tasks to do – but not so many as to disrupt the reading – then even struggling readers might be able to complete a whole text on their own. The accumulated background knowledge from the previous text may help this struggling reader in particular to get into the new text. The rehearsal of having read the class text with peers and teacher may also support an independent reading because of the recent activation of all the various reading skills needed to get through a longer text. Selecting such related texts will challenge and enhance the teacher's knowledge of children's and young people's literature. For *Holes* – possible linked texts can be *Guantanamo Boy* by, Small Steps, the sequel to *Holes*, texts related to racism in the States – *Of Mice and Men, To Kill A Mockingbird, I Know Why the Caged Bird Sings*.

If the class reads six shared readers a year and then another six directly following on from this, then that is twelve novels read a year plus all those related non-fiction texts. From Year 7 to 11 that adds up to an impressive 60 novels read in secondary school (Westbrook, 2008).

Do the maths – how many more words would the students have read? How much cleverer would they be?

A satisfying ending

Children and young people who have normal development and no specific cognitive disabilities such as dyslexia 'get' reading at different ages despite the continuation of age-normed attainment targets. They might be 10 and have been struggling to read more than a few pages or even avoiding reading altogether but see the film *Twilight*, get hold of the book at the local bookstore and be hooked. Or be a skilled reader of scientific texts but only read a whole fiction book in their second year of a physics degree at the age of 21. Or be stuck on Batman comics from 8 onwards, slowly progress to Manga comics and then crime thrillers and plough through the complete works of Conan Doyle. English teachers need to work on a balance between direct instruction of reading skills and giving time for students to practise these newly acquired reading skills independently, and in school.

Further reading

Cunningham, A. and Stanovich, K. (2001) 'What reading does for the mind', *Journal of Direct Instruction*, 1(2): 137–49.
     Together with Stanovich's seminal 1986 paper (see Bibliography) in which he explains why good readers get better and poorer readers worse, known as the Matthew effect, this paper takes the argument still further and shows precisely how avid readers become not only better readers but also cleverer, too, accruing knowledge about the world and texts.

Greenleaf, C. L., Schoenbach, R., Cziko, C. and Mueller, F. L. (2001) 'Apprenticing adolescent readers to academic literacy', *Harvard Educational Review*, 71(1): 79–129.

This article describes a small-scale reading intervention targeted at minority ethnic adolescent readers in the US which worked on the simple premise of giving such students whole texts, mostly non-fiction, that were of direct relevance to them in terms of their cultural background, gave them some reading strategies – and 20 minutes of solid reading a day.

Moss, G. (2007) *Literacy and Gender: Researching Texts, Contexts and Readers*, London: Routledge.

Gemma Moss is good at describing reading patterns in primary schools around struggling and less confident readers, with an analysis of how some boys avoid reading longer non-fiction texts and some girls remain stuck reading fiction books that are too easy for them.

National Literacy Trust website (www.literacytrust.org.uk).

This website gives easy access to statistics around reading and literacy, initiatives for reading in schools and communities and several surveys on reading, in particular on social class and inclusion, the role of fathers in reading and readers' self-perceptions (available online at http://www.literacytrust.org.uk/research/nlt_research).

Chapter 8

From *Beowulf* to Batman

Connecting English and media education

Andrew Burn

Introduction

Media and English have been kissing cousins ever since F. R. Leavis launched what has since been dubbed the 'inoculation' approach to media: the development of critical close reading skills in school students to protect them from the ill effects of the mass media (Leavis and Thompson, 1933). For Leavis, as David Buckingham has emphasised (Buckingham, 2003), these ill effects were cultural; and Buckingham identifies two other kinds of protectionist impulses in media education since. One of these is the aim of radical pedagogy in the 1970s and 1980s to protect children from the ideological effects of the media; the other is the moral protectionism Buckingham associates more with media education in America.

Most media teachers in the UK would not now subscribe to any form of protectionism, taking instead a positive view of young people's media cultures and practices, not least because of a general shift towards forms of creative production enabled by the increasing availability of digital authoring tools. However, they would see themselves as teaching forms of critical awareness, as we shall see later. In this chapter, I will focus on three aspects of media education which can inform English. It seems to me to be important not to produce neat models of media education – media studies, for instance – which emphasise difference from, even incompatibility with, English. Such models lead to media as a tacked-on appendage to the English curriculum at best. More productive, maybe, is to muddle the boundaries, find common ground and use tensions to challenge each field of study to move beyond its limitations and prejudices.

The three areas I will focus on are *cultural distinction, rhetoric/poetics* and *creative production.* They roughly correspond to the key concepts of the English curriculum: Cultural understanding, Critical understanding and Creativity (QCA, 2007a, 2007b). However, my emphasis here will be on media literacy, which is also often understood in terms of this 3-Cs model (see Burn and Durran, 2007). In this model, these concepts are rather differently understood, in ways which can usefully inform English teaching. Running through these I'll use a common theme, which I shall call the *oral-ludic sensibility.* This theme emphasises the textual forms of traditional oral cultures, in contrast to the (print) literary sensibilities traditionally favoured by English syllabuses. I shall argue that it also relates these ancient oral forms to the modern computer game, a kind of media text which offers particular challenges to English teachers, as well as useful new ways to think about narrative, language and performance.

Cultural distinction

The simple way to state the problem here is to say that the English curriculum has traditionally been concerned with 'high' culture (though of course those teachers who come under the category identified in the Cox Report (DES, 1989) as 'cultural analysts' have always contested the literary canon and the values associated with it); while media education is committed to popular culture (though those who emphasise the importance of film sometimes observe their own kind of canon).

However, the curriculum, oddly, renders the question of culture pretty well invisible. A search through versions of the English for references to 'culture' or 'cultural' reveals only rather tokenistic references to multiculturalism, as if culture only becomes visible through contrast between ethnic groups. Contrasts between the cultures of different social classes, which even now might be expected to reveal something of the tension between popular and élite cultural forms and preferences, are not available as a mode of inquiry in the English curriculum. We are enjoined to consider, in short, the meaning of Sujata Bhatt's bilingual tongue, split between English and Gujarati; but not to consider why some teenagers might prefer Marvel comics to Shakespeare, *Call of Duty: Modern Warfare* to the war poets or *Hollyoaks* to Keats. Such contrasts run the risk of reducing the argument to tabloid knockabout of the 'Shakespeare or soaps?' variety, a hoary debate we have had many times before. Nevertheless, it seems important to acknowledge that this kind of cultural distinction still exists, and to consider how to approach this in the classroom. In any case, my argument is that we do not need to choose. We can, and should, have both extremes of the cultural spectrum, and anything in between that suits our purpose.

The ideas of culture which I have found most helpful in scoping out the cultural space of English and media education are those of Raymond Williams, who identified three levels: *lived culture*, the *documentary record* and the *selective tradition* (Williams, 1961). 'Lived culture' was the culture of everyday life, of ordinary people: in effect, a recognition of the vitality of the forms of popular culture which Leavis's approach had represented as debased. Williams recognised the importance of popular music, film, television drama, radio as important parts of this culture, resources to which ordinary people looked for meaning, identity and community, for pleasure, information and entertainment. It is this conception of 'common culture' which has been so influential in the field of cultural studies which Williams effectively founded, and which has profoundly informed the conception of popular culture in media studies and media education.

Williams' 'documentary record' was the residue of past cultures, inaccessible to us now except through the texts, artefacts and buildings left behind. While

Williams' example of ancient Greece is at an extreme distance, we might consider how the media texts of the late twentieth century could be viewed by students as documentary records of the spectacular sub-cultures of the fifties and sixties, the political and social significance of punk, the post-colonial cultures of diaspora or the paranoia of the Cold War. At a greater historical remove, we can consider how the popular cultural texts of modern mass media continue in certain ways the narrative threads, styles, imagery and voice of older popular cultural forms; from the oral tradition of Old English poetry and the mediaeval ballad, through vernacular theatre such as the mystery plays, to the broadsheet ballads, penny dreadful and melodramas of the eighteenth and nineteenth centuries. While the popular culture of the mass media is different in certain ways, particularly in the production regimes out of which it emerges, in many ways these older textual forms and traditions are the direct ancestors of the modern pop lyric, soap opera, horror film and some genres of computer game.

Finally, Williams' 'selective tradition' is the historical process which sifts out some cultural phenomena as more valuable, important, worthy of preservation. It is the process which creates the literary canon, Leavis's Great Tradition. But what we can take from Williams is not the exclusive endorsement of this level of culture above all others, the stance adopted by Leavis (and by successive versions of the National Curriculum for England). Rather, we can interrogate with students the processes by which such texts become valued in this way. Through what mechanisms of commentary, critique, transformation, myth-making, appreciation, did Shakespeare become 'greater' than Marlowe or Ben Jonson? Through what kinds of cultural alchemy did low-budget formula movies like *Casablanca* and *Psycho* become elevated into paramount exemplars of cinematic art? These questions of cultural distinction are not ones which the English curriculum prompts or even allows us to ask, as I have already observed. Interestingly, though, they are not questions prompted by media education either. Both domains duck the question of cultural value, though both are locked solidly into it. Williams' clear-sighted model offers us a way to think about it constructively.

But what might any of this mean in practice? Let us take, as an example, *Beowulf*. An unquestionably canonic text, the best-known of a small surviving group of Old English poetry, it is valorised by academic commentary, and translated/adapted by Seamus Heaney. However, it usefully problematises the idea of literature. It was orally composed and transmitted, is by no known author and conforms to Walter Ong's 'psychodyamics' of oral narrative (Ong, 1982). In particular, the figure of Beowulf himself is what Ong called a 'heavy hero' – characterised by a few simple, memorable qualities; agonistic (solving problems through physical action rather than psychological effort); in short, formulaic, as might be expected from a text composed and transmitted in the oral-formulaic process (Parry, 1930; Lord, 1960).

My point in drawing attention to these characteristics is to show that *Beowulf* is what we now think of as a popular cultural text. This strong, formulaic narrative in which a mighty hero battles fantasy monsters may be the earliest jewel in the crown of English literature, performed in the mead-halls of kings as well as for the common folk; but it resembles the adventures of Spider-Man, Superman and Batman more than it resembles the tortured protagonists of Renaissance drama or the modern novel. This is not to dismiss the psychological insights, descriptive power, social critique and aesthetic innovation that the prose and poetry of the modern era produce. My argument is not to prefer the archaic and fantastic over the modern and naturalistic; again, we can have both. I do want, though, to recall vital cultural forms that may get less attention than they deserve at present, and to point out the lineage which links them with modern mediated popular cultural forms, a lineage we can exploit for the benefit of our students.

In this respect, we can consider what happens when a text like this is adapted into a contemporary media form. *Beowulf* was produced as an animated film in 2007 (Zemeckis, 2007). In comic-book style, scripted by the graphic novelist Neil Gaiman, it represented Beowulf as a muscled superhero (voiced with Cockney bravado by Ray Winstone) and Grendel's mother as a naked temptress (Angelina Jolie).

The popular cultural references to comic-strip narrative and fantasy film will make a connection with the imaginative worlds and media cultures of many students in our classrooms. But this connection is not contrived, superficial or gratuitous. The point of the *Beowulf* movie for the English and media teacher is that it is an example of the continuity of popular narrative, of how its tropes, structures, values and affective charge descend in a discernible line from the archaic worlds of Achilles and Beowulf to the superheroes of Marvel comics. It is the line of descent that can be traced through the transformative threads which take Arthur and the Matter of Britain from early mediaeval verse through Malory's great prose epic to Tennyson's mournful idylls, T. H. White's comic genius, and the profusion of film and animation of the late twentieth century. It is the narrative simplicity and demotic appeal of Robin Hood, utterly transformed yet completely unchanged in his journey from mediaeval ballad cycle to the competing film icons of Errol Flynn, Sean Connery, Kevin Costner and Russell Crowe.

There are plenty of lessons here for the English and media classroom about the form and content of popular cultural narrative. What do superheroes mean, and why are they perennially fascinating to us? What serious themes do they enact, of justice, identity, freedom, revenge, gendered power, behind their fantastic costumes and elaborate weaponry, from Beowulf's sword to Batman's utility belt, Athena's shield to Xena's spinning steel ring? How are these meanings encoded in the poetic forms of successive ages, from alliterative verse and kenning to the chiaroscuro of late-twentieth-century comic-book art, or the rapid editing, CGI effects and condensed scripting of superhero film franchises? These are questions about meaning and representation, but also about semiotic mode and medium, which I will return to below.

For the purposes of this section, there are serious questions about the nature of culture, distinctions between differently valued cultural forms, and the articulation between such texts and the cultural lives of our students. These are questions about which the pedagogies and curricula of English and media remain routinely dumb, each content to outlaw the cultural territory of the other and reify the values of its own terrain. This is not a matter of wilful choice by today's teachers, but of sedimented practice accreted over time, and regressive curriculum policy.

Let us move on, however, and look at the relatively new medium of computer games. The animated film of *Beowulf* has been further adapted into a computer game version (Beowulf, 2007). Game versions have been developed in the cross-media franchises of *The Lord of the Rings*, the Harry Potter stories and the film based on Philip Pullman's *Northern Lights* sequence (where you can wield a Wii-mote and Nunchuk as an armoured bear).

I shall come back to how computer games might help us think in different ways about narrative, language and literacy. Here, the focus is on their cultural status and function. An argument for English teachers to consider is that computer games are particularly well suited to adapt the ancient narratives of oral tradition I have described above. This is partly because they share the popular cultural milieu of their sister media forms. But it is also because they are, literally, formulaic texts, made up of computer code. Suppose you want to describe the death of a warrior in battle. The sensibility of modern literature requires variety and originality – cliché and formula are the enemies. We need different words to describe the warrior's fall each time; different words to describe the sounds of battle; novel ways to render the agony of death. For Homeric texts the opposite was true. The oral poet, performer and audience needed the repetition of the *same* words for these familiar scenarios: words that could be easily remembered, easily re-ordered if the performer needed to alter the narrative and easily recognised by an audience which needed familiar stories. The battlefield slaughter of *The Iliad* follows a well-rehearsed formula of weapon use, disembowelling and the ringing of armour about the fallen warrior. The computer game is not dissimilar. The character is a bundle of audiovisual resources, constant through the game. The actions of killing an enemy will involve triggering the same animation cycle, the same soundtrack, the same range of player options each time. As in the oral performance, significant variations on the theme are possible, such as the way in which these options can be exercised by the player. Although computer games are very different from traditional oral narratives in many ways, both employ formulaic narrative techniques, integral components of the popular aesthetic.

Finally, while popular culture is more than able to explore the serious preoccupations of everyday life, we always know that the fictions we love to spin about these concerns are a kind of game. When we enter Coleridge's 'willing suspension of disbelief', it is very similar to entering the contract about the status of a game – that however dramatic the combat, claws will be sheathed; however convincing the representation, its rules only apply within the magic circle of the game. Above all, it is played for pleasure, a fact never adequately represented in curricular programmes. It is important to consider how such pleasures may fall into different categories, perform different psycho-social roles: the thrill of risk for a teenager aspiring to adulthood; the pleasure of catharsis in tragic narratives;

the pleasure of humorous, subversive, carnivalesque inversions of officialdom (or, for children, of the adult world).

An 'oral-ludic sensibility', then, might have much to offer the cultural work of the English and media classroom, offering a recuperation of ancient stories, styles and values; a dramatic engagement for students with the protagonists of these narratives; a goal-oriented approach to the problems of everyday life and a reminder of the importance of pleasure and play.

Rhetoric/poetics

English and media have quite different approaches to textuality: to communication, representation, lexico-grammar and the aesthetic properties of texts. Approaches to literary texts have often focused on their aesthetic form and have been characterised by what we might call a mode of appreciation. By contrast, media texts have been approached in what we might call a rhetorical mode, exploring the politics of representation, and interrogating the motivations of producers and audiences. These two modes have long histories which can be traced back to Aristotle: we can detect the legacy of his *Poetics* in the English approach to literature and the legacy of his *Rhetoric* in the media approach to the texts that fall within its domain. I simplify here for the sake of contrast; but, both in the habituated practices of the English and media classrooms and in the curricular formations that have constructed literature as an object of reverence and media texts as objects of suspicion, something like this contrast seems stubbornly resistant to change. We need both rhetoric and poetics if we are to attend to the politics of representation in both media and literary texts, as well as to the aesthetic forms in which such representations are framed.

The rhetorical stance of media education is often encoded in the conceptual frameworks used to identify what critical understandings students might be expected to gain. There are several different versions of these but they can generally be grouped under *institutions, texts* and *audiences.*

Institutions

The idea of media institutions is often seen as problematic by media teachers; it is rarely considered in the teaching of literature, though much of Dickens' work was structured by the contingencies of magazine publication, the careers of the women writers of the nineteenth century were at the mercy of male publishers and the literary creations of modern novelists are commonly franchised by multinational media organisations. To move beyond the immediate pleasures of engagement with media texts in order to consider the shadowy regimes of production and distribution that lie behind them can seem dry, remote and hard to pin down. There are also uncertainties: what institutions are we talking about exactly? What do we need to know about them? Why do we need to know it?

Current approaches to media education would support a nuanced attitude to the question of the media industries. Buckingham argues, for instance, that we have moved beyond a paradigm of 'radical pedagogy' in which the role of education is to unmask bourgeois and capitalist ideologies (2000). This is not to say that a degree of healthy scepticism is not warranted. There are good reasons why we might want young people to understand what commercial interests lie behind a MacDonald's advert or a leader in a Murdoch-owned newspaper. But institutions more typically have complex motives and socio-political functions. The practical question is: how might we explore these?

One example comes from a colleague who explored the cross-media Harry Potter franchise by looking at logos on the covers of the book, the DVD box and the game box. The media institutions involved included Bloomsbury, Sony, KnowWonder games, Electronic Arts, *The Times Educational Supplement,* Dolby sound and several more. The complexity of function speaks for itself.

Another example, from a Year 8 game design course, is the simulation of a game development company by the class. They create a name for the company, consider the roles of the people who work on the design, develop the marketing of the game, write the press release for game journals and so on (see Burn and Durran, 2007: ch. 7).

These activities give some sense to young people of the complexity of motives, functions and processes in the production of a media text, whether it be a novel or a computer game. It is routine work for media teachers, and easy enough to imagine as a dimension of literature teaching and learning. This is too brief an introduction; more can be found in books elaborating the theory and practice of media education (Buckingham, 2003; McDougall, 2006; Burn and Durran, 2007).

Texts

A rhetorical approach to texts will centre on the question of *representation*. This is a familiar word in media education and media studies; not so commonly found in English documents or conceptual frameworks. At one level, of course, it means any semiotic act: any utterance, written word, image, dramatic gesture is a representation of some aspect of reality. The question to explore with students is the nature of the relationship between the representation and that 'reality', which is of course multiple, shifting and situated. We may explore Shylock as a representation of Renaissance ideas about Jewishness, but we cannot escape the fact that the actor depicting the role, the director behind him and the audience in the theatre (or cinema) have more recent memories of the Holocaust and the Arab–Israeli conflict. To return to the example of *Beowulf,* we might investigate how the character represents an ideal of the Anglo-Saxon warrior prince. But we can also attend to the meanings of the contemporary superhero which the animated film invokes; or to the gendered significance of the combat mechanics in the computer game.

How, though, might students understand the detailed structure of texts which produce these meanings?

One approach is to focus on the signifying systems of particular media. There is no room here to run exhaustively through all possible media so I will use two examples from film and games. In the first, a Year 8 boy is writing about what he has learned from re-editing a sequence from Baz Luhrmann's *Romeo + Juliet*. The task was to take a sequence of footage from the film, imported into editing software (Adobe Premiere) and to creatively rework it, adding different music, changing the order and duration, but producing their own take on the play using these 'found' resources:

Also, at that point when the camera tracks up, it is the first time there has been any significant movement in it. The camera has stayed still to reflect the movement of the most important character in the sequence: like Mercutio, the camera has witnessed everything, but has done nothing about it . . . The final shot is of a new character to the sequence: Samson. The camera is placed at an oblique angle to him. He is not an important character; he is at the side of the action. His emotion, his expression of fear and anxiety, needs to be acknowledged – not felt – by the audience. He simply watches – he does not act.

This kind of critical work, a fluid mix of technical production, aesthetic choices and critical reflection, is close to the kind of work a student might undertake in analysing literature. Media teachers would recognise it as a thoughtful reading of a filmic text, aware of both the grammar of the moving image and the meanings conveyed by it. English teachers would recognise it as an equally thoughtful reading of a sequence from *Romeo and Juliet*. It can be seen as an aspect of critical literacy and as situated within the conceptual framework of media education. But it also exemplifies the kind of thing I am thinking of as a 'poetics' of media education: an attention to the aesthetic features of dramatic texts which Aristotle codified, adapted for the photographic media of the early twenty-first century.

Here is another example, again by a Year 8 boy – an extract from his proposal for a computer game based on *The Odyssey*, written after learning basic principles of game design using the software MissionMaker:

My game, being largely concerned with narrative, will not contain exceptionally large amounts of rules and economies. One example of a rule, however, is involved in Odysseus's encounter with Scylla (an huge, six-headed monster) and Charybdis (a deadly whirlpool). A rule used in this section states that if the ship enters a special trigger volume by getting too close to Scylla's cave, she flies out and carries away six of Odysseus's men (one for each head), reducing the crew economy by six. This economy is a fairly close equivalent of the standard health economy, in that the game is ended if it gets reduced to zero, although it varies in that the player is hampered when its value is reduced to close to zero, as the ship becomes more difficult to manoeuvre. In this respect, then, it is closer to a strength economy.

This piece of work presents an understanding of narrative but one that is informed by the game concepts learned in the course as well as those he knows from his own experience. The two key concepts of game design which the use of the software has rehearsed – rules and economies – are important in this rendition of *The Odyssey*. The student conceives of game rules, such as the one which states that if the player gets too near to Scylla she will carry off some of the ship's crew. Similarly, he imagines an economy (a quantifiable resource) related to the 'strength' of the ship, depleted by the men carried off by the monster.

In these two examples, work in different media extends the understanding of textual structures that students might learn in English. To the metalinguistic lexicon of clause, sentence, paragraph, narrative, argument and so on is added the grammar of film (shots, camera movement, camera angle) and game design (levels, non-player characters, rules and economies).

However, these new understandings are not simply additive: they can be mutually reinforcing. An English teacher in a media literacy project currently being conducted asked Year 8 students to think about systems of address across book, game and film, first in relation to Harry Potter, then through making their own stories, films and games. In doing so, their understanding of a complex set of ideas such as point-of-view, person, address, focalisation (Genette, 1980) became richer, more robust, less susceptible to reductive formulations. Such semiotic principles run across different modes and media: they are, in short, *multimodal* (Kress and van Leeuwen, 1996).

Attention, then, to the representational strategies and the poetics of texts can be reinforced, enriched, made more complex if it encompasses the semiotic structures of different media.

Audiences

It is now an orthodoxy for English teachers and media teachers to encourage students to create texts for a particular audience. But who that audience might be, or how we might get a concrete idea of them, is a slippery business. We can imagine, for instance, a series of concentric circles, in which the most intimate idea of audience is to ask students to conceive of themselves as audiences: what are their reading/viewing/playing preferences? How do they make particular cultural choices? What kinds of pleasure do they derive from the texts they choose? In what social groups do they engage with these texts? What cultural practices do they engage in as audiences? The second level might be to identify a specific actual audience: making texts for a partner primary school class, for a parents' evening, for a local council meeting, for a visiting VIP. The third level, one often used by media teachers, could be the socio-economic groupings of market research: are they targeting their texts at the A1 or the C2 grouping, for example?

A rather different approach is to explore audience practices, particularly online. To take games as an example again, game fans engage in the following kinds of activity:

- Fanfiction – writing stories, 'spoilers', backstories, poems about their favourite characters. Popular cross-media franchises such as Harry Potter, *Buffy the Vampire Slayer*, *The Lord of the Rings* or The Chronicles of Narnia produce vast quantities of such writing, often carefully crafted, generically disciplined (sometimes parodic), reverential in its attitude to the source-text and highly regulated by its constituent communities.
- Fan art – drawings, paintings, computer-generated artwork, produced in similar ways.
- Walk-throughs – elaborate sets of instructions for playing games. Again, the Harry Potter games provide good examples, often beautifully produced as websites, illustrated with images and screengrabs from the games.
- Mods – modifications of games by fans to produce their own version of a game or a level or even a completely new game based on the game-engine (the programmed 'skeleton') of an existing game.
- Online communities – such as the clans that are supported by online role-playing games such as *World of Warcraft*; or the role-playing groups who develop intricate stories which they act out via their online characters or avatars.

There are, then, many ways to conceive of audiences. Students need to visit these regularly if they are to learn how texts are adopted or rejected, how cultural affiliations are made and broken, how meanings are interpreted, how cultural resources are appropriated and transformed, what pleasures are sought and found and in what social configurations, for what cultural or political purposes, this all happens.

The idea of a critical literacy which detects the workings of media institutions and analyses audience behaviours is only part of the picture, however – a reader who could *only* perform such a reading would be a dull creature indeed. Do we really want a world where there can be no media 'effects'? Of course we do not want an entire generation uncritically swallowing the message that life without Coke or PlayStation is not worth living. But do we want them to be unmoved by the affective charge of horror or romance; unaffected by the polemic of Orwell's *1984* or Lennon's 'Imagine'; unamused by the satirical humour of *The Simpsons*? The great nineteenth-century French magician Jean-Eugene Robert-Houdin argued that he much preferred to perform his illusions to intelligent people than stupid people. Stupid people would always try to see how the trick was done, thereby making his job more difficult and destroying their own pleasure, while intelligent people would allow themselves to be duped, knowing that this was where the enjoyment of the experience lay. We could make the same argument about the media. We can know it is an illusion and still surrender ourselves to its spell. It is the paradox of Coleridge's 'willing suspension of disbelief'.

Creativity: cultural resources, semiotic tools

Creativity in education is a highly contested idea, appearing in a bewildering variety of forms (Banaji and Burn, 2007). Here, I draw on the work of the Russian psychologist Lev Vygotsky, for whom the creativity of children and adolescents was closely related to play (Vygotsky 1931/1998). In playful activity, children learn the meaning of symbolic substitution through the manipulation of physical objects; Vygotsky's well-known example is a child using a broomstick as an imaginary horse. These symbolic understandings become internalised and develop into the mental processes which generate creative work. True creativity for Vygotsky only develops, however, when the imaginative transformations of play are connected with thinking in concepts – in other words, with rational intellectual processes.

What might this kind of creativity look like in the English and media classroom? Figure 8.1 shows a screengrab from a computer game made by Year 9 students. Their task was to devise a game based on *The Tempest*. From a cultural point of view, it juxtaposes the most popular of contemporary art forms and the most elevated of literary-dramatic texts. It can be seen as a practical example, perhaps, of an exploration both of Williams' 'lived culture', the students' familiarity with games and his 'selective tradition', the successive, aggregated cultural commentaries and practices which have promoted Shakespeare's work to the status it currently enjoys.

The four Year 9 girls who have designed this level have used the game-authoring software *MissionMaker*. Their game design involves creating rules – central to the composition and play of videogames (Salen and Zimmerman, 2004) – specifying particular events. These rules construct a sequence in which the player, as Ferdinand, the king's son, must overcome a series of challenges based on events in the play to find his love Miranda and confront the (assumed) anger of her father, Prospero. This screengrab shows the final stage of the game, when the three meet.

While this game design involves a creative transformation of the digital assets of the software (characters, objects, locations), the creation of new rules and the recording and deployment of spoken dialogue, it also, of course, involves a

Figure 8.1 Screengrab from Year 9 computer game adapted from *The Tempest*.

transformation of Shakespeare's original text. The dramatic sequences are converted into the challenge-and-reward structures and win/lose states of the adventure game genre while the characters become the first-person avatar and non-player characters of this genre. Shakespeare purists might express horror at the apparent violence done to this most cherished piece of literary heritage, though Derek Jarman's and Peter Greenaway's films of *The Tempest* emphasise the need to create the play anew for a different cultural moment. More specifically, it can be argued that this 'ludic' approach to the play recognises its similarities to a game: its magical island, the challenges, tests, punishments and rewards Prospero devises; even Prospero's final surrender to the control of the audience, who must decide whether he will finally return to Milan or not.

It is not only the narrative structures of the text which are transformed into the elements of the game, however. The students also pay close attention to the words and imagery of the text. So Ariel's song to Ferdinand, 'Full fathom five thy father lies', is incorporated into the text as a pop-up (Figure 8.2) and voiced by a girl in the group. At the same time, the imagery of the song is transformed into objects in the gameworld: a treasure chest of clues for the player as Ferdinand to open and acquire (Figure 8.3). The objects they found that were most representative of the play-text were a skull, representing Alonso's bones and death; a crown, to indicate his kingship; and a marble (the closest they could get in the menu of objects in the software to the 'pearls that were his eyes').

These objects have twin significance in the game. Adventure games and role-playing games are a combination of narrative structures (events, characters, systems of narration and address, narrative duration and order and so on) and ludic structures (choices, challenges, game objectives, points, assets, alternative routes, win/lose states and so on). This group of girls have constructed these objects with poetic significance, charged with the metaphorical and narrative meanings of Ferdinand's supposed bereavement. But they have also constructed them as ludic objects: they are pick-ups, which the player must drop into an inventory, and use later in

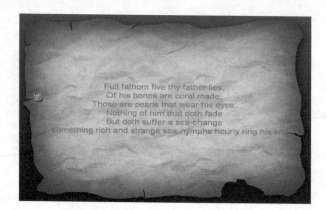

Figure 8.2 Ariel's song as a game pop-up.

Figure 8.3 Objects from Ariel's song as pick-ups in the game.

the game to open a door to the next stage. They have been programmed by the girls to collectively weigh the required amount to open the door when dropped in front of it.

In Vygotsky's terms, there is imaginative work here: a transformation of verbal imagery to visual, of Ariel's song to a game environment, of Prospero to a mad scientist and Miranda to a scantily clad Amazon, of Ferdinand's trials to a series of ludic challenges. Vygotsky's argument that creativity consists of rational, conceptual thought is equally well demonstrated, as these imaginative transformations are regulated by the rational structures of narrative sequence and consequence, ludic coherence and metaphoric representation.

Conclusion: ten principles

The view of media education presented in this chapter, and the notion of media literacy associated with it, offers significant variations on the ideas of culture, criticality and creativity in the English curriculum. Rather than repeat these, here are ten key principles. While they run the risk of omission and reductiveness which all lists court, they may serve as a stimulus for discussion, department meetings, continuing professional development (CPD) sessions and seminars. There is no settled way to resolve these issues, no simple template to adopt. The examples of this chapter can only hope to provoke debate and contribute something to the thinking, reflection and curriculum design which only teachers can carry through.

Ten principles of media education

1. Build on students' experiences and knowledge of the media.
2. Find connections between high culture and popular culture.
3. Find connections between the popular cultures of the past and those of contemporary media.

4. Cultivate orality as well as literacy.
5. Explore the rhetorics of institutions, texts and audiences.
6. Explore semiotic principles, lexicons and grammars across different media.
7. Promote creative production in different media.
8. Connect analytical work with production work.
9. Develop a media poetics, and explore the nature of cultural value and taste.
10. Promote the online distribution of students' work, and explore the meaning of such distribution.

Acknowledgements

Thanks are due to James Durran and Anthony Partington of Parkside Community College, Cambridge, for the examples of media work used in this chapter.

Further reading

Buckingham, D. (2003) *Media Education: Literacy, Learning and Contemporary Culture*, Cambridge: Polity.

Burn, A. and Durran, J. (2007) *Media Literacy in Schools: Practice, Production and Progression*, London: Paul Chapman.

McDougall, J. (2006) *The Media Teacher's Book*, London: Hodder Education.

Chapter 9

The 'real world' of technologies

What kinds of professional development are needed for English teachers?

Caroline Daly

Introduction

Economic and Social Research Council (ESRC) reports (2008a, 2008b) provide evidence that a majority of young people in the UK live in changed social and cultural conditions brought about by technology, and that this has far-reaching implications for schools and teachers. The message is that educational policy-making struggles to keep up with the realities of most learners' lives, and 'the future' is a world which many young people are already experiencing:

> While educationalists are rethinking formal learning environments, young people themselves are using new technologies for informal learning in a far wider array of social settings, public and private, shared and individual.
>
> (ESRC, 2008b: 4)

Where young people have access to technologies outside of formal education, there is a considerable range of evidence which points out the extent of the divide between young people's experiences of learning inside and outside of school. The Horizon Reports (The New Media Consortium and Educause, 2008, 2009, 2010) and the MacArthur Report (2008) have shown the extent of immersion in digital cultures of young people in the USA, examining these as new sites of learning. The MacArthur Report is based on a study which explored the impact of digital cultures on the ways classroom practices need to be re-conceptualised, with huge implications for teacher education: 'New media forms have altered how youth socialize and learn, and this raises a new set of issues that educators, parents, and policymakers should consider' (p. 2).

This chapter argues that in the UK, English teacher education is still far from 'considering' the full impact of the immersion of students in digital technologies. Crucially, the significance of Web 2.0 social communications technology is still peripheral to learning and teaching in most English departments, and practice develops in an *ad hoc* way which is scarcely sufficient to respond to the social environment which young learners now inhabit. Interactive whiteboards and learning platforms are, in fact, less significant for teacher development than learning to harness the real-world technologies which are ubiquitous for most young people and in which they are experienced, though not necessarily critical, users – social networking sites, photo and digital film sharing and mobile technologies.

The persistent problem

Through all stages of compulsory education, the political will and financial investment to embed technologies within the formal educational experience has been present for much of the past decade (the Building Schools for the Future initiative for secondary schools was an example). Prior to the current economic downturn, policy-making in the UK had seen a considerable mobilisation of funding and resources to support the development of 'e-confident' learners and teachers in schools (Becta, 2008; DfES, 2005) who might benefit from fully integrated technological infrastructures for learning. Policy-making, however, has not brought about the anticipated gains that might have been expected. A literature review undertaken as part of a larger study for Becta (Daly *et al.*, 2009a) provides evidence that many effective approaches to ICT CPD (information and communications technology continuing professional development) are in place, but they remain localised and there are insufficient means for ensuring that all teachers can access high-quality professional development in this area. Despite considerable resources being dedicated to developing the use of ICT in schools in recent years, there is a lack of impact on teachers' everyday practice, or what Becta has described as a 'significant deficit' (*Harnessing Technology Review*, 2008). This is despite the vast majority of teachers receiving some form of ICT CPD according to national surveys.

The implications of this pedagogical deficit are serious. For less advantaged sections of society, the pedagogy which exists within schools is crucial to how they gain access to the potentials of these technologies. The *Media Literacy Audit* (Ofcom, 2008) showed that children in the UK are familiar with the use of key media such as television, games consoles and the internet by the age of 5, but differences exist in access to technologies according to socio-economic group. There is a 'digital divide', and poorer students rely on technology in schools to participate in 'media culture' – for example, by having broadband access and use of relatively recent computers. Clearly, this picture changes all the time, as prices come down, but policy-making for schools needs to 'take responsibility to distribute access to these resources fairly and to compensate thereby for their unequal distribution in society' (Daly *et al.*, 2009a: 17).

The divide between young people's experiences and expectations of technology and practice within schools is a persistent challenge. For English teachers, whose work is so closely related to the formation of the cultural practices and social identities of the young people they teach, the challenge is significant. Most books aimed at English teacher education are organised around core 'skills and processes' as defined by the National Curriculum (2007) – speaking and listening, reading and writing, with ICT acknowledged as a linking strand within each, but usually treated as a further area of English subject knowledge and understanding somewhere towards the back of the volume. Hughes and Tolley (2010) argue that this is prevalent in the US as well as the UK and still suggests that 'newer literacy practices are peripheral topics rather than pedagogical frameworks that undergird language and literacy teaching' (p. 7).

In a recent study of initial teacher education in English in the UK, Smith (2010) found that there is 'wide variance' in provision and 'piecemeal' support for English teacher educators. While approximately one-third of teacher educators had received training in such things as making podcasts, the use of Web 2.0 in teaching and digital film, another third had received no training at all, with the remainder taking personal steps to develop their knowledge and skills in some forms of technology. She also found that there is little evidence that schools offer consistent learning experiences in ICT for trainee English teachers and that this is rarely a consideration in placing trainees in schools. In many ways, as technology becomes ubiquitous in schools, the pedagogical issues become invisible. Learning with and through technology is further down the agenda in terms of preparing English teachers – and yet, a significant body of evidence is being amassed which points to the fundamental importance of technologies in young people's identity formation, social relationships, communication skills and engagement with information. As cited elsewhere in this book, the Bullock Report argued in 1975 that:

> No child should be expected to cast off the language and culture of the home as he crosses the school threshold, nor to live and act as though school and home represent two totally separate and different cultures which have to be kept firmly apart.
>
> (DES, 1975: 286)

Given the persisting significance of this statement for principled English teaching, it seems extraordinary that a child's lived engagement with culture via technology outside the school is still considered something to think about 'additionally' rather than acknowledged as a prime factor in how students are oriented to learning in English. The slow rate of change is acknowledged in a NATE (National Association for the Teaching of English) position paper:

> As a profession, we cannot ignore ICT. By far the largest component of ICT is the C: communication. We don't have to embrace every aspect of it, any more than we do of the printed word. But we do need to acknowledge young people's use of Web 2 technology and we need to understand how to harness their creative potential in the classroom.
>
> (2007: 1)

The paper goes on to outline many of the same problems discussed by Scarratt and McInnes (2009) and Daly et al. (2009b) that are outlined in the next section.

A fragmented picture of ICT CPD

A key issue is the lack of a coherent provision for teachers to develop their subject pedagogy once they have qualified. The devolution of control over ICT CPD provision to school leaders in an expanding free-market economy for CPD has meant that an extremely varied pattern of provision exists. Pedagogy is often neglected as other agendas predominate the market for CPD spending. Scarratt and McInnes (2009) argue that a 'complex set of partnerships . . . have emerged between hardware manufacturers, software producers and educational institutions and support agencies.' (pp. 203–4). While English departments may be better equipped than ever before, there is a lack of opportunities for most teachers to access professional development focused on developing criticality in the use of, for example, blogging, film-making and podcasts. There is much inconsistency in reporting on the effectiveness of certain types of provision, especially regarding Local Authorities and higher education institutions. The CPD arrangements with these stakeholders are so varied that it is difficult to generalise about them in terms of their approach and success. The vast majority of CPD takes place within schools, where there is also an extremely varied picture of provision. It is possible for teachers within the same school to have widely differing CPD experiences, depending on the individual department, the relationship between the school and the Local Authority and the degree of teacher motivation. There is a prevalent dissatisfaction with one-off courses and external programmes which do not take account of the specific contexts of the school. There is also, however, dissatisfaction with school-based CPD where it is poorly planned and does not take account of subject differences and 'mixed ability' issues in teachers' technical competence.

Although skills training is clearly vital to being able to integrate technology into teachers' practice, it is very evident that a focus on skills is not sufficient to help teachers to develop their pedagogy. The amount of skills training provided can have misleading consequences by sending the message that a lot of teacher development has taken place, when in fact it makes little impact in itself on the quality of learning activities in classrooms unless it is accompanied by dedicated activities which focus on planning to teach a specific area of the curriculum to a specific class. A great deal of skills training has taken place in recent years, and yet there is a persistent lack of integration of technology into teachers' practice.

Challenges for professional development

The core issue to emerge is that teachers need to be at the centre of their own learning if they are to change their deep-seated beliefs and habits regarding the use of technology. Otherwise, surface-level adoption occurs, by which teachers just have time to learn how to use a technology without deep consideration of how it might be used to address context-specific learning needs of students. Rather than deepening and consolidating understanding of how to use the technology for enhancing learning, teachers frequently find they have to move on to learn how to use another technology or address another priority. Hammond *et al.* (2009) have identified the importance of cultivating 'an inclination' to use ICT in initial teacher education. Deep-seated beliefs continue to affect CPD throughout teachers' careers. Cogill (2008) has identified the importance of a 'learning disposition' which can overcome barriers to developing with ICT, and Hansson (2006) has highlighted that 'motivation' to want to improve professionally through ICT CPD can be cultivated by 'reflecting as a teacher' and asking, 'What is in it for me? How can I improve my teaching using technology? What are the benefits for the students?' (p. 562).

A historical focus on techno-centric aims for practitioner development has been identified as very hard to shift. Centralised training (the New Opportunities Fund), generic skills training, top-down frameworks for training and 'one shot' and 'one shot plus follow-up' approaches (Jimoyiannis and Komis, 2007) have meant that the potential of technology to enhance the learning experiences of students remains largely unfulfilled (see, for example, reports on interactive whiteboard use in the UK, Moss *et al.*, 2007; Preston, 2004). Similarly, there has been relatively little focus on *how* teachers learn with technologies within online collaborative contexts (Dede, 2006; Fisher *et al.*, 2006). The importance of secure subject knowledge and subject-based pedagogical understanding has been highlighted for the effective use of technologies in education (Cox *et al.*, 2003), but there is relatively little that examines how professional development with technologies might be achieved.

The pressure to 'move on', to keep up with the latest technology initiative and remain satisfied with surface-level adoption comes from conflicting priorities for CPD which arise when schools must implement multiple policy initiatives, concerning both ICT and other areas of development. It is difficult for headteachers to devote dedicated CPD time to consolidation and further development of ICT. There is a lack of time to both consolidate and respond to the next new initiative. Consistent, low-profile changes in the quality of teaching have been less visible than other high-profile initiatives such as installing interactive whiteboards in recent years. It is possible for observers to assume that teachers are sufficiently trained because they are 'using' a technology in a visible way, but this is no indication that genuine change has happened in the quality of the learning.

Problem-free access to equipment and specialist technical support are prerequisites for CPD to take effect. Without these, teachers become de-motivated and lack confidence in trying out new ideas. Although this has long been recognised, it is still a prevalent problem in schools, and a shortage of access to equipment which is concentrated in computer suites remains a serious obstacle to professional development.

The Becta study (Daly *et al.*, 2009a) found that teachers are motivated by their subject enthusiasms being catered for but subject-specific pedagogy is not sufficiently explored in ICT CPD provision. Subject-specific needs have been met by access to outside experts, subject associations and peers in other schools. This is especially important for secondary school teachers who do not get sufficient access to stimulating CPD which is informed by the latest subject developments

(Smith, 2008). Senior management have a critical role in ensuring that CPD involving external stakeholders is successful, and their active and focused investment in the CPD from the start is critical to its success. This is not only in supporting staff to gain access to externally provided CPD but also in ensuring that time is provided in school for implementation. The co-operative link between the school and external programmes is extremely important (Pachler, Daly and Turvey, 2010; Smith, 2008). Smith (2008), Daly et al. (2009b) and Cordingley et al. (2007) have all emphasised the importance of *judicious* external input to school-based professional development. Such input can come from a range of stakeholders – higher education institutions, Local Authorities or commercial companies, but the important thing is a deep and sustained engagement over time in a learning project which allows teachers to prioritise their own development focus, pace their development and take risks.

English teachers reported the importance of personal pedagogical beliefs about the learning and teaching of English in developing work with technologies (Pachler et al., 2010). In analysing a case of English teachers, they report on one teacher who typifies the need for collaborative practice and an environment which encourages risk-taking:

> A major factor . . . is the sharing of practice with colleagues she trusts and in situations where she feels free to experiment and 'play around on my own'. She says at one point that she needs to 'believe in the learning' before she feels 'pushed to find out more about the technology' and it is clear that her belief in [working with a virtual learning environment] begins with a view of learning before the practice becomes an integral part of her professional life as an English teacher.

Further evidence from Hughes and Tolley (2010) suggests that judicious intervention by English higher education tutors with their trainees as they learn to use technologies can model practice in English classrooms:

> Our role became like that of butterfly catchers – briefly interacting to study them and offer support and guidance, but releasing them quickly, careful not to damage their own innate beauty or creativity. So how much of our teaching should be the exploration of knowledge by the students themselves and how much should be directed by the teacher?
>
> (p. 9)

They advocate the teaching of what they term 'visual essays' as a means of encouraging school students to 'think about who they are and what they want to represent to the world through, not only what they say, but also how they say it' (p. 18). Crucial to this was allowing trainees to explore for themselves the potential of a range of Web 2.0 technologies for the creation of visual essays and make choices about the application in classrooms of what they developed.

A major problem, however, is that the majority of teachers do not get access to external sources of professional development. The 'landscape' for CDP (see Figure 9.1) identified by Daly *et al.* (2009b) represents the range of models for ICT CPD which are current in schools today. There is doubt about whether familiar 'models' of ICT CPD can have any particular value without first dedicating time to helping teachers to see how technologies can make a difference in their own particular contexts. This seems to be the most important factor which underpins success in a range of widely differing approaches. Holmes *et al.* (2007) argue:

> Time after time . . . the traditional forms of continuing professional develop-ment (the 'training', 'deficit' and 'cascade' models for example) have proven to be ineffective. Concentrating more effort on seeking convergence between the teachers' values and their perceptions of the utility of the ICT professional development, before beginning the conventional professional development activities, should ensure that more teachers have the necessary readiness and receptiveness to be committed to engaging with change.
>
> (p. 402)

The argument is that CPD should focus on developing 'readiness' to learn to teach with technologies and 'receptiveness' to new ideas. Rather than identifying a set of relatively fixed models for how to 'do' ICT, it seems important to build principles into the design of professional development which can be flexibly applied in a range of settings. Each school and English department is unique, as are all the teachers who work in them. Teachers experience the same provision differently (Holmes *et al.*, 2007), which affects their perceptions of whether the time it takes to learn how to use ICT is a worthwhile investment. The effectiveness of various types of provision is affected by a range of factors, including teachers' previous experience of technologies, personal attitudes to change, deep-held beliefs about learning and being exposed to informal opportunities to develop skills which are learned formally. It is, therefore, not surprising that the literature offers contrasting, and sometimes even contradictory, findings regarding the effectiveness of particular types of provision within small-scale studies. Teachers may experience effective professional development from external providers who meet needs where expertise is not available within the school, or where there is a more motivated impetus pro-vided by committed outsiders rather than less enthusiastic school-based colleagues. At the same time, teachers can find that external provision does not take account of the specific issues the teachers deal with on a day-to-day basis in their schools, with their particular learners and resources. The sheer complexity of this picture is acknowledged (Rae and O'Brien, 2007) and the focus needs to be on identifying principles of effective CPD which can be achieved in diverse contexts.

Professional development in using technologies in English therefore needs to be recognised as a complex, social, intellectual and practical activity which brings about change in teachers' beliefs and understandings in relation to chang-ing practice and developing skills. It takes place within a range of locations and

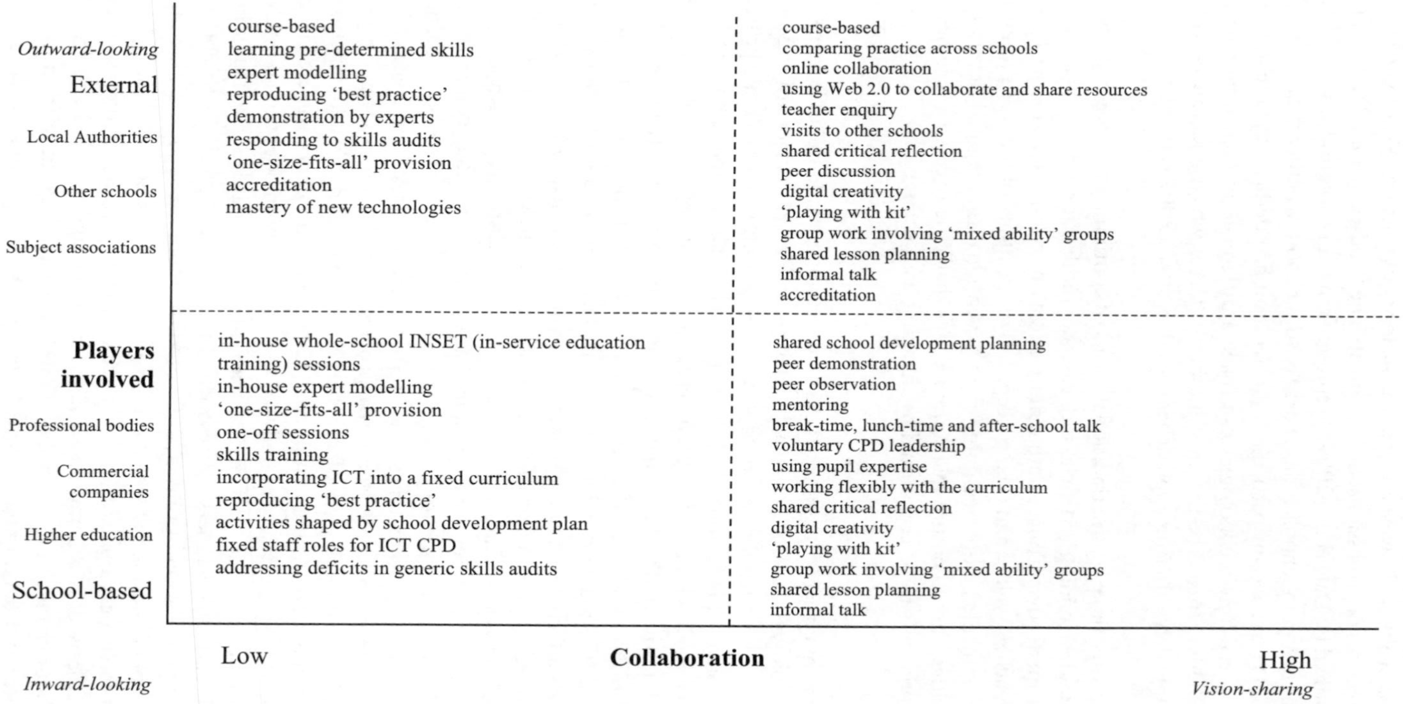

	Low	**High** *Vision-sharing*
Outward-looking **External** Local Authorities Other schools Subject associations	course-based learning pre-determined skills expert modelling reproducing 'best practice' demonstration by experts responding to skills audits 'one-size-fits-all' provision accreditation mastery of new technologies	course-based comparing practice across schools online collaboration using Web 2.0 to collaborate and share resources teacher enquiry visits to other schools shared critical reflection peer discussion digital creativity 'playing with kit' group work involving 'mixed ability' groups shared lesson planning informal talk accreditation
Players involved Professional bodies Commercial companies Higher education **School-based** *Inward-looking*	in-house whole-school INSET (in-service education training) sessions in-house expert modelling 'one-size-fits-all' provision one-off sessions skills training incorporating ICT into a fixed curriculum reproducing 'best practice' activities shaped by school development plan fixed staff roles for ICT CPD addressing deficits in generic skills audits	shared school development planning peer demonstration peer observation mentoring break-time, lunch-time and after-school talk voluntary CPD leadership using pupil expertise working flexibly with the curriculum shared critical reflection digital creativity 'playing with kit' group work involving 'mixed ability' groups shared lesson planning informal talk
		Collaboration

Figure 9.1 The ICT CPD landscape (Daly et al., 2009a: 72).

modes which provide cultural contexts in which to learn. It involves re-evaluating learner–teacher roles and overall classroom pedagogies. It brings changes in aspects of professional identity. For these reasons, simplistic models are not helpful – it is highly situated and success is subject to many inter-related human and social factors which vary across locations, strategies and relationships. From the factors identified in the literature, a pattern emerges of professional development taking place within two types of frameworks which have key features. The features do not necessarily determine success or failure. They interact with other features of both frameworks, and they have effects on each other within an ecological view of how teachers learn. This means that CPD depends on how different aspects interact with each other, bearing in mind all the time that the English teacher is a vital element within the ecology. The frameworks are *pedagogical frameworks* and *frameworks of players*.

Pedagogical frameworks are characterised by the degree of collaboration and hierarchical approaches which underpin the learning design of the provision. This determines the relationships, roles and responsibilities of the various players involved. It shapes the design of CPD, in terms of engagement, activity, duration and intellectual commitment. It is essentially about the extent to which a 'vision' of ICT pedagogy is developed *with* staff or is 'delivered' by others who may be internal to the school (a headteacher or subject ICT coordinator or advanced skills teacher) or external (a body which provides a course). This determines the way CPD activities are designed and the degree of autonomy, relevance and differentiation which teachers may experience.

Frameworks of players are characterised by the degree to which CPD involves a range of players. It determines the various roles of people involved, the importance attributed to different types of expertise and choices about where expertise comes from. Frameworks of players determine how far the CPD is inward- or outward-looking, in terms of the school environment. It describes the extent to which teachers engage with CPD which involves external sources of help and advice which can ensure that the sources of knowledge on which ICT is based have a broader and more informed perspective. This is not just about whether the CPD is provided 'in-house' or at an external location. It is possible for an 'in-house' school-based CPD programme to involve much outside support and help from the Local Authority or a local higher education institution.

Figure 9.1 shows these frameworks. The diagram consists of two axes. One represents the 'collaboration' aspects (horizontal axis) of pedagogical frameworks for CPD, ranging from 'high' to 'low' collaboration. The other shows the 'players involved' (vertical axis) in frameworks of players and aspects of those, ranging from exclusively school-based to fully engaged with external players. Where the frameworks are more or less collaborative and more or less involved with external players, different features of ICT CPD appear within the diagram. The diagram, therefore, offers a way of seeing the current landscape. Four key areas represent the patterns of provision which exist where the two frameworks intersect. These areas show the features of CPD which frequently appear, in the form of four models:

- High Collaborative School-Based
- Low Collaborative School-Based
- High Collaborative External Players
- Low Collaborative External Players.

These are not intended to represent deterministic models for CPD affecting English teachers. They are descriptive, and several features of the models will appear to greater or lesser extents, and cross boundaries. They are intended as a guide to considering the core features of professional development which are consistent with prevalent types of provision.

Changing personal–public boundaries

Boundaries between the private and the public world dissolve in many ways as a consequence of increased flexibility and user-control over the locus of work-related and private communication. One key affordance of new technologies, for example, is that they allow users to exercise control and determine whether a 'space' for communication is private or public. Users do not just generate their own content but also generate the contexts for their learning in and across formal and informal settings (Pachler, Daly and Turvey, 2010). 'Spaces' for social networking and online participation continually evolve in ways which classrooms have never been able to do, and are certainly controlled in ways which reflect a completely different set of power relations between participants than those found in a conventional classroom. This user-centred and agentive perspective is still a long way from the experience of most learners in schools and further and higher education settings – including those which are rich in technology. The MacArthur Report (2008) claims that 'notions of expertise and authority have been turned on their heads' (p. 2) and English departments need to capitalise far more on the informal, collaborative, peer-learning networks which their students inhabit. This would constitute a considerable shift in the ways that formal education has been organised to date.

Conclusion

Electronic mobile devices, especially mobile phones with a wide range of functions, are more and more central features of our everyday lives. Yet, they remain mostly excluded from schools. While media use in everyday life and formal education belong to separate socio-cultural practice domains, the devices and services prevalent in everyday life offer considerable potential as learning resources. This we consider to be one of the main challenges in coming years for educational institutions which have been slow, on the whole, to incorporate the divergent social and cultural realities of students' lives into learning practices.

There is rich potential for technologies to become embedded in English departments in the UK – the technological infrastructure is there in most cases, and creative curriculum possibilities have begun to re-emerge. But the counter-forces at work appear to ensure that there is ongoing tension between policy and implementation, between skills agendas and professional knowledge and understanding and between technology-driven priorities and a learning agenda.

Further reading

Hughes, J. and Tolley, S. (2010) 'Engaging students through new literacies: The good, bad and curriculum of visual essays', *English in Education*, 44(1): 5–26.

This journal article is an extremely accessible account of a research project into trainee English teachers' development of practice using technologies to create 'visual essays' with their students. It locates their development in conceptual work on multimodal literacies.

Pachler, N., Daly, C. and Turvey, A. (2010) 'Teacher professional development practices: The case of the Haringey Transformation Teachers Programme', in O. Lindberg and A. Olofsson (eds), *Online Learning Communities and Teacher Professional Development*, Hershey, PA: IGI Global, pp. 77–95.

This chapter presents research into a collaborative programme of professional development for teachers in a London borough, and analyses the findings in relation to its impact on English teachers.

Website

National Association for the Teaching of English, 'English and ICT'. Available online at http://www.nate.org.uk/index.php?page=44 (accessed 27 October 2010).

These web pages contain the policy and position papers which underpin innovative and fully informed development of English teaching using ICT, as well as a range of exemplar material to support the development of critically informed English teaching involving technologies.

Chapter 10

Creativity in English teaching and learning

Sue Dymoke

Introduction

The word creativity originated in the nineteenth century as a 'creative power or faculty; ability to create' (Brown 1993: 544) and has increasingly come to the fore in educational policy terms in the last 15 years, both in England and internationally. This chapter considers different ways of defining creativity, the contexts in which the emergence of this term has occurred and how creative practices have been/ are being shaped by political considerations. Furthermore, it looks at potential opportunities for creativity within the English curriculum and its associated assessment frameworks and introduces some key research and reflections on the subject. Throughout, the chapter raises issues and questions for readers to explore with reference to their own developing experiences of English teaching and learning.

Definitions of creativity

Many writers have attempted to define creativity, for example:

- 'Creativity is the essence of learning itself . . . Creative imagination is not a by product of our interactions with the world but the basis of them' (Smith *et al*. 1984: 151, as cited Harrison 1994).
- 'Creativity is the ability to see relationships where none exist' (Thomas Disch (n.d.), poet and science fiction writer).
- 'Creativity, it has been said, consists largely of re-arranging what we know in order to find out what we do not know' (George Kneller (1965)).
- '[An] ability to produce something new through imaginative skill, whether a new solution to a problem, a new method or device, or a new artistic object or form' (Britannica Concise Encyclopedia (2006)).
- 'Creativity is essentially a form of problem-solving. But it is a special type of problem-solving – one that involves problems for which there are no easy answers: that is, problems for which popular or conventional responses do not work. Creativity involves adaptability and flexibility of thought . . . Creativity goes beyond possession and use of artistic or musical talent' (James D. Moran III (1988)).

Some of these definitions emphasise an originality of thought and a flexibility of mind that enables the creative person to create something (either in concrete or abstract form) which is completely new and paves the way for others. Some appear to be describing the work of geniuses in their particular fields and arguably distance ordinary members of society from the act of creativity and, importantly, from the perception that they could ever be creative themselves.

Perhaps a more helpful definition, certainly with regard to teaching and learning English, has been developed by Anna Craft, one of the foremost academics researching in this field, in her description of 'little c creativity' or 'LCC' as she often calls it (Craft 2001: 45). LCC is different from the highly creative acts demonstrated by artists, scientists, composers, child prodigies and other people of exceptional creative skill in that it is not concerned with choreographing a new ballet, composing a startlingly original epic poem or discovering the patterns of DNA. Instead it pertains to how we live our lives, how we identify and actively initiate or respond to the challenges and contexts in which we find ourselves, how we innovate, make choices or affect changes in order to move on. In placing emphasis on the personal, Craft also presents a challenge to teachers to think beyond rigid subject definitions and barriers in order to consider the place of creativity and the creative processes involved in all areas of knowledge and skills development, not just those traditionally labelled as 'arts' or 'creative subjects'.

Margaret Boden also distinguishes between personal everyday acts of creativity that might be new *psychologically* significant experiences for the individuals concerned, but which are not ground-breaking or original, with those creative acts which are of a lasting *historical* significance. She describes these as 'P-creative' and 'H-creative' acts (Boden 2005: 43).

The emphasis in *All Our Futures: Creativity, Culture and Education*, the report from National Advisory Committee on Creative and Cultural Education (NACCCE), is that, given the right opportunities, we are all creative, or have the potential to be creative, to varying degrees. In preferring this more democratic approach, to 'sectoral' or 'élite' definitions (1999: 28) which privilege arts-based practitioners or highly talented individuals, the report has much that is of interest to English teachers and students. Its authors define creativity as consisting of four characteristics:

> First, they always involve thinking or behaving imaginatively. Second, overall this imaginative activity is purposeful: that is, it is directed to achieving an objective. Third, these processes must generate something original. Fourth, the outcome must be of value in relation to the objective.
>
> (NACCCE 1999: 29)

These characteristics result in creativity as 'imaginative activity fashioned so as to produce outcomes that are both original and of value' (1999: 29). This notion of value was reiterated some seven years later in an entertaining Technology, Entertainment, Design (TED) lecture given by the chairperson of NACCCE, Sir

Ken Robinson, in which he succinctly describes creativity as 'the process of having original ideas that have value' (Robinson 2006).

Before moving on, it might be worth pausing to reflect on the above definitions and their potential applicability to the work of English teachers. For example, where and how, in the context of an English lesson, could a teacher devise opportunities to engage students in developing 'original ideas that have value' (Robinson 2006)? Is this a laudable aim? Is it realistic? What sort of English activities would students participate in to develop original and valuable ideas? In exploring Craft and Boden's conceptualisations of creativity, how could creativity be identified or nurtured in the lives of learners? Although there is not the space in this short chapter to explore definitions of creativity in greater depth or across a range of different subject areas, useful reviews in Loveless (2002) and a special issue of the *Cambridge Journal of Education* (vol. 36, no. 3) on creativity provide further opportunities to investigate this aspect more fully.

Contextual overview: how and what sort of creativity has come to the fore in education?

Creativity became something of a catchphrase towards the end of the 1990s, a decade that had previously been characterised by its focus on 'high-stakes testing' and standards agendas and from which many educators and creative practitioners were anxious to escape. It might appear, therefore, that creativity in education is a recent phenomena. However, as early as 1962 Jerome Bruner wrote, 'there is, alas, a shrillness to our contemporary concern with creativity' (p. 17). Bruner recognised the need for what he called 'a metaphoric understanding of creativity' (1962: 30, as cited in Harrison 1994), while at the same time emphasising the danger of making exaggerated claims that one educational movement could provide all the solutions.

Nine years later, in his celebrated study *Playing and Reality*, Winnicott reflected on origins of creativity and the enforced state of compliance in which people can live their lives. He perceives this as a listless state, disarming individuals of choices and opportunities for access to or engagement in creative existence or actions. He comments: 'It is creative apperception that more than anything else that makes the individual feel life is worth living' (Winnicott 1971: 65).

More recently, the publication of *All Our Futures: Creativity, Culture and Education* (NACCCE 1999) focused attention on the need to support and encourage the creative potential of individual learners. Following in its wake, government-funded programmes and initiatives, such as the National College for School Leadership's (NCSL) creative leadership seminars and creative partnerships, came into being. A number of influential research seminar series took creativity and aspects of English or education as their focus.[1] In addition, inspectors from the Office for Standards in Education (Ofsted) have put creativity in schools under the spotlight in their reports of school inspections (Ofsted 2010).

Anna Craft charts the heightened interest shown by policy makers worldwide in establishing creativity as a phenomena and the shift from the 'performative' culture (Craft 2006: 340) of heavily monitored 1990s classrooms. Although this change has largely been welcomed by those working in education and creative fields, it is important to remember that this latest creative emphasis is underpinned by economic incentives and driven by societal pressures to succeed in a global market-place. What could be called an appropriation of creativity for economic ends has become enshrined, in England at least, within the five outcomes of Every Child Matters policy in that children are to be supported to 'achieve economic well being' (DfES 2004a:1). Furthermore, this emphasis has permeated the National Curriculum. Its creativity and critical thinking section states:

> Creative activity is essential for the future wellbeing of society and the economy. It can unlock the potential of individuals and communities to solve personal, local and global problems. Creativity is possible in every area of human activity – from the cutting edge of human endeavour to ordinary aspects of our daily life.
>
> (QCDA 2010a)

Contextual overview: creativity in the English curriculum

At the time of its introduction in 2001, fears were raised by educators about the Secondary English Framework's (DfEE 2001) impact on creative classroom approaches and opportunities for the development of sustained writing. Arguments about the need for a creative curriculum have continued ever since in a period when increasing managerialism of schooling has resulted in a decreased autonomy for teachers (Jones 2003). In some schools, learners have been 'hustled from one skills-based-task to another' (Marsh and Millard 2000: 61) and given dwindling opportunities for risk-taking or creativity by their teachers who are trying to meet targets, climb value-added league tables, keep friendly with their management teams and keep under the Ofsted radar. Operating within an education marketplace, English teachers have been increasingly seen to deal in knowledge rather than meaning-making (Kress *et al.* 2004) being expected to 'deliver' the goods rather than to teach young people to engage in deep learning. Ofsted have written of texts being used as 'manual[s]' (2005: 23). To take this analogy further, I suggest that this utilitarian approach to English teaching opened the door to an IKEA-style subject in which flat-packed (specification compliant) framework responses to texts could be reassembled and transformed into 'personalised' learning outcomes.

Fortunately, however, this bleak picture did not reflect the situation in every classroom. Creative English teachers continued to find ways to teach imaginatively and to inspire young readers using active approaches. Support for their creative approaches was also at hand as intense debates about the need for flexibility and creativity finally began to have an influence on some aspects of curriculum development. A statement by the then English poet laureate Andrew Motion, published during QCA's English 21 consultations about the future of the curriculum, high-lighted issues of creative entitlement. He wrote: 'Every child has the right to read and write creatively and we believe that creativity should become a central part of formal education' (QCA 2005a: 1). This paper provoked other produc-tive discussions among artists, educators, subject associations and researchers and proposals for a Creative Writing AS (Advanced Supplementary) exam specifica-tion.[2] Subsequent *Playback* and *Taking English Forward* publications (QCA 2005b, 2005c) reinforced a desire from many quarters for increased creative curriculum opportunities. The discussions also acknowledged the merits of creative activities in English as being good preparation for imaginative problem-solving in the workplace and elsewhere (QCA 2005b). In 2006 Ken Robinson contributed to this debate with the warning: '[W]e are educating people out of their creative capacities'. In the same lecture he contended that 'creativity now is as important in education as literacy, and we should treat it with the same status' (Robinson 2006).

To some extent the revised content of the Primary Strategy documentation (DfES 2006c) and the National Curriculum (QCA 2007a) both aimed to reflect these growing concerns. A greater focus on creativity within the 2007 National Curriculum orders provides some grounds for optimism that there will be more time for creative, non-exam-focused work in future. But in an education system where core subjects, a new emphasis on functional skills and a testing regime (albeit a slightly less straitened one) continue to dominate, is it possible that creativity could or should have an equal footing with literacy? I now want to consider where creativity is currently located within what Mission and Morgan call 'schooled English' (2006: 107) and how it is defined in assessment terms.

Within the programmes of study for the 2007 iteration of Secondary National Curriculum English, creativity is named as the second of four key concepts. (The other concepts are 'competence, cultural understanding and critical understanding' (QCA 2007b).) It is interesting to observe how the descriptors of what constitutes creativity vary across Key Stages 3 and 4. Within Key Stage 3 English creativity is conceptualised as:

- Making fresh connections between ideas, experiences, texts and words, draw-ing on a rich experience of language and literature.
- Using inventive approaches to making meaning, taking risks, playing with language and using it to create new effects.
- Using imagination to convey themes, ideas and arguments, solve problems, and create settings, moods and characters.
- Using creative approaches to answering questions, solving problems and devel-oping ideas.

(QCA 2007a: 1.2)

Whereas at Key Stage 4, the second and third statements above change to:

◻ Experimenting with language, manipulating form, challenging conventions and reinterpreting ideas.
◻ Using imagination to create effects to surprise and engage the audience.

(QCA 2007b: 1.2)

It appears that 11- to 14-year-olds are encouraged to take a more original approach to different aspects of the subject. Key Stage 3 offers more opportunity for playfulness before the more serious business of writing for assessment takes hold in Key Stage 4.

The Key Stage 3 concept also dovetails quite neatly with the newly developed Primary Curriculum (which was to be implemented from 2011) in that one of the Learning and Thinking skills primary-aged children were to work on was to '*create and develop*, using their imagination to explore possibilities and generate ideas. They try out innovative alternatives, looking for patterns, recognising differences and making generalisations, predicting outcomes and making reasoned decisions' (QCDA 2010b). These skills were intended to be integrated within their work in all aspects of the curriculum, including literacy. If this curriculum is eventually made statutory in some form,[3] it will be interesting to see how great an emphasis is placed on development of creativity in primary classrooms and the impact that this could have on teaching and learning in English as the first cohort of children move into secondary education.

Creative speaking and listening

The arrival of a new curriculum model has a greater focus on spoken language at both primary and secondary level. The National Curriculum for English clearly states the importance of spoken language study in all four of its 'key concepts'. The development of students' knowledge about how language functions to create meaning is a key element within all the above curriculum requirements. Students will be in a better position to explore how meaning is created if the approach to planning and teaching begins with contexts and situations that they have experienced. For example, students need to be able to 'use a range of ways to structure and organise their speech to support their purposes and guide the listener' (QCA 2007a: 2.1b). This could, for example, involve asking a class to think about their construction of a very short piece of spoken informational text – a joke. In his work on the art of common talk, Carter has acknowledged that even young children have 'the capacity for telling and receiving jokes which depend for their effect on a recognition of the creative play with patterns of meaning' (Carter 2003: 18). He comments on the creativity of everyday talk with its 'wordplay, puns and formulaic jokes' (2003: 18). Such a rich and accessible field is ideal for student investigations.

Creative reading

Reading is a highly creative act. Rosenblatt memorably describes how a text is created in the space between what the writer provides on the page and what the reader brings to the text. Each text provides a 'blueprint' (1978: 88) which is made real by each individual reader as they bring themselves, their associations, feelings and experiences to the page. Each text 'event' stimulates the reader's creativity. Rosenblatt distinguishes between efferent, non-aesthetic reading, in which the reader has an impersonal relationship with a text (and is primarily concerned with information retrieval), and aesthetic reading, where an individual's 'attention is centred directly on what he is living through during his relationship with a particular text' (Rosenblatt 1978: 25).

During my doctoral research on the teaching of poetry I interviewed a head of English who abhorred the pressure he felt under with his GCSE (General Certificate of Secondary Education) classes to 'produce kids who can write responses rather than kids who can write poems' (Dymoke 2002: 88). During the last ten years he has undoubtedly felt under even greater pressure. There has been increased emphasis on an efferent approach to studying all kinds of texts; one could say that students and teachers are becoming ever more conversant with acronyms such as PEE (point, evidence, explain) at the expense of developing an understanding of the creative processes which have shaped texts in the first place. Could it be that the act of devising increasingly elaborate acronyms has in fact become the most creative aspect of English teaching?

Creative writing and teacher confidence

The proposed development of an A level in creative writing and the introduction of an increased creative writing element within A-level English are both helping to focus attention once again on English teachers' levels of confidence in teaching creative processes. Although this is likely to be a concern for teachers who are new to the profession, the concern is not exclusive to this group by any means. Research tells us that many pre-service English teachers (training to teach across the 5–19 age range) have, for example, had very limited experience of writing poetry themselves either at school or in their first degree (Ray 1999; Dymoke 2009). Nevertheless, in many countries including the UK and Canada they would be expected to model themselves as writers and readers of poetry and other types of texts in the classroom (see, for example, the curriculum policy documents Saskatchewan Education 1998 and DCSF 2008a). Although the expectation, that the teacher should also be a writer in their classroom, is not embedded within curriculum policy documents in all anglophone nations, the potential impact of teacher-writer on the development of students' composition skills has been a topic for debate internationally for many decades. For example, poet Kenneth Koch's accounts of teaching poetry writing in a New York public school (1970, 1973) and Donald Graves' investigations of young children's writing in New Hampshire and his use of classroom writing conferences

(1981, 1983) have been widely discussed and imitated. Many UK-based research-ers have commented on the need for teachers to model themselves as both writers and readers of poetry (Stibbs 1981; Dunn *et al.* 1987, Nicholls 1990, Yates 1999). Nicholls observes that 'children need to know that adults too, struggle with words' (1990: 27). Stibbs views teachers' encouragement of writing by writing as a moral obligation and a vital element of a child's classroom experience: '[U]nless teachers do that they are tailor's dummies in a nudist colony – very bad manners' (1981: 49). Yates writes whenever possible with students. He comments, 'what I write won't necessarily be any good, but that's not important; writing is about taking chances and trying things out' (Yates 1999: 2). Clearly, those who are new to the teaching profession may not yet have the confidence to struggle, bare all or take such chances. They may well need to be given supported opportunities, early in their training, to take risks, experiment with creative approaches (including poetry writing activities) and to develop a critical awareness of creative writing pedagogy which will sustain them throughout their teaching careers, which will, in turn, enable them to develop their creative selves.

Cremin (2006) draws on a survey of primary teachers and student teachers to suggest that modelling often focuses on pre-prepared sections of text and lacks the 'struggle' or reflection on that struggle which the creative process may have originally involved. She questions the extent to which 'real modelling, encompass-ing spontaneity and risk' (2006: 417) actually takes place in classrooms and reflects on the limiting and overtly instructional nature of writing pedagogy as directed by the National Literacy Strategy (DfEE 1988). This investigation led her and her colleagues to support greater risk-taking by a small group of teachers and their students and to develop their creativity in writing (see Grainger *et al.* 2005).

Innovative schemes including Writing Together,[4] Poetry Places,[5] Poetryclass,[6] Creative Partnerships[7] and We're Writers[8] strive, in their various ways, to strengthen links between creative practitioners and learning communities. Some national schemes such as Poetryclass, Writing Together and the residential writing courses run by the Arvon Foundation can provide tailored opportunities for teachers to develop confidence to write creatively for themselves but such opportunities sadly remain limited and are subject to the vagaries of funding. Creative Partnerships describes itself as 'the flagship creative learning programme, designed to develop the skills of children and young people across England, raising their aspirations, achievements, skills and life chances' (Creative Partnerships 2010). The impact of such creative projects can be very short-lived and the outcomes not always as was intended (see, for example, Thomson *et al.* 2006). However, in the most successful projects there now appears to be a greater emphasis on teacher development to ensure that creative work is carefully planned for and has a lasting impact on the participants. In such cases they can be a powerful force for creative renewal in a school and for professional development across a department team (Arts Council 2003, Ofsted 2010).

Creativity within public examinations for English

GCSE

Alongside this overarching curriculum, it is important to consider the opportunities that exist for creative approaches to speaking, listening, reading and writing within public examinations. New specifications for GCSE English (for first teaching in autumn 2010) contain some acknowledgement of the increased emphasis on creativity within the National Curriculum. However, these acknowledgements could appear to be rather token nods towards creativity. An examination of the two examples of tasks below (or those from other specifications) raises such questions as: What creative processes will students be engaged if they carry out these tasks? How genuinely creative could these assessed activities be? To what extent could they develop students' understanding of the texts they are making and/or reading through their completion?

For example, Assessment and Qualifications Alliance's (AQA) Language Unit 3b (AQA 2009a) includes a section on 'Producing creative texts (creative writing)'. The guidance word limit is 1,200 words for two different tasks. These should be produced under formal supervision with a maximum time for completion of 4 hours. (AQA stress the need for texts to be of suitable lengths for their intended purpose and that they do not have to be completed at the same time.)

Two of the illustrative tasks provided on the AQA website are:

a)   Look at the poem 'Sister Maude' by Christina Rossetti (from the literary heritage section of the AQA Anthology). Transform this text into one of your own by writing a non-fiction or journalistic piece based on the content or ideas in the poem.

b)   The web host of a creative writing web site approaches you to submit some writing for it. This month's theme is 'Change'. You have complete freedom in your choice of form, but are asked not to make what you submit longer than 1000 words. Write your piece for the web site.

The objective assessed in this part of AQA's Unit 3 is AO4 Writing:

◻   Write to communicate clearly, effectively and imaginatively, using and adapting forms and selecting vocabulary appropriate to task and purpose in ways that engage the reader.
◻   Organise information and ideas into structured and sequenced sentences, paragraphs and whole texts, using a variety of linguistic and structural features to support cohesion and overall coherence.
◻   Use a range of sentence structures for clarity, purpose and effect, with accurate punctuation and spelling.

(AQA 2009a)

AQA advise that 'at least one-third of available credit for AO4 should be awarded for the use of a range of sentence structures for clarity, purpose and effect, with accurate punctuation and spelling.

(AQA 2009a)

Clearly, these examples raise questions about how and where creativity features within the specification, the balance of the weightings and about the teaching GCSE English as it is constituted in the different specifications on offer.

A-level English Literature

Within the A-level English Literature assessment objectives, creativity features in AO1, which assesses candidates' ability to '[a]rticulate creative, informed and relevant responses to literary texts, using appropriate terminology and concepts, and coherent, accurate written expression' (QCA 2006a). Barbara Bleiman considers that post-16 English courses do offer 'new opportunities for responding to texts in creative ways, following similar developments in many higher education literature courses' (2008a: 37). She observes that most of the English Literature A-level specifications allow for one recreative-style written piece within their internal assessment. Nevertheless, when looked at more closely, it would appear that these pieces (which include text transformation and imitative writing) offer limited creative scope for students. It is also interesting to note that the majority of creative opportunities are within the AS year (first year) of the course. Lack of a creative element, for the most part, within A2 courses could imply that examiners do not consider creative writing tasks will elicit sufficiently rigorous outcomes for assessment in the final year of the course. Alternatively, this could suggest that the creative writing skills developed in AS are perceived as building blocks to support in-depth textual analysis by A-level candidates rather than as a means to an end in themselves.

A-level English Language

In contrast, assessment of creativity is to the fore throughout the modules offered in A-level English Language specifications both at AS and A2. It is also a compulsory element for all candidates. Audience, purpose and contextual factors are stressed within the types of activities exemplified. AO4 states that students should '[d]emonstrate expertise and creativity in the use of English in a range of different contexts, informed by linguistic study' (QCA 2006b). The ways in which this AO has been interpreted by the different examination boards arguably limits students' creativity by dictating specifically the range of forms and topics that may be chosen. For example, WJEC candidates are categorically told that the 'original writing' section of their AS paper 'should consist of a single, continuous, extended piece of creative, original writing in a fictional, 'literary' mode. **Candidates must not submit poetry, or any writing which is purely informative/factual/vaguely descriptive**' [original bold]. They are given a choice of forms (which include a short story, an extract from a novel or a generic fictional style, a dramatic monologue, a play script, a piece of satire or parody); however, this choice must be restricted to forms or genres that they have previously studied. While it is undoubtedly pleasing to note that students are being given a bit more scope to set their own coursework tasks, it is clear that much will depend on the choices made for them or (better still) negotiated with by their own English teachers. Levels of teacher confidence in preparing their students for creative writing tasks will have a significant role to play here. In addition, the way the WJEC coursework task is framed seems to imply creativity is reserved for writers of fiction – albeit in a variety of forms. Creative non-fiction (an increasingly popular option in university creative writing degree courses) is not considered suitable and poetry is another no-go area. This pigeonholing of certain types of writing as being more appropriate and, perhaps in the case of poetry, less daunting for assessment purposes should be scrutinised: if students are to be encouraged to be truly creative then surely they need to be given opportunities to make genuine, informed choices about which genre might be most suited to the ideas they want to express.

Critical commentaries

Candidates who are studying for most of the English Language specifications are also required to write a critical commentary to accompany their creative work in which they must justify aspects such as the linguistic and structural choices they have made in creating their piece, their intended effects and the distinctiveness of the piece. In many cases the commentary element can be almost as long as the original work. The stipulation that original work should be accompanied by a commentary has been a contentious issue within secondary English teaching for many years. In the early 1980s, when 'alternative' approaches to A-level English coursework were first instituted,[9] the value or necessity of a commentary was, in my experience, a frequently discussed issue among teachers at Associated Examining Board (AEB) consortium meetings for the 660 syllabus.

It is possible to see that, given appropriate guidance and assessment criteria, commentaries can enable writers to review the drafting and redrafting processes they have undertaken in ways which can inform their future development as writers. (For examples of this refer to Atkinson *et al.*'s 2001 model for assessment of creative writing portfolios and examples of GCSE students' commentaries on their poetry coursework in Dymoke (2003) and NAWE (2008).) Unfortunately, a focus on drafting does not appear to be the underlying reason for the use of commentaries within the A-level specifications. Primarily, they seem to serve as a means of assessing a student's knowledge about language. Examination boards justify the inclusion of commentaries by saying, for example, that they will

> enable candidates to: communicate their knowledge and understanding of how language works; use appropriate linguistic terminology; show knowledge of the key constituents of language.
>
> (WJEC 2009:14)

One could question what the actual original piece of creative writing has enabled the candidates to achieve if not all of the aspects listed above. Creativity is seen as subservient to knowledge.

A-level English Language and Literature

Within English Language and Literature A level, the focus on creativity again rests with AO4 which requires students to '[d]emonstrate expertise and creativity in using language appropriately for a variety of purposes and audiences, drawing on insights from linguistic and literary studies' (QCA 2006c). For the several specifications, including Assessment and Qualifications Alliance (AQA) A and WJEC, this objective has a weighting of a mere 17.5 per cent across the whole A level. This is by far the smallest weighting of the four AOs in the specification. As with GCSE English, it is worth noting the weightings allocated to creative components across all three types of English A level. A-level teachers might want to explore with other colleagues which balance of weightings might best suit the students in their school or college. In the vast majority of their specifications, the examination boards have fought shy of awarding high weightings.

The AQA English Language and Literature (ELLA) specification A offers an unusual creative feature in that it includes a formal written examination to assess creative writing skills. This AS unit (ELLA 1) is a language production task which requires candidates to 'write in a particular style, register or voice, based on a thorough knowledge of the text. They will be assessed on language use appropriate to the set task and on technical accuracy' (AQA 2009b: 3). The labelling of creative responses to texts as 'production tasks' is a further indicator of the restricted nature of creativity within the specifications. However, beyond this one wonders if creativity can ever be effectively assessed within a summative assessment framework. Would Alan Bennett have written a scene of his highly acclaimed *The History Boys* (a set text on the paper in question) if had not been able to draw on the influence of other texts including popular songs and redraft in rehearsal? Does he describe as a 'production task' or a play? Would Emily Brontë have written *Wuthering Heights*, drawing inspiration from the moorland beyond her parsonage window, if she had had to 'produce' an extract from it in 50 minutes in an examination? Creative ideas and original texts take varying amounts of time and thought to gestate. The type of texts students are asked to produce for this paper range through letters, newspaper articles, reports and narratives offering different characters' points of view. Although some of these do appear to offer significant challenges to the candidates and students' potential creative achievements should not be underestimated, the value of such tasks is questionable. The nature of the examination environment and the constraints of responding to a studied author's text in a specified way will inevitably limit what could be achieved.

Creative and media diplomas

Instigated in 2009 in England and Wales, diplomas are qualifications for 14- to 19-year-olds developed, in conjunction with employers, to support progression to further study, training or employment. Those teaching media or working in the communications faculty of a school or college with a post-16 centre are likely to have some involvement in these courses. Each diploma is offered at three levels and includes opportunities for students to develop and practise work-related skills within a chosen employment sector. The creative and media diplomas were one of first tranche of diplomas to be introduced. The 'principal learning' that underpins them is structured around four core themes:

1. creativity in context
2. thinking and working creatively
3. principles, processes and practice
4. creative businesses and enterprise.

These themes inevitably promote a conceptualisation of creativity that is most keenly geared to economic productivity.

Although the explicit introduction of creativity into the assessment objectives and units at GCSE and A level should in many respects be celebrated, the cautious approach taken by the exam boards underlines their anxiety both about assessing creative work and/or prioritising this approach above other aspects of English which still dominate many examinations. In reviewing the place of creativity within English, readers might want to consider where and how they could influence the assessment choices made in their departments.

Conclusion

In 1985 Freire observed:

> Teaching kids to read and write should be an artistic event. Instead, many teachers transform these experiences into a technical event, into something without emotions, without creativity – but with repetition. Many teachers work bureaucratically when they should work artistically.
>
> (1985: 79)

In 2001 Bethan Marshall commented on the need to reassert the centrality of English within the arts in education. She stresses that educators should celebrate 'the radical edge to creativity' (Marshall 2001: 125), exemplified in the poetry of Keats, Blake and many others, that is most feared by those in power.

In 2010 Ofsted advise that 'in curriculum planning, [schools should] balance opportunities for creative ways of learning with secure coverage of National Curriculum subjects and skills' (Ofsted 2010: 7).

In their different ways, all three of these quotations point to challenges which continue to confront English teachers and their students as they teach and learn English in the twenty-first century and underline that creativity should be at the heart of English. The suggestion that creativity presents a potential, uncontrollable threat to the status quo reinforces the power of our subject and the responsibility of English teachers to support the development of students' expressive, creative selves.

This chapter poses a number of questions about the place and nature of creativity within English. In developing further reflections on this topic, readers might want to consider creativity in relation to the English departments they have observed or taught in so far or texts read and used in the classroom and to think about the following issues:

❏ Conditions in which creativity actually occurs in everyday life can be said to be very different from English students' artificial classroom experiences. Where is the struggle of the creative process laid bare? Does the form of modelling promoted by government initiatives militate against genuine creativity or even indicate a demonstrable lack of understanding of it?

❏ Is it possible to assess students' creative responses to/creations of texts within existing assessment frameworks? Is it worth arguing for a separate creative writing qualification at GCSE or A level or should such opportunities be embedded within existing examinations?

❏ Has the term creativity been watered down or even hijacked by policy makers?

What creative solutions could be found to these questions and what other questions should now be asked about creativity in English?

Notes

1 For example: *ESRC Seminar Series Creativity in Education* (papers available online at http://opencreativity.open.ac.uk/recent.htm#previous_papers); *Creativity and Digital Literacies* (papers available online at http://www.bishopg.ac.uk/?_id=865 &page=70); AHRC, *Transitions and Transformations* seminar series (see account of the series by Snapper *et al.*, 2008, pp. 8–9).

2 For details of this proposal including draft assessment objectives go to: http://www.nawe.co.uk/metadot/index.pl?id=35894&isa=Category&op=show (accessed 28 August 2010).

3 The primary curriculum lost out in the 'wash-up' process when an election was declared in the UK in April 2010 and did not pass into law.

4 Writing Together: Writers in Schools Research Programme, 2006–9, available online at http://www.nawe.co.uk/metadot/index.pl?id=24926 (accessed 13 June 2010).

5 Poetry Places: available at http://www.poetrysociety.org.uk/content/archives/places/ (accessed 13 June 2010).

6 Poetryclass: available at http://www.poetryclass.net/ (accessed 13 June 2010).

7   Creative Partnerships: available at http://www.creative-partnerships.com/ (accessed 13 June 2010).
8   We're Writers: available at http://www.everybodywrites.org.uk/projects/case-study-details/were-writers-developing-teacher-and-pupil-autonomy/ (accessed 13 June 2010).
9   For an account of the development of 'alternative' syllabuses developed in 1970s and 1980s refer to Greenwell, B. (n.d) *Alternatives at 'A' level*, Sheffield: NATE.

Further reading

Craft, A., Jeffrey, B. and Leibling, M. (eds) (2001) *Creativity in Education*, London: Continuum.
    Essential reading for those researching at Masters level.
Cambridge Journal of Education, 36(3), (2006).
    This special creativity issue, edited by Pamela Burnard, begins with her editorial 'Reflecting on the creativity agenda in education' (pp. 313–18) and contains international perspectives on the topic from key researchers in the field of creativity.
English, Drama, Media, 12, (2008) 'Back to the future: Creativity, coursework and poetry at A level'.
    This issue of *EDM*, edited by Gary Snapper, focuses on creativity in aspects of A-level English Language and Literature teaching. It includes articles by Barbara Bleiman, Ben Knights, Rob Pope and Joan Swann.

Please also refer to footnote i) for details of web materials and papers from creativity-focused research seminar series.

I should like to thank Amy Weaver for sharing her reflections on the A-level English specifications which have helped me to develop my ideas about this aspect of the chapter.

Chapter 11

English and inclusion

John Yandell

Introduction

Arguments over inclusion are generally located in relation to school admissions policies and in the vexed issue of pupil grouping. These are important questions of policy and practice, but they are not the main focus of this chapter.[1] Beyond such concerns, it might appear that there is nothing to debate about inclusion and English. After all, we all aspire to be inclusive, don't we? What I want to suggest in what follows is that issues around inclusion are not reducible to questions of organisation and access, but are, crucially, questions of pedagogy: what inclusion means and how it can be instantiated in practice in the classroom is, therefore, fundamentally important to the work of English teachers.

Subject knowledge: the aim of schooling?

There is a fairly widespread view that what makes a good teacher is subject knowledge. Those who hold this view have tended to be dismissive of educational theory, regarding it as at best superfluous and at worst a distraction from the real purpose of schooling, which is the transmission both of bodies of knowledge (the proper academic disciplines represented in school subjects) and of an enthusiasm for this knowledge; practical skills such as classroom management are best acquired on the job, by working with more experienced colleagues.

This position was vociferously championed 20 years ago by the 'New Right' (Furlong *et al.* 2000), a loose grouping of academics and politicians whose support for alternative routes into teaching was underpinned by the conviction that what counted, above all else, was teachers' commitment to their subject (Lawlor 1990). It is this same conviction that has informed more recent policy interventions that have sought to address issues of teacher quality by regulating the intake of initial teacher education provision (House of Commons Children, Schools and Families Committee 2010; Gove 2009). The assumption is that the better qualified (graduates with second- or first-class degrees in the subject that they are to teach, those with higher grades in English and maths GCSE (General Certificate of Secondary Education)) will become better teachers: already-acquired subject knowledge, in other words, is regarded as, at the very least, the precondition of effective teaching. From this perspective, what matters is that the person at the front of the English class knows a thing or two about Shakespeare, the subordinate clause and the correct use of the semicolon (or, in slightly more ecumenical versions of the subject, about Scorsese or Soyinka).

An important concomitant of this view has been an impatience with anything that might get in the way of the transmission of subject knowledge, and hence with other conceptions of schooling and its function in relation to the wider society. The 'New Right' were sharply critical of anti-racist and anti-sexist initiatives in education in the 1970s and 1980s (O'Hear 1988; The Hillgate Group 1989). And an echo of these older arguments can be heard in Frank Furedi's lengthy critique of the education policies of the New Labour government (Furedi 2009). Furedi's main line of argument runs something like this: There is a crisis of authority, and more particularly of adult authority in relation to children. This crisis is manifested in schools and in government education policy in a variety of different ways, in a failure of discipline and in a loss of confidence in, and respect for, the academic disciplines. Under New Labour, the role of teachers and of schools has been reconfigured: their primary responsibility is no longer the transmission of established (authoritative) bodies of knowledge – the subject knowledge that was formerly the defining characteristic of the good teacher – but rather a more diffuse (and ever-changing) set of social and ethical duties. Schools, in Furedi's view, are now being expected to address a spectrum of social ills, from obesity to the lack of community cohesion. This is, he argues, asking simultaneously too much and too little of the education system: too much, because schools simply cannot take on the burden of society's disorders; too little, because this reconfiguration of the role of the school betrays a loss of confidence in the capacity of education to effect real change in the lives and life chances of individuals – the kind of change that might be achieved if schools were to concentrate on transmitting legitimate content.

Furedi's view of teaching and of the subjects that are taught is essentially conservative. I return to this point below, to take issue with the premises from which Furedi is arguing. First, though, it is worth saying that Furedi is correct in identifying a shift in education policy over the past decade or so. I want to explore this shift in a little more detail, focusing on the moment that exemplifies it most clearly.

The government Green Paper *Every Child Matters* (DfES 2003) was published as a response to the Laming Report into the tragic death of Victoria Climbié, but it was much more than that. Had it been intended to address the specific issues raised by the Laming Report, it might have focused on improving and systematising the coordination of aspects of welfare provision; it might, more particularly, have suggested a bigger role for schools in the care of children at risk. But, from Green Paper onwards, *Every Child Matters* has been a disproportionate response to the events that ostensibly produced it. *Every Child Matters* has become a long-term intervention in schooling: an element in school inspections and in the standards that entrants into the profession are required to meet before they can be granted qualified teacher status (TDA 2007). It offers a different vision of schooling, a fundamentally different conception of the place of the school, a different set of priorities for teachers. Embodied in *Every Child Matters* would appear to be an understanding of the needs of the whole child and the need to look at children's development holistically. Its five outcomes, taken as a package, a coherent whole, emphasise the interrelatedness of health, safety, economic well-being, active citizenship, enjoyment and achievement. Schools are thus presented as the hub of community life, the centre of a closely articulated network of multi-agency social provision.

It is far from easy to equate this conception of the school with the paradigm that had been dominant at least since the 1988 Education Reform Act – the legislation that introduced both the National Curriculum and testing, local management of schools and open enrolment. The paradigm of schools as small businesses, competing with each other in the education marketplace, invites all interested parties to judge schools, to determine both their worth and their effectiveness, according to the exam results achieved by their students; the *Every Child Matters* paradigm, on the other hand, places on schools the responsibility for ensuring the welfare of the whole child and judges their effectiveness by the contribution that they make to the well-being of individuals and of the communities they serve. (And this fundamental change in perspective can be seen to be mirrored in the rebranding – and reorientation – of the government department responsible for the oversight of schools: from Department for Education and Skills to Department for Children, Schools and Families. Schools, thus, become sandwiched between children and families, schools' role defined as meeting the needs of children and their families.)

When one looks at the academic and educational literature that makes reference to *Every Child Matters*, what is striking about it is that there is a fairly consistent knot of meanings that have clustered around the phrase. In contributions to debates about pastoral teaching, about the shifts in the meaning of multiculturalism and the competing claims of gender and religious identity, in arguments about the rights of LGBT (lesbian, gay, bisexual and transgendered) students and about fundamental values in education, *Every Child Matters* is used to gesture at and to assert a commitment to principles of equity and equality, to human rights and to social justice (see, for example, Biddulph 2006; Hunt 2006; Patel 2007; Stern 2007). This does not mean, however, that these principles are embedded in *Every Child Matters* as an identifiable government policy or intervention, nor that the effect of the ECM agenda on schools has been transformative in the way that might be inferred from Furedi; merely that the phrase has entered into the discourse of education in a way that enables it to stand for a set of much more widely held commitments.[2]

What is at stake here is a fundamental question for all involved in education. It is the question of what schooling is for. One's attitude to initiatives such as *Every Child Matters* will depend, very largely, on one's answer to the bigger question of the function and purposes of schooling itself. For Furedi, the answer is very simple:

> The ascendancy of the social inclusion agenda is symptomatic of a loss of faith in the project of providing an intellectually challenging education for children

from different social backgrounds. In previous times, the emphasis of reform-ers was on the elimination of the social barriers that prevented children from gaining access to quality education. Today, the social engineering imperative of inclusion takes precedence over the content of schooling. That is why a growing number of policy-makers and curriculum experts regard academic education as a barrier to be overcome. . . . the social engineering perspective does not take the content of education seriously.

(Furedi 2009: 139)

I have spent some time on Furedi's critique because it is the most clearly articulated version of the position that regards inclusion as, in effect, inimical to education. In what remains of this chapter, I want to mount a defence of inclusion as both a necessary and a worthwhile aim of education. The argument I want to pursue, however, is about inclusion not as a set of additional demands placed on schooling, the consequence of policies such as *Every Child Matters*, but rather as the necessary corollary of certain conceptions of learning and of English as a school subject.

What does learning look like?

The view of schooling that I started this chapter with is one that I have described as conservative. What I mean by this is not primarily an ascription of party-political affiliation; I want to draw attention, rather, to its underlying assumptions about knowledge and about pedagogy. The model is conservative in that the relevant knowledge – subject knowledge – already exists, in the teacher's head, before the lesson begins; what happens within the lesson is that this knowledge is transferred to the students. This notion of the teaching episode as transmission – the passing on of a pre-existing entity – is one that Furedi explicitly endorses. 'Adults', he insists, 'must assume responsibility for the world as it is and pass on its cultural and intellectual legacy to young people' (Furedi 2009: 49). Culture, like knowledge, is thus seen as a stable entity, passed on in time but, presumably, existing outside history. The teacher is thus the fount of knowledge, while the learner is positioned as the passive recipient of this legacy, an empty vessel waiting to be filled.

This seems to me to be a fundamental flaw in Furedi's position. Students do not start learning when they enter the classroom; they started learning at birth, if not several months earlier (Tomasello 1999; Hobson 2002). Learning is not accomplished by the acquisition of bite-sized chunks of information, handed out by the teacher. It is more complex and a great deal messier than that. Right from the start, learning is an irreducibly social process – a process that involves not just the brain but the whole body too, a process in which there is no neat separation of intellect and affect, a process of active meaning-making. To treat school learning as an entirely different category from learning in the world, and all that we know about it, is wholly unwarrantable. In making this claim, I am attempting neither to deny the existence or the usefulness of particular bodies of knowledge or ways of knowing nor to argue that schooling does not have an important part to play in making these available to young people. What I am suggesting, however, is that learning within the classroom happens most effectively and most powerfully when school students are encouraged to draw on the resources that they already possess, their 'funds of knowledge' (Moll 2000).

What I am alluding to here is a body of research and scholarship within a Vygotskian socio-cultural tradition. Lev Vygotsky, the Soviet psychologist whose work from the 1920s and early 1930s has become increasingly widely known over the past half century, provides us with a set of insights into learning that are immensely powerful.[3] Of central importance to the current argument are three aspects of Vygotskian theory. First, there is the emphasis on the social, on learning happening in the interaction between people and on that learning being mediated through culture and history. Learning, in other words, is not something that occurs in isolated individuals. Second, there is the understanding that the relationship between thought and semiotic activity is a complicated one: language enables the development of thought, gives learners access to resources beyond their immediate experience, but the process whereby learners develop a full sense of a word is a lengthy one. To be given a dictionary definition – the meaning – of a word is not enough; learners need time to explore the connotative dimensions that have accreted around the sign as it is used, and has been used, and to fill out for themselves the semiotic potential of that sign (see Gregory 1996: 16–18). The third aspect, closely related to the complexity of the relationship between thought and sign, is the complexity of the process whereby 'scientific concepts' are acquired. What Vygotksy meant by scientific concepts was, very loosely, school knowledge – the kind of codified, abstract ways of understanding the world that are represented in subject disciplines. What Vygotsky insisted on was the necessity of a dialectical relationship between scientific and everyday (or spontaneous) concepts: the latter, the concepts that learners bring with them from their lives outside school, are the intellectual resources that enable them to make sense of the scientific concepts that they are presented with in the school curriculum, the ideas that will be reorganized and transformed through the processes of schooling. To suggest that there is a dialectical relationship between everyday and scientific concepts, however, is to make a further claim – namely, that the everyday knowledge that the students bring may also transform and reorganise the curricularised knowledge of schooling.[4] As Vygotsky was at pains to emphasise, these theoretical insights are confirmed by teachers' practical experiences:

> No less than experimental research, pedagogical experience demonstrates that *direct instruction in concepts is impossible*. It is pedagogically fruitless. The teacher who attempts to use this approach achieves nothing but a mindless learning of words, an empty verbalism that simulates or imitates the presence of concepts in the child. Under these conditions, the child learns not the concept but the word, and this word is taken over by the child through memory rather than thought. Such knowledge turns out to be inadequate in any meaningful application. This mode of instruction is the basic defect of

the purely scholastic verbal modes of teaching which have been universally condemned. *It substitutes the learning of dead and empty verbal schemes for the mastery of living knowledge.*

(Vygotsky 1987: 170, this author's emphases)

And to suggest this means having to re-conceptualize the notion of access. No longer is it enough to throw open the school gates and allow the students to enter. As the authors of the Bullock Report acknowledged, a very long time ago:

No child should be expected to cast off the language and culture of the home as he crosses the school threshold, nor to live and act as though school and home represent two totally separate and different cultures which have to be kept firmly apart.

(DES 1975: 286)

Inclusion, I am arguing, is not just about admissions policies or even about pupil grouping arrangements within the school or the individual classroom. It is also about knowledge itself – about whose knowledge counts, whose voice is heard.

In part, this argument is about the practicalities of pedagogy. School students will, whether one likes it or not, arrive in the classroom with all sorts of other experiences, with histories that will inform their school identities and the sense that they make of school knowledge. They will have particular interests in the knowledge that the school has to offer – and, because they can learn a great deal from each other, they need to be provided with structured opportunities for collaborative learning.

In part, though, this argument is about the ethical implications for teachers' practice. Following the line taken by the Bullock Report, I am suggesting that part of the respect that teachers owe to their students is to attend to their lives, cultures, histories and experiences beyond the school gates, to see these out-of-school identities as integral to the students' identities within the classroom. And this does mean that teachers should make it their business to find out about their students, to find out about their other languages and literacies, to find out about the 'funds of knowledge' that are valorised within their communities. Teachers' knowledge of their students is, of course, a very different kind of knowledge from the subject knowledge acquired through a degree course – but it is just as vital an ingredient in teaching. On the PGCE (Postgraduate Certificate in Education) course on which I teach, student teachers are introduced to this idea in their first lecture, where it is presented as a question to be addressed throughout the course, and beyond: *Who are the learners and what do they know?*

One of the texts that we encourage our students to read is *Exiting Nirvana*, Clara Claiborne Park's magnificent account of her autistic daughter, Jessy (Park 2001). In tracing Jessy's life over 20 years and the slow, partial and uneven course of her socialisation, the book stands as testimony to her mother's meticulous observation and documenting of a vast body of evidence – evidence of how the world appears to Jessy, of the meanings that she makes. Park's work is, therefore, a model of attentiveness over time – and is presented to our students as an example of what can be learned by paying detailed attention to learners.

This conception of a teacher's role is significantly different from that envisaged in *Every Child Matters*, where the emphasis is on remediation – the teacher as social worker, as it were – rather than what I am proposing here, which is teachers as ethnographers, finding out about the histories, cultures and values of their students. The model involved in *Every Child Matters* is, in effect, one of deficit, to be addressed through a range of interventions; the model that can be traced back to the Bullock Report is one of dialogue.

What is being outlined here is the view that processes of learning necessarily involve culture and history – or cultures and histories – and that any account of schooling that neglects these forces is inadequate. This argument is by no means limited to the field of English studies. Science teachers have to engage with the fact that their students will arrive at the classroom or laboratory with very different attitudes to Darwinian theory, for example. To acknowledge this is not to argue that creationism should be taught alongside theories of evolution; it is to suggest that the science teacher needs to be prepared to recognise the different perspectives that might be encountered and to engage in what can be a very productive epistemological debate about scientific method.[5]

What's in a name?

To explore in a little more detail the implications of Vygotskian ideas about learning and learners, I want to address the ways in which policies and practices in relation to inclusion can (and should) be informed by ongoing debates around bilingual learners. It might be as well to start with an explanation about the term I have chosen to use and what I mean by it. I include within the category of bilingual learners all those students who operate in more than one language as part of their daily lives 'with some degree of self-confidence' (Miller 1983: x). It is important to note what is not included in this definition. There is no assumption here about the attainment of fluency or of some external measure of competence: the term attempts to be descriptive, rather than evaluative. Much more commonly used, both in the discourse of policy (for example, QCA 2007a, 2007b) and in teachers' conversations, is the term 'EAL' (English as an additional language). In practice, the label EAL tends to be applied to those learners who have yet to attain full fluency in English. It is, therefore, a label that gestures at what the learners cannot yet do, and at a sub-set of all bilingual learners, whereas the looser, more all-encompassing term 'bilingual' serves to acknowledge the existence of different areas of linguistic knowledge and expertise. Further, EAL emphasises the orientation towards the acquisition of English and hence tends to imply a monolingual norm. It is common for students to cease to be categorised as EAL once it is deemed that they are no longer in need of additional support. Although not usually explicitly articulated as such, the perspective that informs such practice is an assimilationist one, in which difference is identified as deficit. There is, therefore, a relationship between the term that is used and an underlying pedagogic attitude to the 'funds of knowledge' that students possess: EAL assumes a deficit model, while 'bilingualism' encourages the teacher to find out more about what students already know and can do, and to explore how this existing knowledge, acquired beyond the school gates, might be exploited as a resource for learning within the classroom.

There are good reasons for all teachers to be interested in the languages that their students speak. It was from a Congolese student, with whom I was working in a GCSE maths class, that I learned about the difference between the lexis of *Belgian* French and *French* French, as it were. Whereas a Parisian would use *soixante-dix*, *quatre-vingts* and *quatre-vingts-dix* for 70, 80 and 90, a francophone Congolese would, because of the legacy of Belgian imperialism, say *septante*, *octante* and *nonante*. The difference is of interest within the maths classroom because the Belgian/Congolese forms are more logical within a decimal counting system: what this opens up is the possibility of students exploring the relationship between arithmetic concepts and the language in which they are expressed. (In English, of course, there is a parallel in the difference between 'eighty' and 'fourscore'.) What I also remember, most vividly, is my Congolese student's look of withering scorn, directed at me for my ignorance on these matters.

For English teachers, there might be particularly strong reasons to provide opportunities for students to explore and share their linguistic expertise. English teachers might be expected to be interested in literacy and the acquisition of literacy. In the recent past, it has become fashionable to conceptualise the development of literacy as the acquisition of more or less separate skills and to regard these skills as existing outside any context or culture (DfEE 2001). At the same time, however, the growth of ethnographic interest in situated literacies (Heath 1983; Barton *et al.* 2000; Street 1984, 1995, 2001) has made it increasingly difficult to accept the adequacy of a model of literacy that fails to take account of context and culture. Bilingual students are often not merely aware of different literacy practices but active and daily participants in a range of different literacy practices (Gregory 1996, 2004; Gregory and Williams 2000; Purewal and Simpson 2010).

To recognise that bilingualism is not a learning difficulty is important (Levine 1996). It makes a difference to the provision that is made for bilingual learners in mainstream classes. It positions both the student and the teacher differently in relation to knowledge and power (think of my Congolese student and of how the moment I described shifted the relationship between her and me). It can also enable the teacher to question assumptions that might otherwise be made about what an appropriate curriculum might look like. For example, the common-sense view – which I have often heard expressed by both new and experienced English teachers – is that Shakespeare is too hard for 'EAL students': since they have yet to acquire full fluency in modern, idiomatic English, how can they be expected to cope with something so linguistically demanding and so different from the vernacular? One of the assumptions in this 'double barrier' thesis is that the acquisition of

fluency in the vernacular is a necessary intermediate stage on the route to engagement with Shakespeare.[6] But why should that be the case?

Vernacular English sometimes helps with Shakespeare, but it also can be a hindrance: Shakespearean lexis often causes difficulties for a modern audience precisely
because we think we know what a word means when what it meant then is different from any of the meanings attached to it now (Crystal and Crystal 2002).
When Tybalt calls Romeo a 'villain' it is very hard for us to recuperate the force
of the insult partly because we live in a different society, in which class prejudices
are differently articulated, but also because the word Tybalt uses is familiar to
us. Our sense of the word is different from Tybalt's, or from how it would have
been understood by an Elizabethan audience. Precisely because they are used to
operating in more than one language, bilingual learners are less prone to assume
a simple correlation between signifier and signified, less inclined to expect a text
to deliver up instantly apprehensible meaning. This metalinguistic awareness can
make them better prepared to deal with linguistic difficulty.

The 'double barrier' thesis also tends to isolate language from culture. It assumes
that language exists outside culture and that the difficulties of understanding and
interpretation that are posed by a Shakespeare play are primarily linguistic. Often, I
would want to argue, they are not – these difficulties relate to culture and history.
My experience of teaching *Romeo and Juliet* to Year 9 students in Hackney, most
of whom were of Turkish or Kurdish heritage, was that the students found it much
easier to make sense of the world of the play, and particularly of the Capulet family
relationships and the position that Juliet finds herself in, than I did: the forms of
patriarchy that are represented in the play were, in some ways, much closer to their
lived experience than they were to my own, either now or in my adolescent past.

When I first started teaching, I was placed in a school where almost all the
students were of Bangladeshi heritage. With a class of 12-year-olds, I developed
a scheme of work around oral storytelling. To start things off, I thought I should
tell a story. I chose *King Lear*. I had not got much further than 'A long time ago
there was a king who had three daughters . . .' when I had to stop. 'We know this!'
the class shouted, as one. 'It's an old Bengali story.' Graciously, they allowed me
to continue, only interrupting occasionally when my version strayed too far from
the one with which they were familiar. In recounting this now, I am not suggesting
that my 12-year-olds knew all there was to know about *Lear*; what I would want to
argue is that their existing 'funds of knowledge' constituted a resource that enabled
them to make meaning out of my (more or less) canonical text. What the anecdote
also indicates is that the very fact that Shakespeare plays tend to be tissues of old
tales is part of what makes them accessible – and endlessly reworkable.

The 'double barrier' thesis is also problematic because it tends to ignore those
aspects of doing Shakespeare in the classroom that make it particularly accessible
to all. Plays involve more and different semiotic resources than novels, both in the
layout of the script (the cues provided by characters' names and stage directions)
and in the opportunities for enactment (Gibson 1998; Franks 2003; Yandell 2008).
Moreover, there is ready access to a range of interpretations (filmic, visual and

so on) that enable all learners to experience the text in performance and that can foreground questions of interpretation (Yandell and Franks 2009).

Texts or readers: where is meaning made?

Attitudes to inclusion are, as I have argued thus far, inextricably connected with debates about the aims and purposes of formal education (schooling), as well as with debates about the processes of learning. For teachers within the field of English studies, the issue of inclusion also intersects with long-running debates about the nature of the subject itself.

Issues of inclusion have most commonly manifested themselves in relation to English in debates about which texts should be read in the classroom. These debates have been valuable, to the extent that they have foregrounded the question of representation. As Robert Scholes has argued:

> Understanding the category of literature as a problem – and a problem with a history – is part of what every serious student of English should know. . . .
>
> As a discipline, English needs both the cool rigor of theory and a passionate commitment to particular texts and ideas. Even as individual readers, we need them both. The political enters the study of English primarily through questions of representation: who is represented, who does the representing, who is object, who is subject – and how do these representations connect to the values of groups, communities, classes, tribes, sects, and nations?
>
> (Scholes 1998: 151, 153)

These questions are important. They provide a means of interrogating the selection of texts that is a necessary constituent in the process of constructing a curriculum. To ask which texts should be included in the curriculum necessarily entails a consideration of what has been excluded, and what are the criteria. What is central, what is marginal? Who decides? These questions matter at the level of statutorily enforced national curricula; they matter, too, in relation to the books that are in a departmental stockroom. My argument, though, is that the selection of text is only one element in processes of inclusion and exclusion. What matters more is how these texts are read: whose readings count?

Something of this is suggested by the approach taken above to Shakespeare, where I have made the assumption that what students bring to the text is worth attending to because it makes a difference to the meanings that are made. If one takes the view that texts are stable repositories of meaning and that, therefore, the task of the reader is merely to uncover that meaning, then the question of what the reader brings to the text is a trivial one. If, on the other hand, one considers that meanings are made by readers in interaction with text, and that these interactions are shaped by the circumstances in which they happen, then one is more inclined to adopt a contingent theory of meaning, and hence to position school students as agentive, as makers of meaning, not merely as recipients of pre-existent, pre-packaged meanings. My objective here is not to offer a potted history of literary theory, but rather to make the point that literary theory, because it confronts the relationship between reader and text, has an important bearing on inclusive practice in the classroom. If meaning is stable and the student's role is merely to assimilate it, then the teacher-dictated annotation of text makes perfect sense as classroom practice. But if students should be encouraged to deploy the full resources of culture and history that they have at their disposal, if textual meaning is construed as irreducibly intertextual, dependent on and arising out of the readers' experience of other texts, then classroom practice might reasonably be expected to include opportunities for more active and collaborative approaches to text.[7]

I have focused on this theoretical question about where and how meaning is made because it seems to me to be a question of fundamental importance to practice in the classroom. For English teachers, this must involve debates about the choice of text and how texts are read, but it must also involve a consideration of students' lives beyond the classroom, of students' cultural making across an increasingly broad range of modes and media. To do so means taking seriously Raymond Williams' notion of culture as 'a whole way of life' (Williams 1958), as well as heeding the Bullock Report's advice by finding room within the curriculum for students to draw on and explore the diversity of their engagements in wider cultural activity. Now that really would look like an inclusive version of English!

Notes

1 For a lucid introduction to these matters, see Hart *et al.* (2004), ch. 2.
2 For a more accurate sense of what the policy intervention might represent, see Hartley (2007).
3 This is, of course, an oversimplification. Vygotsky did not work alone and his work took place in a particular context – the aftermath of the Russian Revolution of 1917. His exploration of problems in relation to how children learn was given an urgency by the revolutionary context of his work: the aim was to make a new society, and education had a key role to place in its construction. Equally, Vygotsky's ideas have a history that extends back over centuries of Western thought. For a more detailed account of this intellectual history, see Van der Veer and Valsiner (1991); Hardcastle (2009).
4 Since the rediscovery of Vygotksy in the 1960s, his intellectual legacy remains a subject of fierce contestation. It is clear that his ideas were developing, and there are internal tensions and contradictions in what is available to us. What I am presenting here is a necessarily simplified account. It is also one that contests a number of readings of the Vygotsky that I find somewhat reductive. For a fuller account of these debates, see Britton (1987); Daniels (2001); Gillen (2000); Kozulin *et al.* (2003).
5 The argument I am making here is the one that was advanced by Professor Michael Reiss (2008). The furore that greeted Reiss's argument – a controversy that led to his resignation as director of education at the Royal Society (see Smith and Henderson 2008) – seems to me almost entirely to miss the point of Reiss's argument, which was an argument about pedagogy.
6 For a recent expression of this view, see Kearns (2009).

7 What I suggest about texts here has a parallel in the turn in linguistics – the move from a Saussurean focus on *langue* – the fairly stable structure of language-as-system – to the sociolinguistic interest in *parole* – language in use. Of particular interest to teachers, in this respect, is the work that Ben Rampton has done to demonstrate the complexity of school students' linguistic choices and appropriations (Rampton 2006).

Chapter 12

Literacy and social class

Jon Davison

> Two nations; between whom there is no intercourse and no sympathy; who are as ignorant of each other's habits, thoughts, and feelings, as if they were dwellers in different zones, or inhabitants of different planets . . .
> —Benjamin Disraeli, *Sybil, or The Two Nations*

It would be tempting to believe that Disraeli's description of society in *Sybil, or The Two Nations* might be an account of a world that disappeared in the nineteenth century. However, such a thought is disabused by recently published photographs of some of the undergraduate members of the notorious 200-year-old Bullingdon Club at Oxford, whose £3,000 uniform comprises a tailcoat of dark navy blue with a matching velvet collar and brass monogrammed buttons, a mustard waistcoat and a sky-blue bow tie. The undergraduates depicted in these photographs are the current UK prime minister, David Cameron; chancellor of the exchequer, George Osborne; and mayor of London, Boris Johnson. The Club was satirised by Evelyn Waugh in *Decline and Fall* (1928) as the Bollinger Club whose drunken revels were characterised by 'the sound of English county families baying for broken glass'. After Club dinners in 1894 and 1927 Bullingdon members smashed almost all the glass of the lights and 468 windows in Peckwater Quad at Christ Church, Oxford. However, the effects of social class on an individual's educational and life chances are far from fictional and even less so humorous.

Consistently, academic attainment tends to be low in schools with high proportions of pupils from low-income homes: 'In 2001, only a fifth of pupils in schools with the poorest intakes achieved five GCSE (General Certificate of Secondary Education) passes at grades A*–C, compared with 50% nationally' (Lupton, 2004). Poor examination results at the end of secondary schooling preclude the opportunity to engage in further and higher education by attending college or university. UK government figures produced in 1991 showed that only 5 per cent of children from skilled manual home backgrounds attended university and, despite a claimed 30 per cent increase in access to university, in 1998 only approximately 5 per cent of those at university came from the poorest post-coded areas (Halsey, 1998). And data in 'The widening socio-economic gap in UK higher education' shows that, far from improving, matters are actually getting worse:

> [T]he gap between rich and poor, in terms of HE [higher education] participation, has widened during the 1990s. Children from poor neighbourhoods have become relatively less likely to participate in HE since 1994/5, as compared to children from richer neighbourhoods. This trend started before the introduction of tuition fees. Much of the class difference in HE participation seems to reflect inequalities at earlier stages of the education system.
>
> (Galindo-Rueda *et al.*, 2004)

The last decade of the twentieth century began with a Conservative prime minister announcing that society did not exist and drew to a close with a New Labour prime minister announcing that we are now all members of the middle class. In the twenty-first century it has become unfashionable to discuss social class and education, as is seen by the Coalition prime minister's comment: 'I think this country has moved beyond class and all that sort of stuff' (BBC, 2010). There appears to be an underlying assumption that it is now passé to do so: the debate has moved on; social class is an irrelevance.

However, despite the inception of a National Curriculum in England, Wales and Northern Ireland in 1990, designed to ensure an equal curricular entitlement for all pupils, children from working-class backgrounds have continued to underachieve compared with children of the middle classes. 'Parental background continues to exert a significant influence on the academic progress of recent generations of children' (Blanden and Machin, 2007: 4). Furthermore, for ten years from 1997 the New Labour government's Widening Access and Increasing Participation initiative aimed at reaching a target of 50 per cent university attendance from all social groups, but '[i]nequalities in degree acquisition meanwhile persist across different income groups. While 44 per cent of young people from the richest 20 per cent of households acquired a degree in 2002, only 10 per cent from the poorest 20 per cent of households did so' (Blanden and Machin, 2007: 3).

This chapter explores some of the reasons for educational underachievement and the role that the teaching of English has played in promoting success or creating failure in pupils. A second aim of this chapter is to consider the importance of discursive practice in the social construction of knowledge and the need to make educational discourses *visible* to pupils. Finally, the chapter argues the need for developing in pupils an empowering literacy.

Cultural capital and cultural reproduction

The terms 'cultural capital' and 'cultural reproduction' stem from the work of Bourdieu (see, for example, Bourdieu, 2007). Bourdieu proposes that different social groups have different 'cultural capital', which may be seen as the knowledge, experience and connections an individual has and develops over time that enable a person to succeed more so than someone with knowledge, experience and connections that is seen in society as being of less value. Further, particular groups of people, notably social classes, act to reproduce the existing social structure in order to legitimate and preserve their social and cultural advantage.

Put simply, cultural reproduction is the process through which existing cultural values and norms are transmitted from generation to generation, thereby ensuring continuity of cultural experience across time. Cultural reproduction, therefore, often results in 'social reproduction' – the process through which facets of society, such as class, are transferred from generation to generation.

Education as an agent of cultural reproduction

> Dominant social and cultural groups have been able to establish their language, and their knowledge priorities, learning styles, pedagogical preferences, etc., as the 'official examinable culture' of school. Their notions of important and useful knowledge, their ways of presenting truth, their ways of arguing and establishing correctness, and their logics, grammars and language as institutional norms by which academic and scholastic success is defined and assessed.
>
> (Lankshear *et al.*, 1997: 30)

Brown (1973), Bourdieu (1973) and Bowles and Gintis (1976) propose that it is the stratification of school knowledge that reproduces inequalities in cultural capital. Bourdieu argues that the structural reproduction of disadvantages and inequalities are caused by cultural reproduction and are recycled through the education system, as well as through other social institutions. The education system, therefore, is an agent of cultural reproduction biased towards those of higher social class, not only in the curricular content of subjects taught but also through what is known as the 'hidden curriculum', which includes the language, values and attitudes located in, and which an individual acquires from, the discourse of curricular subjects and all aspects of school life that contribute to an individual's socialisation through the education process. An individual's success or failure within the formal education system is determined by the ability to achieve formal educational qualifications *and* to acquire the appropriate language, values, attitudes and qualities through the process of socialisation within the system. The ability to complete successfully all aspects of schooling correlates strongly to an individual's capacity subsequently to enjoy high cultural capital such as, *inter alia*, adequate pay, occupational prestige and social status in adult life.

The chapter will now consider some specific causes of educational underachievement related to social class.

Social class and underachievement

In the latter half of the twentieth century a variety of aspects of school life were examined in order to identify the causes of pupil underachievement, such as access, institutional structures and the nature of school knowledge. For example, Hargreaves (1967), Lacey (1970) and Ball (1981) cited the institutional structures of schools, such as streaming and banding, as being influential in determining the performance of working-class pupils: a disproportionate number of whom were found to be represented in the lower streams and bands.

It is well documented that, despite the intentions of education Acts from 1944 to 1988, children from the working class in the UK continued to underachieve at school. The '11-plus' examination was created by the 1944 Education Act, which proposed the establishment of a tripartite system of secondary schooling comprising 'modern', 'technical' and 'grammar' schools. Success or failure in the 11-plus examination determined the type of school an individual attended. Floud *et al.* (1966) exposed massive under-representation of working-class boys at grammar schools. The 11-plus examination included an Intelligence Quotient (IQ) test (see below). Douglas (1964) showed how working-class pupils with the same IQ scores as middle-class children were failing to gain grammar school places, because of the class bias of teachers in primary schools.

Of equal concern is how both working-class and middle-class girls were institutionally discriminated against in the 11-plus examination. It is now well known that the 11-plus examination scores of all girls were adjusted down because they were far outstripping boys' achievement. Thousands of girls who passed the 11-plus and should have, therefore, attended grammar schools were prevented from doing so because their scores were downgraded. It was feared that all grammar schools were otherwise going to be filled with far more girls than boys (see *The Report of the Task Group on Assessment and Testing* (TGAT) (DES, 1987: 40–53) for a discussion of these issues in relation to the establishment of the National Curriculum).

The 11-plus and IQ tests were criticised for a middle-class bias in their content, their use of middle-class cultural references, their vocabulary and language register. The 11-plus was seen as culturally biased towards the middle-class children (for example, a question might be related to classical composers, something a middle-class child would be more likely to answer correctly than would a child from the working class because of social and cultural differences in their home backgrounds):

> [W]ithin societies like our own there is a tendency for forms of literacy to prevail which effectively maintain patterned inequalities of power within the social structure.
>
> (Lankshear, 1987: 79–80)

Additionally, in *Class, Codes and Control*, Basil Bernstein (1971) showed marked differences in the language use of members of different social classes, with middle-class children having access in their language to a more formal 'elaborated code' while working-class language was characterised as operating within a simple 'restricted code'. However, many researchers, including Trudgill (1974), Boocock (1980) and Bennett and LeCompte (1990), criticised Bernstein as a proponent of 'deficit theory':

> Bernstein's theory of codes does not suggest that the academically success-
> ful are merely *perceived* as smarter or more capable, due to the marketability
> of their particular talents. Rather, it implies that the academically successful
> really are smarter, ready to engage in a discourse capable of expressing 'uni-
> versal meaning,' eschewing the fragmentation and 'logical simplicity' of the
> underclass. . . . In such a society, the oppressed are required to climb the
> ladder of 'equal opportunity.' The higher they get, the more they resemble
> the oppressors and the more their efforts are rewarded.
>
> (MacSwan and McLaren, 1997: 334–40)

For Ball *et al.* (1990), Gee (1991), Lankshear (1987) and Lankshear *et al.* (1997) the challenge for those who would wish to address such issues lies in the development of an alternative to the dominant model of English and in inculcating a 'proper' literacy that will empower pupils.

Social class and educational policy makers

If there are such determinants that militate against success of working-class children in the education system, how were these structures and systems put in place? The answer, of course, is that they are, *inter alia*, the results of a combination of national and local education policy, which is espoused in the discourse of dominant social and cultural groups.

The quotation earlier from Lankshear *et al.*'s *Changing Literacies* (1997: 30) states that dominant social and cultural groups have been able to establish the 'official examinable culture of school'. However, he goes on to say that the determination of the official examinable culture of the school by dominant social and cultural groups is not necessarily a conscious process and far less a conspiracy:

> It is simply what tends to happen, with the result that discourse and discourses
> of dominant groups become those which dominate education, and become
> established as major legitimate routes to securing social goods (like wealth
> and status).
>
> (Lankshear *et al.*, 1997: 30)

The Board of Education

For Gossman (1981: 352) state education, introduced by the 1870 Education Act (the Forster Act), was 'advocated in a hard-headed way as a means of social control' and an examination of twentieth-century government education documents highlights the antipathetic attitudes to the working class displayed by educational policy makers:

> Many persons, most prominently social and economic leaders and social reformers, grasped the uses of schooling and the vehicle of literacy for the promotion of values, attitudes and habits considered essential to the maintenance of social order and the persistence of integration and cohesion.
>
> (Graff, 1987: 7)

Concerns about the level of literacy among working-class children were addressed by the Board of Education's *Circular 753* (BoE, 1910), which was instrumental in establishing the nature of English as it came to be in school: '[I]nstruction in English in the secondary school aims at training the mind to appreciate English Literature and at cultivating the power of using the English Language in speech and writing' (para. 2). Successive circulars and reports promulgated beliefs in the power of English to civilise the masses. 'Pure English is not merely an accomplishment, but an index to and a formative influence over character' (para. 2).

The importance of spoken English

The first major report into *The Teaching of English in England* was suspicious of the growing working class. The Newbolt Report (BoE, 1921), as it tends to be known – after its chair, Oxford professor of poetry Sir Henry Newbolt – was sympathetic to elementary school teachers who had 'to fight against evil habits of speech contracted in home and street' (para 167). One senses the vehemence here in the choice of adjective to describe pupils' spoken English, which is referred to as 'disfigured' (para. 167). The report's hostility to working-class children is confirmed when it describes the teacher's battle, which is 'not with ignorance but with a perverted power' (para. 59). Children who do not use Standard English are more than just untutored, they are 'disfigured', 'evil' and 'perverted'.

There is not space here to discuss them in detail, but similar attitudes are to be found in subsequent reports produced throughout the twentieth century. In the early years of the century, *Circular 753* lamented that pupils 'fall helplessly back on slang, the base coin of the language' (BoE, 1910: para. 2), while a decade after the Newbolt Report, in the *Report on Secondary Education*, the Spens Report (BoE, 1938), pupils' spoken English is described as 'slovenly, ungrammatical, and often incomprehensible to a stranger' (p. 220): presumably a middle-class stranger, for one assumes that the working-class children would understand each other perfectly. Half a century later, *English from 5 to 16* believed that pupils should '[s]peak clearly, audibly and pleasantly, in an accent intelligible to the listener(s)' (HMI, 1984: 10).

Three years after the inception of the National Curriculum, the draft proposals for a rewritten National Curriculum *English 5–16* (DES, 1993) stated that, from

Key Stage 1, pupils 'should speak clearly using Standard English' and 'should be taught to speak accurately, precisely, and with clear diction'. Examples of accuracy and precision cited in the proposals include: 'We were (not was) late back from the trip'; 'We won (not winned) at cricket'; 'Pass me those (not them) books'; 'Clive and I (not me) are going to Wembley'; 'We haven't seen anybody (not nobody)' (pp. 9–23). In relation to the spoken language of working-class children it is clear that for almost 100 years there has been considerable continuity in the attitudes expressed and that they have all been negative.

The threat of the unions

For the members of the Newbolt Committee, not only were working-class children perceived as potentially dangerous but so too were members of 'organised labour movements', because they 'were antagonistic to, and contemptuous of literature . . . a subject to be despised by really virile men'. The writers of the report learned that 'a large number of thinking working men' believed literature to be as useful and relevant to their lives as 'antimacassars, fish-knives and other unintelligible and futile trivialities of middle-class culture', and that it was taught in schools only 'to side-track the working movement' (para. 233). Writing elsewhere, Newbolt Committee member George Sampson (1921) further stereotypes 'the extravagant British workman' and his 'moral, intellectual and emotional level', whose habits lead him to 'the newest and nudest revues' and who ends by 'being divorced'. Sampson believed that working-class children would only be saved by the correct teaching of English, because it would serve to educate them intellectually, morally and spiritually and 'very especially it will cover all that we at present leave naked and barbarous' (Sampson, 1921: 104–5). The teaching of correct English would do nothing to address the glaring social inequalities in society other than 'cover' them: an attitude which re-emerged in the *Report on Secondary Education*, the Spens Report: '[I]t should be possible for the spread of a common habit of English teaching to soften the distinctions which separate men and classes in later life' (BoE, 1938: 222).

Popular culture

Most education policy documents produced in the twentieth century were antipathetic to popular culture. *Circular 753* (BoE, 1910) was dismissive of popular, or working-class, culture: 'Boys and girls will read of their own accord many books – chiefly fiction. These . . . are only of transitory interest, and involve little or no mental effort' (para. 17).

Policy makers espoused an almost evangelical approach to the teaching of 'Great Literature', believing that nothing was more valuable, or, indeed, more civilising, than pupils connecting with the great minds of the past such as Milton, Wordsworth, Coleridge, Swift and the like, in order to 'appreciate' the 'divine nature' of such texts (Davison and Dowson, 2009: 24). Therefore, pupils 'should be taught to understand, not to criticise or judge' such great works (BoE, 1910: para. 36). Thus, a version of English teaching that had as its purpose an induction into high culture, by definition, must be antipathetic to popular culture.

It is unsurprising, therefore, that elsewhere the adverse effects of cinema were deplored: '[T]he mental effect upon the children was to make them more fond of noise, ostentatious display, self-advertisement and change. The pictures excited their minds and created a love of pleasure and disinclination for steady work and effort' (*The Times Educational Supplement*, 1915). Such attitudes pervade education documents throughout the twentieth century: 'The pervading influences of the hoarding, the cinema and a large section of the public press, are (in this respect as in others) subtly corrupting the taste and habits of the rising generation' (BoE, 1938: 222–3). Antipathy to the indulgence in popular culture by children can be traced to present-day educational documents: from cinema through radio, television and video, to computer games. For example, although the Bullock Report, *A Language for Life* (DES, 1975) helped to pave the way for media education, it contains the same attitudes displayed by the dominant social groups half a century earlier:

> Between them, radio and television spread the catch-phrase, the advertising jingle, and the frenetic trivia of the disc-jockey . . . it is clear that the content and form of much radio and television utterance makes the teacher's job a great deal more difficult.
>
> (para. 2.8)

Twenty years later, at the Conservative Party conference on 7 October 1992, Secretary of State for Education John Patten railed against '1960s theorists', 'the trendy left' and 'teachers' union bosses', who were destroying 'our great literary heritage'. In a speech that attacked not only the trades unions but also popular culture, he warned: 'They'd give us chips with Chaucer. Milton with mayonnaise. Mr Chairman, I want William Shakespeare in our classrooms, not Ronald McDonald' (Patten, 1992).

Similar hostility to popular culture came in the 1990s from Her Majesty's Chief Inspector of Schools (HMCI), Mr Chris Woodhead, and his comments mirror educational documents almost 100 years previously: 'The best schools struggle to outdo the influence of peer pressure, and the teenage culture created by the pop and fashion industries, but struggle they must' (Woodhead, 2000). Although the Bullock Report, *A Language for Life* (DES, 1975), began the slow process that led to the establishment of media studies, Woodhead has been resolute in his criticism of the study of popular culture: 'Media Studies has always been a nonsense – now it has degenerated into a farce. Students ought to be exposed to interesting and worthwhile figures and issues' (Woodhead, 2008). Dominant high-cultural criticisms of working-class culture are very much evident in the twenty-first century.

The problem of 'naturalisation'

Even from this cursory examination of the development of the subject it would appear that Lankshear's assertion is correct. For a century, dominant views about the nature of the subject have held sway. Particular 'notions of important and useful knowledge' and clearly defined 'ways of arguing and establishing correctness' have formed the basis of school curricula, examination syllabuses and the National Curriculum for English, which, in their assessment methodology, have established the 'institutional norms by which academic and scholastic success is defined and assessed'.

John Patten's speech fully endorses the view of English as the great literary tradition. The 1995 National Curriculum maintained the importance of Standard English as the means of teaching and learning. Such attitudes have at their heart what has become the 'traditional' view of English teaching. For a century, a dominant version of the subject has prevailed, which with the exception of a brief period during the 1960s and 1970s has been, for the most part, accepted rather than challenged. With the passing of time, the reiteration of a dominant view leads to the belief that the status quo is the natural order of things by some universal right: particular curricular content, attitudes, values and practices are accepted as the very 'nature' of English itself, rather than interrogated to determine the underpinning value systems:

> A particular set of discourse practices and conventions may achieve a high degree of *naturalisation* – they may come to be seen as simply 'there' in a common-sense way, rather than socially put there.
>
> (Fairclough, 1989: 9)

Forms of English as a school subject

The Cox Report (DES, 1989: para. 2.21–25) identified five broad versions of English its writers found in schools: 'Personal Growth'; 'Cross-curricular'; 'Adult Needs'; 'Cultural Heritage' and 'Cultural Analysis'. Ball *et al.* (1990: 76) propose four main versions of the subject which have emerged since 1900: 'English as Skills'; 'English as the Great Literary Tradition'; 'Progressive English' and 'English as Critical Literacy'. For Ball *et al.*, it is the first two models that have dominated.

Ball *et al.* go further and usefully link these versions of the subject to questions of power and conceptions of literacy, which they locate on a two-by-two matrix (see Figure 12.1). The horizontal axis (Self–Not Self) concerns relationships between people and portrays the distance between a focus on the personal, private needs of the individual and the formal, rule-governed situations to which the individual might be subject – the essence of an individual living in a society. Put simply, individual needs versus collective need. The vertical axis concerns sources of power and the relationship between polarised authorities: Authority–Authenticity. In essence, the polarity of power lies in the fact that it can be 'top-down' or 'bottom-up' – dictatorial or democratic. A top-down model is characterised by direction and prescription, whereas in a bottom-up model power is developed through negotiation and participation. Figure 12.1 is adapted from Ball *et al.* (1990) and shows the versions of English as a subject mapped into the sectors.

The 'English as Skills' version of the subject has at its heart the development of functionally literate individuals. There is a strong link here with the perceived needs of industry and commerce for individuals who are able to function in the workplace and earn an income. State education acts on behalf of employers and manufacturers by providing a functionally literate workforce of active consumers. Much of the drive for the introduction of the National Literacy Strategy came from a belief that workers in the UK were less literate than their European counterparts – most notably those in Germany – and were, therefore, not only a symptom of but also part of the cause of, the decline in British manufacturing industries.

Similarly, many were the cries from employers that the level of literacy among school leavers was in steady decline. This perception is, however, hardly surprising

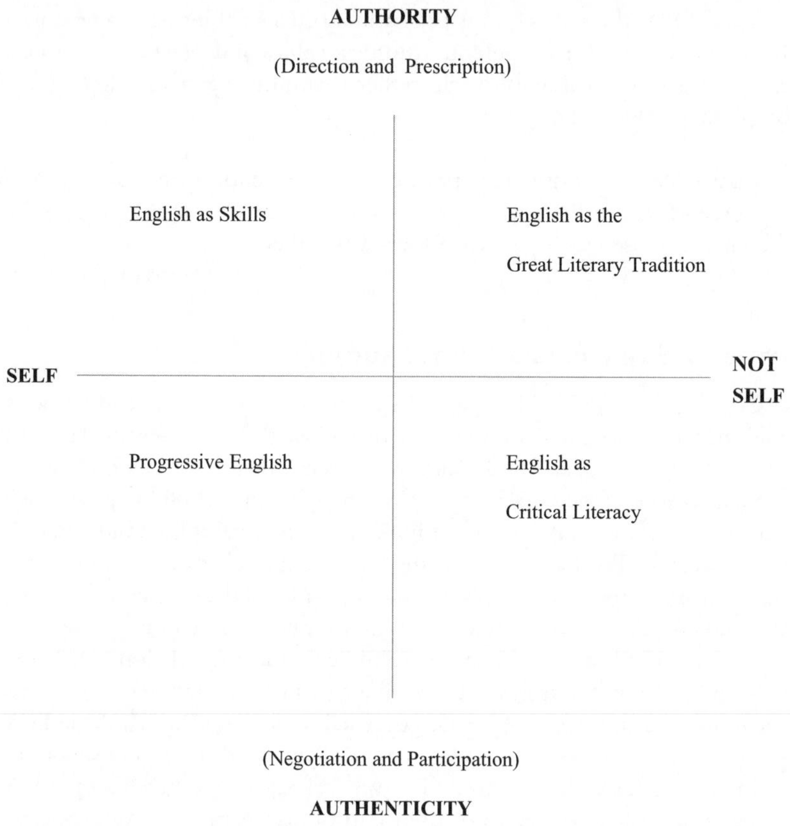

AUTHORITY

(Direction and Prescription)

<table>
<tr><td></td><td></td></tr>
<tr><td>English as Skills</td><td>English as the
Great Literary Tradition</td></tr>
<tr><td>**SELF**</td><td>**NOT SELF**</td></tr>
<tr><td>Progressive English</td><td>English as
Critical Literacy</td></tr>
</table>

(Negotiation and Participation)

AUTHENTICITY

Figure 12.1 Versions of English.

when we consider the social changes that have occurred since, say, 1960, and the growth in the literacy demands on individuals. For example, exponential growth in advertising has led to a need to decode sophisticated, complex advertisements in print alone; increasingly, the demands made upon applicants for even the lowest status jobs have increased during a period of high unemployment; as a consumer, the individual has had to develop complex skills brought about by the transition of corner grocery shops into out-of-town supermarkets filled with a plethora of signs and aisle guides, with shelves containing an abundance of groceries in sophisticated packaging bearing complex instructions. Similarly, the 'packaging' of political messages in the 'infomercial', increasing delivery into the home of political pamphlets through the use of the mailshot and sophisticated, enigmatic poster campaigns, all have placed increasing literacy demands on the individual. While in the home, every major electrical appliance comes complete with its 48-page guide in six languages. Lankshear observes:

> Even if schools improved their current performance to the point where they matched the functional demands of the present day, changes occurring *outside* the school – in technology, economic production, commerce, communications, consumerism, cultural life, etc., – would tend towards creating a rate of illiteracy in the future by simply continuing to raise the minimum required level of print competence.

(1987: 135)

The National Literacy Strategy can be seen as a prime manifestation of the English as Skills version of English: a top-down model of prescription and direction, and one which, in its emphasis on print-based literacy, is, in Lankshear's analysis, doomed to failure. Patten's (1993) *Literacy in the Opportunity Society* is a useful example of the discourse that promotes this version of English.

The version of 'English as the Great Literary Tradition' is likewise constructed on direction and prescription. Ultimately, the high-cultural model is anti-democratic. A selected elite agree the canon of great works into which educated members of society are inducted. As we saw earlier, this is the literacy of morality. The great texts speak of the divine nature of human kind, the virtues, duty, citizenship. They cultivate the intellectual, emotional and moral aspects of life. It is in this version, too, that an emphasis on correctness, on grammar and Standard English is located, because the 'standard form is identified with cultivation and national identity and acts as a form of social closure and social exclusion' (Ball *et al.*, 1990: 79). A prime treatise on this version of English can be found in Marenbon's (1987) *English Our English*.

Both versions of English are underpinned by models of what Lankshear (1987) and Lankshear *et al.* (1997) call 'improper literacy' because the learner is passive – the individual is not empowered or invited to engage in the construction of knowledge, nor to debate it. The individual simply learns to conform to a defined set of rules; to regurgitate a predetermined set of attitudes about a prescribed body of texts; to appreciate rather than to critique; to acquire rather than to actively generate knowledge.

'Progressive English', or the 'Personal Growth' model as Cox referred to it, places an emphasis on the development of the individual and the link between language and learning: the English of self-expression, the personal voice, of creativity and discovery. Here, literature is a source for the development of the individual's imagination and aesthetic sensibilities. Personal responses to stimuli are valued and developed. During the 1960s and 1970s the development of 100 per cent coursework examinations, of Mode 3 CSEs (Certificate of Secondary Education), which were set and marked by teachers in schools, the development of materials by the Inner London Education Authority's English Centre, the work of the London Association of the Teaching of English, all helped to develop a more democratic version of the subject. Contemporary culture, mass media, youth culture and popular cultural artefacts were regarded as objects of study as equally valid as 'traditional' literary texts. John Dixon's *Growth through English* (1967) was particularly influential in promoting this version of English.

'English as Critical Literacy' is a 'radical' version of the subject. Unquestionably, it acknowledges the political nature of the subject and of schooling. Schooling and education (two different things) are problematised and debated. 'This version of English is assertive, class-conscious and political in content. Social issues are addressed head on. The stance is oppositional, collective aspirations and criticisms become the basis for action . . . The critical gaze is turned upon the school itself and the processes of schooling' (Ball *et al.*, 1990). It is a model that closely matches Lanshear's 'proper literacy': 'Literacy is essential for generating and transmitting information, and for organising, lobbying, articulating grievances and so on' (Lankshear, 1987: 144). Chris Searle's *Stepney Words* (1971) and *Heart of Sheffield* (1995) are testaments to the power of a radical version of English teaching.

Discourse and schooling

Gee (1991) makes a distinction between what he calls 'primary' and 'secondary' Discourses and between 'Discourses' and 'discourses'. He defines 'discourses' as the 'connected stretches of language that make sense, like conversations, stories, reports, arguments, essays' as such, they may be found within, appropriate to and different across, Discourses (Gee, 1990: 143). For Gee, Discourse is always greater than language and incorporates beliefs, values, ways of thinking, of behaving and of using language.

An individual's primary Discourse is most often acquired through socialisation into the family: the acquisition of thoughts, values, attitudes, ways of using language that create a world view; engagement here most likely to be one-to-one, face-to-face. Because Discourses incorporate beliefs, values, ways of thinking, of behaving and of using language, different social groups are likely to have very different primary Discourses.

It is important to recognise that there may not be a congruence between an individual's primary Discourse and secondary Discourses encountered in the process of schooling. Secondary Discourses may be in complete contrast, or in direct opposition, to primary Discourses and as such have relevance to the earlier discussion of working class underachievement, because it is likely that such a clash of primary and secondary Discourses will 'effectively maintain patterned inequalities of power within the social structure' (Lankshear, 1987: 79–80). Furthermore, such a situation is likely to be exacerbated precisely because the ground rules of the secondary 'educated' Discourse remain invisible.

For Freire (1972, 1976), human beings develop through a process of reflection upon action: a conscious objectification of their own and others' actions through investigation, contemplation and comment. By engaging in such a process, they become historical and cultural agents, which is an active, rather than passive, role. This 'becoming', however, is not achieved in isolation, but through a process of 'dialogue' (Freire 1985: 49–59):

> [B]ecoming is the ontological vocation of human beings: of *all* humans equally. To deny any human beings the right to name the world on equal terms is to dehumanise those people, to subvert their ontological vocation, to rule them out of the process of becoming.
>
> (Peters and Lankshear, 1994: 67)

One context of dialogue is in the meeting of primary and secondary Discourses. Secondary Discourses are encountered through engagement in different social institutions: schools; churches; societies; clubs; through being a football supporter; through participation in aspects of popular culture, etc. Such secondary Discourses also involve uses of language, ways of thinking, believing, valuing and behaving, which offer human beings new and different ways of seeing the world:

> Education, socialisation, training, apprenticeship and enculturation are among the terms we use to refer to processes by which individuals are initiated into the Discourses of their identity formations . . .. Initiation into Discourses is cultural activity, and the Discourses themselves are, simultaneously, means and outcomes of cultural process.
>
> (Lankshear *et al.*, 1997: 17)

Schools are discourse communities: in Mercer's (1995) terms, they are the site of 'educational discourse'. The language, values, ways of being and membership of various facets of the school, whether by staff or pupils, define and are defined by individuals' engagement with Discourses – in Gee's terms above, 'ways of using language, of thinking, and of acting' that identify the individual as a member of a socially meaningful group' (Gee, 1990). Furthermore, each curriculum subject will have its own particular Discourse (for example, mathematics or science) and the 'official discourse' (Mercer, 1995) of any classroom will result from the teachers' interaction in a 'dialogue of educational discourses' that will determine their position on teaching and learning (Arthur *et al.*, 1997). As Kress (1988: ii) observes, 'social structures and linguistic forms are intimately intermeshed'. Engagement with learning will result from an induction into 'educated discourse', success in which will determine future acquisition of social 'goods'; for example, particular employment paths, higher education, power, status, wealth and so on.

Awareness, or 'knowledge of Discourses is not innate' (Lankshear *et al.*, 1997: 17). While, in general terms, a school may make statements concerning ethos and values, the very values, beliefs and ways of thinking which underpin the Discourse of the version of English which pupils encounter in the classroom, for example, are rarely, if ever, made explicit. Coupled to the fact that much of what comprises classroom interaction arises from versions of English which are in the top two quadrants of Figure 12.1 – versions underpinned by prescription and direction – it is unsurprising that socially inequalities are maintained, precisely because pupils are not 'becoming' in Freirean terms; they are not empowered through critique and debate; they are not active subjects engaging in 'dialogue' to generate knowledge, but are passive objects, who might engage in 'educated discourse' by taking notes, writing essays, reports, etc., without learning.

Literacy and empowerment

In New Zealand research by Jones (1986) clearly exemplifies the problems raised in the previous paragraph. Jones studied two streamed classes of girls – 5M and 5S. Girls in both were committed to work hard in order to achieve academic success, which they perceived to be the route to better life chances. The 5M class comprised working-class girls of a low-to-middle academic ability, while 5S girls were overwhelmingly middle-class, higher-ability girls. Unsurprisingly, the two groups had very different views of the work, corresponding to two very different views of how to operate language within learning based upon two contrasting primary Discourses.

Within their primary Discourse, 5M girls' model of education was hierarchical, top-down: the teacher was seen as the source of authority and knowledge. Such a view demanded an academic and examination-oriented literacy characterised by gaining the knowledge the teacher held about texts through assiduous note-taking:

> [T]hey had no apparent idea that claims advanced as knowledge/information should be checked for accuracy and sense against recognised authoritative sources. Yet this is an essential aspect of enacting the appropriate 'saying(writing)-believing-valuing-doing combinations' involved in academic-exam literacy specifically and academic Discourse generally.
>
> (Lankshear *et al.*, 1997: 28)

Consequently, if teachers attempted discursive practice in the class through, for example, question and answer, 5M did not value it as 'real work' and tended to be disruptive. Therefore, by relying heavily upon dictation as a means of control, teachers reinforced the girls' view of teacher-as-authority, teacher-as-source-of-knowledge. In complete contrast, however, within their primary Discourse, 5S girls saw the teacher as just one of the sources of knowledge available to them and insisted that sessions were structured by discussion and critique that challenged their teachers' assertions. The 5S class played an active role in the construction of knowledge through discussion and debate in the classroom. Ultimately, 5S students passed their School Certificate examinations precisely because the attitudes, values and belief enshrined in the Discourse official examinable culture of the school was closer to their experiences within their primary Discourse, whereas, almost without exception, 5M girls, whose view of education was the product of a contrasting primary Discourse, failed:

> The kinds of difference in language and literacy in Jones's study are closely associated with systematic patterns of academic success and failure . . . Scholastic achievement draws heavily on discursive practices and associated language use which emphasise developing positions and viewpoints by demonstrating flair in arguing a point of view; manipulating and relating abstract ideas; and assuming detached standpoints when matters of objectivity or hypothesis arise.
>
> (Lankshear *et al.*, 1997: 29–30)

The modes of thinking, writing and speaking, appropriate registers, come much more easily to those students in the same social groupings as 5S. The difficulty for 5M students was that in adopting a 'scholastic pose' doing or appearing what is believed to be educationally literate (or, indeed, doing what *they* believed to be scholastic activity, i.e. taking notes) without an understanding of the underlying principles and values, the activities, such as note-taking, become an end in themselves. By devolving all power and responsibility to the teacher as fount of all knowledge, the class was not learning or understanding (Lankshear, 1987: 164). As knowledge of discourse is not innate and nobody had ever made the ground rules visible, 5M students were much more likely to fail. They simply did not control the secondary language uses of the secondary Discourse. Whereas 5S students were more able to 'own' the dominant literacy of written exams precisely because their primary Discourses and cultural capitals privileged them in relation to students from the same social grouping as 5M students, whose parents did not have access to secondary Discourses.

The guided construction of knowledge

Research in the United Kingdom carried out by Mercer (1995) confirms Gee's assertions and suggests a way in which to facilitate access to secondary Discourses. In *The Guided Construction of Knowledge*, Mercer examines language as a social mode of thinking. He argues that while, in Vygotskyan terms, language can be described as a psychological tool it is also, essentially, a cultural tool. The two

functions of language – the psychological (thinking) and the cultural (communication) – are inextricably conjoined and enable each of us to make sense of the world
(in Freirean terms, enabling us to 'become'): 'Language is therefore not just a
means by which individuals can formulate ideas and communicate them, it is also
a means for people to think and learn together' (Mercer, 1995: 4).

Mercer envisages the classroom as a 'discourse village . . . a small language
outpost from which roads lead to larger communities of educated discourse'. The
teacher is a 'discourse guide', who uses 'educational discourse to organise, energise
and maintain a local mini-community of educated discourse'. Mercer goes on to
exemplify the key role of the teacher:

> [T]eachers have to start from where the learners are, to use what they already
> know, and to help them go back and forth across the bridge from 'everyday
> discourse' into 'educated discourse'.
>
> (Mercer, 1995: 83–4)

While Mercer's terminology, perhaps, simplifies the linguistic complexities of the
classroom – 'everyday discourse' is, in fact, likely to be a dialogue of a multiplicity
of multicultural primary Discourses, and 'educated discourse' is a complex web of
the secondary Discourses of teaching and learning – Mercer's extended metaphor
is describing the process of induction, in Gee's terms, from primary to secondary Discourses. What is of particular interest is that Mercer's research describes a
methodology through which the secondary Discourse is made visible to learners
by making visible not only the language structures but also, significantly, the values
and beliefs inherent in the secondary Discourse.

Based on the examination of classroom talk in problem-solving situations, Mercer
typifies three ways of talking and thinking: 'disputational talk', characterised by
disagreement and individualised decision-making; 'cumulative talk', characterised
by speakers' uncritical positive support of each other to construct a 'common
knowledge' by accumulation; and 'exploratory talk', characterised by a critical,
constructive engagement with each other's ideas. Exploratory talk is of particular
significance because 'knowledge is made more publicly accountable and reasoning
is more visible in the talk' (Mercer, 1995: 104).

Through his analysis, Mercer elaborates these models of talk into three 'distinctive social modes of thinking' by using three levels of analysis to describe and
evaluate the types of talk: the 'linguistic level', the 'psychological level' and the
'cultural level'. This chapter cannot attempt to relate Mercer's analysis in full.
Therefore, this part of the chapter will focus only on the 'cultural' level of analysis,
because it involves a consideration of the nature 'of "educated" discourse and of
the kinds of reasoning that are valued and encouraged in the cultural institutions
of formal education' (Mercer, 1995: 106).

Mercer's analysis highlights the importance of exploratory talk:

> It typifies language which embodies certain principles – of accountability, of
> clarity, of constructive criticism and receptiveness to well-argued proposals

– which are highly valued in many societies. In many of our key social institutions – for example, the law, government, administration, research in the sciences and arts, and the negotiation of business – people have to use language to interrogate the quality of the claims, hypotheses and proposals made by each other, to express clearly their own understandings, to reach consensual agreement and make joint decisions . . . it is language in which reasoning is made visible and in which knowledge is made accountable – not in any absolute terms, but in accord with the 'ground rules' of the relevant discourse community.

(ibid.)

Here Mercer identifies the beliefs and values that underpin the secondary Discourses of education and schooling. Having exemplified the ground rules of exploratory talk, the next part of the research involved making pupils aware of them in order to encourage exploratory talk, thereby enabling them to enter the secondary Discourse. These ground rules included sharing relevant information; providing reasons for any assertions or opinions; asking for reasons where appropriate; reaching agreement; accepting that the group, rather than any individual, was responsible for decisions and actions and ultimately for any ensuing success or failure (Mercer, 1995: 108).

The results of Mercer's research have shown that, not only did the quality of classroom talk improve and not only was collective problem-solving more successful but also pupils' scores in tests of non-verbal reasoning improved significantly – establishing a tangible link between thinking and learning (Mercer *et al.*, 1999). Further, such learning also exemplifies Gee's claim that '[t]he learning they are doing, provided it is tied to good teaching, is giving them not the literacies, but the meta-level cognitive and linguistic skills that they can use to critique various discourses throughout their lives' (Gee, 1992: 26).

Powerful literacies

Gee defines literacy as 'control of secondary uses of language (i.e. uses of language in secondary discourses)'. Thus, he argues, 'there are as many applications of the word "literacy" as there are secondary discourses'. He goes on to define 'powerful literacy' as:

[C]ontrol of a secondary use of language used in a secondary discourse that can serve as a meta-discourse to critique the primary discourse or other secondary discourses, including dominant discourses.

(Gee, 1992: 25–6)

Powerful literacy, then, is not a particular literacy, per se, but a particular use of a literacy. Pupils are empowered through learning the meta-level linguistic cognitive and linguistic skills, as opposed to acquiring the language of the secondary

Discourse. The differences between the success of 5S and 5M ably demonstrate this difference. Lankshear sums up the importance of this meta-level knowledge as:

> [K]nowledge *about* what is involved in participating in some Discourse(s). It is more than merely knowing *how* (i.e. being able) to engage successfully in a particular discursive practice. Rather, meta-level knowledge is knowing about the nature of that practice, its constitutive values and beliefs, its meaning and significance, how it relates to other practices, what it is about successful performance that makes it successful, and so on.
>
> (Lankshear *et al.*, 1997: 72)

Lankshear further argues that such knowledge empowers in at least three ways. First, it enhances the individual's level of performance within the Discourse and increases the chances of access to social 'goods'. It is easy to relate this mode of empowerment to success in the education system. Second, the ability to control secondary language uses provides the means by which a Discourse may be analysed to see how skills and knowledge may be used in new ways and directions within that Discourse. Finally, the meta-level knowledge of a secondary Discourses makes it possible to critique and transform a secondary Discourse. Critical awareness of alternative Discourses allows the possibility of *choice* among them. To be enabled to critically choose among Discourses rather than simply to acquire or to reject Discourses without such learning and understanding is to be empowered: it is the essence of powerful literacy.

Conclusion

The dominant Discourse of government documents that established the education system in England and Wales was high-cultural and displayed an antipathy to working-class children and to popular culture. The central metaphor of the National Curriculum is 'delivery'. Eisner (1984) reminds us that the metaphors we use shape our understanding of the concepts we study. A curriculum to be 'delivered' by a teacher is disempowering of pupils and teachers alike (see Davison, 2008). It is a view of knowledge that is hierarchical, top-down and is characterised by prescription and direction. Consequently, it is unsurprising that the 'official examinable culture' of school – the language, knowledge priorities, learning styles, pedagogical preferences – is that of dominant social and cultural groups. It is also well documented that children from the working class underachieve disproportionately.

The National Literacy Strategy was a product of the dominant Discourse: it epitomised the official examinable culture of the school described above and, while its aim was to provide higher SATs (Standard Assessment Tasks) scores for the government, how far did it empower pupils? The work of Gee, Lankshear, Mercer and others offers teachers the possibility of empowering pupils through developing powerful literacies – through participation, collaboration and negotiation; by making Discourses visible; by exposing the ground rules, the underpinning values and beliefs. As a result, pupils and teachers are more likely to recognise, critique and value aspects of their primary Discourses and less likely to uncritically take on the language and attitudes of secondary Discourses they encounter:

> Learning should lead to the ability for all children . . . to critique their primary and secondary discourses, including dominant secondary discourses. This requires exposing children to a variety of alternative primary discourses and secondary ones (not necessarily so that they acquire them, but so that they learn about them). It also requires a realising explicitly that this is what good teaching and learning is good at.
>
> (Gee, 1992: 27)

Further reading

Lankshear, C. with Lawler, M. (1987) *Literacy, Schooling and Revolution*, London: Falmer Press.

The book explores the politics of education in relation to the way in which reading and writing are shaped and transmitted within dominant discourses. The inherently political character of literacy is argued and assumptions about the nature and value of reading and writing are challenged.

Shannon, P. (ed.) (1992) *Becoming Political: Readings and Writings in the Politics of Literacy Education*, Portsmouth, NH: Heinemann.

This book contains seminal readings on the politics of literacy education by authors such as Gee, Brice Heath, Bloome and Giroux and is an excellent starting point for anyone interested in the issues related to literacy and power.

Bibliography

Abraham, J. (1993) *Divide and School: Gender and Class Dynamics in Comprehensive Education*, London: Falmer Press.

Adams, A. and Brindley, S. (eds) (2007) *Teaching Secondary English with ICT*, Maidenhead: Open University Press.

Aitchison, J. (1991) *Language Change: Progress or Decay?*, Cambridge: Cambridge University Press.

Alexander, R. J. (2001) *Culture and Pedagogy: International Comparisons in Primary Education*, Oxford: Blackwell.

— (2008) *Towards Dialogic Teaching: Rethinking Classroom Talk* (4th edn), York: Dialogos.

Alexander, R., Armstrong, M., Flutter, J., Hargreaves, L. Harrison, D., Harlen, W., Hartley-Brewer, E., Kershner, R., Macbeath, J., Mayall, B., Northen, S., Pugh, G., Richards, C. and Utting, D. (eds) (2010) *Children, Their World, Their Education: Final Report and Recommendations of the Cambridge Primary Review*, London: Routledge.

Alexander, R., Willcocks, J. and Nelson, N. (1996) 'Discourse, pedagogy and the National Curriculum: Change and continuity in primary schools', *Research Papers in Education*, 11(1): 81–120.

Allen, N. (2002) 'Too much, too young? An analysis of the Key Stage 3 National Literacy Strategy in practice', *English in Education*, 36: 5–15.

Altinyelken, H. K. (2010) 'Curriculum change in Uganda: Teacher perspectives on the new thematic curriculum', *International Journal of Educational Development*, 30: 151–61.

Anderson, H. (1995) 'Monsterous plans? Standard English in the National Curriculum and Norwegian in the "Monsterplan"', *English in Education*, 29(1): 14–19.

Andrews, R. (2003) 'Where next in research on ICT and literacies?' *English in Education*, 37(3): 28–42.

— (2010) *Re-framing Literacy: Teaching and Learning English and the Language Arts*, New York: Routledge.

Andrews, R. and Smith, A. (2011) *Writing Development: Teaching and Learning in the Digital Age*, Maidenhead: McGraw-Hill/Open University Press.

Appleyard, J. A. (1985) *Becoming a Reader: The Experience of Fiction from Childhood and Adulthood*, Cambridge: Cambridge University Press.

Arnold, M. (1869) *Culture and Anarchy* (1969 edn), London: Penguin.

— (1979) *Selected Poetry and Prose*, ed. D. Thompson, London: Heinemann.

Arthur, J., Davison, J. and Moss, J. (1997) *Subject Mentoring in the Secondary School*, London: Routledge.

Arts Council (2003) *Ambition for the Arts 2003–2006*. London: Arts Council England.

Atkinson, A., Cashdan, L., Michael, L. and Pople, I. (2001) 'Analysing the aesthetic a new approach to developing criteria for assessment of creative writing in higher education', *Writing in Education*, 21(Winter): 26–8.

AQA (Assessment and Qualifications Alliance) (2009a) *General Certificate of Secondary Education: English Language 4705 Specimen; Controlled Assessment Tasks*. Available online at http://www.aqa.org.uk/resource-zone/english/overview.php (accessed 31 March 2010).

— (2009b) *A-level English Language and Literature Specification A*. Available online at http://web.aqa.org.uk/qual/gce/english/eng_lang_lit_a_materials. php?id=02&prev=02 (accessed 13 April 2010).

Bakhtin, M. M. (1981) *The Dialogic Imagination*, Austin: University of Texas Press.

Baldick, C. (1983) *The Social Mission of English Criticism*, Oxford: Oxford University Press.

Ball, S. (1981) *Beachside Comprehensive: A Case Study of Secondary Schooling*, London: Cambridge University Press.

— (1985) 'English for the English since 1906', in Goodson, I. (ed.), *Social Histories of the Secondary Curriculum: Subjects for Study*, London: Falmer Press.

— (1987) 'English teaching, the state and forms of literacy', in Kroon, S. and Sturm, J. (eds), *Research on Mother Tongue Education*, Enschede, The Netherlands: Advisory Committee for Curriculum Development.

— (1999) 'Labour, Learning and the Economy: A "policy sociology" perspective', *Cambridge Journal of Education*, 29(2): 195–206.

Ball, S., Kenny, A. and Gardiner, D. (1990) 'Literacy, politics and the teaching of English', in Goodson, I. and Medway, P. (eds), *Bringing English to Order: The History and Politics of a School Subject*, London: Falmer Press.

Balls, E. (2007) 'Every Child Matters', speech at Business Design Centre, Islington, for National Children's Bureau, 18 July 2007.

Banaji, S. and Burn A. (2007) *Rhetorics of Creativity: A Review of the Literature*, London: Creative Partnerships and Arts Council of England.

Barber, M. and Mourshed, M. (2007) *How the World's Best Performing School Systems Come Out on Top*, McKinsey & Company. Available online at http://www.mckinsey.com/clientservice/Social_Sector/our_practices/Education/Knowledge_Highlights/Best_performing_school.aspx (accessed 3 September 2010).

Barnes, D., Barnes, D. and Clarke, S. (1984) *Versions of English*, London: Heinemann.

Barthes, R. (1976) *Pleasure of the Text*, trans. Richard Miller, New York: Hill & Wang.

Barton, D. (1994) *Literacy: An Introduction to the Ecology of Written Language*, Oxford: Blackwell.

Barton, D., Hamilton, M. and Ivanic, R. (2000) *Situated Literacies: Reading and Writing in Context*, London: Routledge.

BBC (2010) David Cameron interview, *Today*, BBC Radio 4, 7 January 2010.

Beard, R. (2000a) 'Research and the National Literacy Strategy', *Oxford Review of Education*, 26(3/4): 421–36.

— (2000b) 'Long overdue? Another look at the National Literacy Strategy', *Journal of Research in Reading*, 23: 245–55.

— (2003) 'Not the whole story of the National Literacy Strategy: A response to Dominic Wyse', *British Educational Research Journal*, 29: 917–28.

Beard, R., Myhill, D., Riley, J. and Nystrand, M. (eds) (2009) *The Sage Handbook of Writing Development*, London: Sage.

Bearne, E. (2003) 'Rethinking literacy: Communication, representation and text', *Reading Literacy and Language*, 37(3): 98–103.

Becta (2008) *Harnessing Technology Review 2008*, Coventry: Becta.

Benner, P. (1984) *From Novice to Expert: Excellence and Power in Clinical Nursing Practice*, Menlo Park: Addison-Wesley, pp. 13–34.

Bennett, A. (2004) *The History Boys*, London: Faber & Faber.

Bennett, K. P. and LeCompte, M. D. (1990) *The Way Schools Work: A Sociological Analysis of Education*, New York: Longman.

Bernstein, B. (1971) *Class, Codes and Control*, London: Paladin.

Beverton, S. (2000) 'Implementing the National Literacy Strategy: How are teachers managing?', *Topic*, 23(Spring): 1–7.

— (2003) 'Can you see the difference? Early impacts of the primary National Literacy Strategy on four secondary English departments', *Cambridge Journal of Education*, 33: 217–45.

Biddulph, M. (2006) 'Sexualities equality in schools: Why every lesbian, gay, bisexual or transgender (LGBT) child matters', *Pastoral Care in Education*, 24(2): 15–21.

Bissex, G. (1980) *GNYS AT WRK: A Child Learns to Write and Read*, Harvard: Harvard University Press.

Blake, J. and Shortis, T. (2010) *The PGCE English Preparedness Survey*, London: British Association for Applied Linguistics.

Blake, R. and Cutler, C. (2003) 'African American vernacular English and variation in teachers' attitudes: A question of school philosophy?', *Linguistics and Education*, 14(2): 163–94.

Blakemore, S. J. and Frith, U. (2005) *The Learning Brain: Lessons for Education*, Oxford: Blackwell.

Blanden, J., Gregg, P. and Machin, S. (2005) *Integrational Mobility in Europe and North America*, London: Centre for Economic Performance, London School of Economics.

Blanden, J. and Machin, S. (2007) *Recent Changes in Intergenerational Mobility the UK*. Available online at http://www.suttontrust.com/annualreports.asp (accessed 28 August 2010).

Bleiman, B. (2008a) 'The new English A level: Further thoughts on the new 2008 specifications', *English Drama Media*, 10(February): 37–44.

— (2008b) 'Back to the future: Creativity, coursework and poetry at A level', *English Drama Media*, 12(October): 11–15.

BoE (Board of Education) (1910) *Circular 753*, London: HMSO.

— (1921) *The Teaching of English in England* (Newbolt Report), London: HMSO.

— (1938) *Report on Secondary Education* (Spens Report), London: HMSO.

Boden, M. (2005) *The Creative Mind: Myths and Mechanisms* (2nd edn), Oxford: Routledge.

Boocook, S. (1980) *Sociology of Education: An Introduction* (2nd edn), Boston: Houghton Mifflin.

Bourdieu, P. (1973) 'Cultural reproduction and social reproduction', in Brown, R. (ed.) *Knowledge, Education and Social Change*, London: Tavistock.

— (2007) *Distinction: A Social Critique of the Judgment of Taste*, trans. R. Nice, Harvard: Harvard University Press.

Bowles, S. and Gintis, H. (1976) *Schooling in Capitalist America: Education and the Contradictions of Economic Life*, London: Routledge & Kegan Paul.

Boyle, A. (2010) 'The dialogic construction of knowledge in university classroom talk: A corpus study of spoken academic discourse', unpublished PhD thesis, Belfast: Queen's University.

Brice Heath, S. (1983) *Ways with Words: Language, Life and Work in Communities and Classrooms*, Cambridge: Cambridge University Press.

Britannica Concise Encyclopedia, 'Creativity'. Available online at http://www.answers.com/topic/creativity (accessed on 24 March 2010).

Britannica Concise Encyclopedia (2006) London: Encyclopaedia Britannica (UK) Ltd.

Britton, J. (1987) 'Vygotsky's contribution to pedagogical theory', *English in Education*, 21(3): 22–6.

Brontë, E. (2004) *Wuthering Heights*, London: Penguin Classics.

Brown, L. (ed.) (1993) *The New Shorter Oxford English Dictionary*, Oxford: Clarendon Press.

Brown, R. (ed.) (1973) *Knowledge, Education and Cultural Change*, London: Tavistock.

Bruner, J. (1962) *On Knowing: Essays for the Left Hand*, Cambridge, MA: Harvard University Press.

Bryan, H. (2003) 'Constructs of teacher professionalism within a changing literacy landscape', *Literacy*, 38(3): 141–8.

Bryson, B. (1990) *Mother Tongue*, London: Penguin.

Buckingham, D. (2000) *The Making of Citizens: Young People, News and Politics*, London: Routledge.

— (2003) *Media Education: Literacy, Learning and Contemporary Culture*, Cambridge: Polity.

Burn, A. and Durran, J. (2007) *Media Literacy in Schools: Practice, Production and Progression*, London: Paul Chapman.

Butler, D. (1995) *Babies Need Books*, Harmondsworth: Penguin Books.

Cain, K., Oakville, J., Barnes, M. and Bryant, P. (2001) 'Comprehension skills, inference-making ability and their relation to knowledge', *Memory and Cognition*, 29(6): 850–59.

Cameron, D. (1995) *Verbal Hygiene*, London: Routledge.

Cameron, D. and Bourne, J. (1988) 'No common ground: Kingman, grammar and the nation', *Language and Education*, 2(3): 147–60.

Camp, D. (2000) 'It takes two: Teaching with twin texts of fact and fiction', *The Reading Teacher*, 53(5): 400–8.

Campbell, R. (1999) *Literacy from Home to School: Reading with Alice*, Stoke on Trent: Trentham Books.

Carter, R. (2003) *Language and Creativity: The Art of Common Talk*, London: Routledge.

Carter, R. and McCarthy, M. (2006) *Cambridge Grammar of English*, Cambridge: Cambridge University Press.

Cazden, C. (2001) *Classroom Discourse: The Language of Teaching and Learning*, Portsmouth, NH: Heinemann.

Chabbott, C. (2006) *Accelerating Early Grades Reading in High Priority EFA Countries: A Desk Review*, US Agency for International Development, Cooperative Agreement No. GDG-A-00-03-00006-00.

Cheshire, J. and Edwards, V. (1993) 'Sociolinguistics in the classroom: Exploring linguistic diversity', in Milroy, J. and Milroy, L. (eds), *Real English: The Grammar of English Dialects in the British Isles*, London: Longman.

Clark, A., Kjorholta, T. and Moss, P. (2005) *Beyond Listening: Children's Perspectives on Early Childhood Services*, Bristol: Policy Press, University of Bristol.

Clark, C., Osborne, S. and Dugdale, G. (2009) *Reaching Out with Role Models: Role Models and Young People's Reading*, London: National Literacy Trust.

Cogill, J. (2008) 'Primary teachers' interactive whiteboard practice across one year: Changes in pedagogy and influencing factors', unpublished doctoral dissertation, Kings College, University of London.

Cordingley, P., Bell, M., Isham, C., Evans, D. and Firth, A. (2007) 'What do specialists do in CPD programmes for which there is evidence of positive outcomes for pupils and teachers?' Research Evidence in Education Library London, EPPI-Centre, Social Science Research Unit, Institute of Education, University of London.

Costa, A. L. and Garmston, R. J. (1994) *Cognitive Coaching: A Foundation for Renaissance Schools,* Norwood: Christopher-Gordon.

Cox, B. (1991) *Cox on Cox: An English Curriculum for the 1990s*, London: Hodder & Stoughton.

— (1992) *The Great Betrayal: Memoirs of a Life in Education*, London: Hodder & Stoughton.

— (ed.) (1998) *Literacy Is Not Enough: Essays on the Importance of Reading*, Manchester: Manchester University Press.

Cox, M., Webb, M., Abbott, C., Blakeley, B., Beauchamp, T. and Rhodes, V. (2003) *ICT and Pedagogy: A Review of the Research Literature*, London: Becta for the DfES.

Craft, A. (2001) 'Little c creativity', in Craft, A., Jeffrey, B. and Leibling, M. (eds), *Creativity in Education*, London: Continuum, pp. 45–61.

— (2006) 'Fostering creativity with wisdom', *Cambridge Journal of Education*, 36(3): 337–50.

Creative Partnerships (2010) 'How we work'. Available online at http://www.creative-partnerships.com/howwework/ (accessed on 13 June 2010).

Cremin, T. (2006) 'Creativity, uncertainty and discomfort: Teachers as writers', *Cambridge Journal of Education*, 36(3): 415–33.

Crouch, L., Korda, M. and Mumo, D. (2009) *Improvements in Reading Skills in Kenya: An Experiment in the Malindi District*, Washington, DC: USAID.

Crowley, T. (2003) *Standard English and the Politics of Language*, London: Palgrave Macmillan.

Crystal, D. (1995) *The Cambridge Encyclopedia of the English Language*, Cambridge: Cambridge University Press.

— (2004) 'A twenty-first century grammar bridge', *Secondary English Magazine*, June: 24–6.

Crystal, D. and Crystal, B. (2002) *Shakespeare's Words: A Glossary and Language Companion*, London: Penguin.

Cunningham, A. and Stanovich, K. (2001) 'What reading does for the mind', *Journal of Direct Instruction*, 1(2): 137–49.

Daly, C., Pachler, N. and Pelletier, C. (2009a) *ICT CPD for School Teachers: Literature Review*, Coventry: Becta.

— (2009b) *Continuing Professional Development in Information and Communications Technology for School Teachers: Report 2*, Coventry: Becta.

Daniels, H. (2001) *Vygotsky and Pedagogy*, New York and London: RoutledgeFalmer.

David, T. (2007) 'What is early childhood for?', in Goouch, K. and Lambirth, A. (eds), *Understanding Phonics and the Teaching of Reading: Critical Perspectives*, Maidenhead: Open University Press.

David, T., Goouch, K., Powell, S. and Abbott, L. (2003) *Birth to Three Matters: A Review of the Literature*, Nottingham: DfES Publications.

David, T., Raban, B., Ure, C., Goouch, K., Jago, M., Barriere, I. and Lambirth, A. (2000) *Making Sense of Early Literacy: A Practitioner's Perspective*, Stoke on Trent: Trentham Books.

Davison, J. (2008) 'Why we shouldn't have it all off Pat', *The Times Educational Supplement*, 14 March.

Davison, J. and Dowson, J. (2009) *Learning to Teach English in the Secondary School* (3rd edn), London: Routledge.

Day, C., Sammons, P., Stobart, G., Kington, A. and Gu, Q., (2007) *Teachers Matter: Connecting Work, Lives and Effectiveness*, Maidenhead: Open University.

Dede, C. (2006) *Online Professional Development for Teachers*, Cambridge, MA: Harvard Education Press.

De Klerk, V. A. (1995) 'The discourse of postgraduate seminars', *Linguistics and Education*, 7: 157–74.

DCSF (Department for Children, Schools and Families) (2007) *The Early Years Foundation*, London: HMSO.

— (2008a) *Assessing Pupils' Progress in English*, London: DCSF.

— (2008b) *Teaching for Progression: Writing*, London: DCSF. Available online at http://nationalstrategies.standards.dcsf.gov.uk/node/154838 (accessed 17 May 2010).

— (2009) *The Simple View of Reading*. Available online at http://nationalstrategies.standards.dcsf.gov.uk/node/20162 (accessed 21 February 2010).

DfEE (Department for Education and Employment) (1993) *English in the National Curriculum*, London: HMSO.

— (1998) *The National Literacy Strategy: Framework for Teaching*, London: DfEE.

— (2001) *Key Stage 3 National Strategy: Framework for Teaching English: Years 7, 8 and 9*, London: HMSO.

DfES (Department for Education and Skills) (2003) *Every Child Matters*, Norwich: The Stationery Office.

— (2004a) *Every Child Matters: Change for Children in Schools*, London: DfES.

— (2004b) *Aiming High: Understanding the Educational Needs of Minority Ethnic Pupils in Mainly White School*, London: DfES

— (2005) *Harnessing Technology: Transforming Learning and Children's Services*, London: DfES.

— (2006a) *Independent Review of the Teaching of Early Reading* (Rose Review), London: DfES.

— (2006b) *Five-Year Strategic Plan: Primary and Secondary National Strategies*, London: DFES.

— (2006c) *The Primary Framework for Literacy and Mathematics*, London: DFES. Available online at http://nationalstrategies.standards.dcsf.gov.uk/primary/primaryframework/literacyframework (accessed 13 June 2010).

— (2006d) *Departmental Report*, London: DfES

DES (Department of Education and Science) (1975) *A Language for Life* (Bullock Report), London: HMSO.

— (1984) *English 5–16, Curriculum Matters 1*, London: HMSO.

— (1986) *English from 5 to 16: The Responses to Curriculum Matters 1*, London: HMSO.

— (1987) *The Report of the Task Group on Assessment and Testing* (TGAT), London: HMSO.

— (1988) *Report of the Committee of Enquiry into the Teaching of the English Language: The Kingman Report*, London: HMSO.

— (1989) *English for Ages 5–16* (Cox Report), London: HMSO.

— (1990) *English in the National Curriculum*, London: HMSO.

— (1993) *English 5–16*, London: HMSO.

Dillon, J. (1994) *Using Discussion in Classrooms*, Milton Keynes: Open University Press.

Disch. T. (n.d) 'Creativity quotes'. Available online at http://www.mycoted.com/Creativity_Quotes (accessed 24 March 2010).

Disraeli, B. (1845) *Sybil, or The Two Nations* (1998 edn), Oxford: Oxford.

Dixon, J. (1967) *Growth through English*, Oxford: Oxford University Press.

Douglas, J. (1964) *The Home and the School*, London: MacGibbon & Kee.

Dreyfus, S. L. and Dreyfus, H. L. (1986) *Mind over Machine: The Power of Human Intuition and Expertise in the Era of the Computer*, New York: Simon & Schuster.

Dunn, J., Styles, M. and Warburton, N. (1987) *In Tune with Yourself*, Cambridge: Cambridge University Press.

Dymoke, S. (2002) 'The dead hand of the exam: The impact of the NEAB anthology on GCSE poetry teaching', *Changing English*, 9(1): 85–93.

— (2003) *Drafting and Assessing Poetry*, London: Paul Chapman.

— (2009) *Teaching English Texts 11–18*, London: Continuum.

Eagleton, T. (1975) *Literary Theory: An Introduction*, Oxford: Blackwell.

— (1983) *Literary Theory: An Introduction*, Oxford: Blackwell.

Earl, L., Watson, N., Levin, B., Fullan, M. and Torrance, N. (2003) *Watching and Learning 3: Final Report of the External Evaluation of England's National Literacy and Numeracy Strategies*, Toronto: University of Toronto.

ESRC (Economic and Social Research Council) (2008a) *Theorising the Benefits of New Technology for Youth: Controversies of Learning and Development*, No. 1, The Educational and Social Impact of New Technologies on Young People in Britain, Oxford: University of Oxford.

— (2008b) *Changing Spaces: Young People, Technology and Learning*, No. 2, The Educational and Social Impact of New Technologies on Young People in Britain, Oxford: University of Oxford.

Edwards, C., Gandini, L., Forman, G. (eds) (1998) *The Hundred Languages of Children: The Reggio Emilia Approach – Advanced Reflections* (2nd edn), Greenwich, CT: Ablex Publishing.

Ehri, L. C. (2002) 'Phases of acquisition in learning to read words and implications for teaching', *British Journal of Educational Psychology Monograph Series II, Learning and Teaching Reading*, 1: 7–28.

Eisner, E. W. (1984) *Cognition and Curriculum*, London: Longman.

— (1985) *The Educational Imagination: On the Design and Evaluation of School Programmes*, New York: Macmillan.

Ellis, V. (2003) 'The love that dare not speak its name? The constitution of the English subject and beginning teachers' motivations to teach it', *English Teaching: Practice and Critique*, 2(1) May: 3–14.

— (2007) *Subject Knowledge and Teacher Education: The Development of Beginning Teachers' Thinking*, London: Continuum.

Elyot, Thomas (1531) *The Book Named the Governor* (1962 edn), ed. S. E. Lemberg, Letchworth: Everyman.

English Association. Available online at http://www.queens-english-society.com (accessed 28 August 2010).

English, E. (2003) 'All change! The National Literacy Strategy and its influence on the teaching of reading', *Studies in Training and Learning*, 4: 18–23.

English, E., Hargreaves, L. and Hislam, J. (2002) 'Pedagogical dilemmas in the National Literacy Strategy: Primary teachers' perceptions, reflections and classroom behaviour', *Cambridge Journal of Education*, 32: 9–26.

Eraut, M. (1994) *Developing Professional Knowledge and Competence*, London: Falmer Press.

— (1995) 'Developing professional knowledge within a client-centred orientation', in Guskey, T.R. and Huberman, M. (eds), *Professional Development in Education*, New York: Teachers College Press, pp. 227–52.

Fairclough, N. (1989) *Language and Power*, London: Addison-Wesley Longman.

Farrel, T. C. and Tan Kiat Kun, T. (2007) 'Language policy, language teachers' beliefs, and classroom practices', *Applied Linguistics*, 29(3): 381–403.

Fisher, T., Higgins, C. and Loveless, A. (2006) 'Teachers learning with digital technologies: A review of research and projects', *Futurelab* series, No. 14. Available online at http://www.futurelab.org.uk/research/lit_reviews.htm#lr14 (accessed 28 August 2010).

Floud, H., Halsey, A. and Martin, F. (1966) *Social Class and Educational Opportunity*, Bath: Chivers.

Franks, A. (2003) 'Palmers' kiss: Shakespeare, school drama and semiotics', in Jewitt, C. and Kress, G. (eds), *Multimodal Literacy*, New York: Peter Lang.

Franzak, J. K. (2006) 'Zoom: A review of the literature on marginalized adolescent readers, literacy theory, and policy implications', *Review of Educational Research*, 76(2): 209–48.

Freire, P. (1972) *Pedagogy of the Oppressed*, Harmondsworth: Penguin.

— (1976) *Education: The Practice of Freedom*, London: Writers & Readers Publishing Cooperative.

— (1985) *The Politics of Education: Culture Power and Liberation*, London: Macmillan.

— (2000) *Pedagogy of the Oppressed*, trans. M. Ramos, London: Continuum.

Freire, P. and Macedo, D. (1987) *Literacy: Reading the Word and the World*, London: Routledge & Kegan Paul.

Furedi, F. (2009) *Wasted: Why Education Isn't Educating*, New York and London: Continuum.

Furlong, J., Barton, L., Miles, S., Whiting, C. and Whitty, G. (2000) *Teacher Education in Transition: Re-forming professionalism?* Philadelphia and Buckingham: Open University Press.

Galindo-Rueda, F., Marcenaro-Gutierrez, O. and Vignoles, A. (2004) 'The widening socio-economic gap in UK higher education', *National Institute Economic Review*, 190(1): 75–88.

Galton, M., Hargreaves, L., Comber, C., Wall, D. and Pell, T. (1999) *Inside the Primary Classroom: 20 Years On*, London: Routledge.

Gardner, D. (2004) 'Vocabulary input through extensive reading: A comparison of words found in children's narrative and expository reading materials', *Applied Linguistics*, 25(1): 11–37.

Gaskell, J. (1985) 'Course enrolment in high school: The perspective of working class females', *Sociology of Education*, 58: 48–59.

Gee, J. P. (1990) *Social Linguistics and Literacies: Ideology in Discourses*, London: Falmer Press.

— (1991) 'What is literacy?', in Mitchell, C. and Weiler, K. (eds), *Rewriting Literacy: Culture of the Discourse and the Other*, New York: Bergin & Garvey.

— (1992) *The Social Mind: Language, Ideology and Social Practice*, New York: Bergin & Harvey.

Genette, G. (1980) *Narrative Discourse: An Essay in Method*, trans. Jane Lewin, Ithaca: Cornell University Press.

Gibson, H. and Patrick, H. (2008) 'Putting words in their mouths: The role of teaching assistants and the spectre of scripted pedagogy', *Journal of Early Childhood Literacy*, 8(1): 25–41.

Gibson, R. (1998) *Teaching Shakespeare*, Cambridge: Cambridge University Press.

Gillen, J. (2000) 'Versions of Vygotsky', *British Journal of Educational Studies*, 48(2): 183–98.

Giroux, H. (1988) 'Critical theory and the politics of culture and voice: Rethinking the discourse of educational research', in Sherman, R. and Rodman, W., *Qualitative Research in Education: Focus and Methods*, London: Routledge.

Goodson, I. and Ball, S. (eds) (1984) *Defining the Curriculum: Histories and Ethnographies*, London: Falmer Press.

Goodson, I. and Medway, P. (eds) (1990) *Bringing English to Order*, London: Falmer Press.

Goodwyn, A. (1992a) 'English teachers and the Cox models', *English in Education*, 28(3): 4–10.

— (1992b) *English Teaching and Media Education*, Buckingham: Open University Press.

— (ed.) (1995) *English and Ability*, London: David Fulton.

— (1997) *Developing English Teachers: The Role of Mentorship in a Reflective Profession*, Milton Keynes: Open University Press.

— (2001) 'Who wants to be a super teacher? The perils and pleasures of recognising expertise in English teaching', *English in Australia*, 129–130, December 2000/ February 2001: 39–50.

— (2004a) 'What's in a frame? The English Framework – three years on', *English Drama Media*, (2): 39–43.

— (2004b) *English Teaching and the Moving Image*, London: Routledge.

— (2008) 'Student teachers and literary reading', paper presented at BERA, Manchester, September.

— (2009a) 'The status of literature teaching in England', paper presented at BERA, Manchester, September.

— (2009b) 'Expert teachers and innovative uses of technology', paper given at the annual conference of the New Zealand Association for the Teaching of English.

— (2010) *The Expert Teacher of English*, London: Routledge

Goodwyn, A., Adams, A. and Clarke, S. (1997) 'The great god of the future: Views of current and future English teachers on the place of IT in English, *English in Education*, 31(2), September: 54–62.

Goodwyn, A., and Findlay, K. (1999) 'The Cox models revisited: English teachers' views of their subject and the National Curriculum', *English in Education*, 33(2), Summer: 19–31.

— (2001) 'Media studies and the establishment', *International Journal of Media Education*, 1(1), Autumn: 23–40.

— (2002) 'Secondary schools and the National Literacy Strategy', in Goodwyn, A. (ed.), *Improving Literacy at KS2 and KS3*, London: Paul Chapman, pp. 45–64.

— (2003a) 'Shaping literacy in the secondary school: Policy, practice and agency in the age of the National Literacy Strategy', *British Journal of Educational Studies*, 51(1): 20–35.

— (2003b) 'Literature, literacy and the discourses of English teaching: A case study, *L1-Educational Studies in Language and Literature*, 3(2), Autumn: 221–38.

Goodwyn, A. and Fuller, C. (eds) (1998) 'Broadening the literacy horizon', in Goodwyn, A. (ed.), *Literary and Media Texts in Secondary English*, London: Cassells, pp. 1–23.

— (2000a), 'Texting: Reading and writing in the intertext', in Goodwyn, A. (ed.), *English in the Digital Age*, London: Continuum, pp. 78–96.

— (2000b), '"A bringer of new things": An English Teacher in the computer age?', in Goodwyn, A. (ed.) *English in the Digital Age*, London: Continuum, pp. 1–21.

— (2001) 'Second-tier professionals: English teachers in England', *L1-Educational Studies in Language and Literature*, 1(2), Autumn: 149–61.

— (2003b), 'Literacy or English: The struggle for the professional identity of English teachers in England', in *English Teachers at Work: Narratives, Counter-narratives and Arguments, Australian Association for the Teaching of English /Interface*, Kent Town: Wakefield Press.

— (2003c) 'Breaking up is hard to do: English teachers and that LOVE of reading, *English Teaching, Practice and Critique*, 1(1), September: 66–78.

— (2004b) 'Learning to read critically in language and literacy education', in Goodwyn, A. and Stables, A. (eds), *Literacy Versus English: A Professional Identity Crisis*, London: Sage, pp. 192–205.

— (2011) *The Great Literacy Debate*, London: Routledge.

Goouch, K. (2007a) 'Parents' voices', in Goouch, K. and Lambirth, A. (eds), *Understanding Phonics and the Teaching of Reading*, Maidenhead: Open University Press.

— (2007b) 'Understanding educational discourse: Attending to multiple voices', in Goouch, K. and Lambirth, A. (eds), *Understanding Phonics and the Teaching of Reading: Critical Perspectives*, Maidenhead: Open University Press.

— (2010) *Towards Excellence in Early Years Education: Exploring Narratives of Experience*, London: Routledge.

Goouch, K. and Bryan, H. (2006) 'Pedagogical Connections, Boundaries and Barriers: the place of travel in teachers' professional development'. *NZ Research in Early Childhood Education*, 9.

Goouch, K. and Lambirth, A. (2010) *Teaching Early Reading and Phonics*, London: Sage.

Goouch, K. and Powell, S. (2010) 'The baby room', unpublished report to the Esmee Fairbairn Foundation.

Gorard, S., Taylor, C. and Fitz, J. (2000) *Education and Social Justice*. Cardiff: University of Wales.

Gopnik, A. (2009) *The Philosophical Baby*, London: The Bodley Head.

Gopnik, A., Meltzoff, A. and Kuhl, P. (1999) *How Babies Think*, London: Weidenfeld & Nicolson.

Gossman, L. (1981) 'Literature and education', *New Literary History*, 13: 341–71.

Goswami, U. (2007) 'Learning to read across languages: The role of phonics and synthetic phonics', in Goouch, K. and Lambirth, A. (eds), *Understanding Phonics and the Teaching of Reading: Critical Perspectives*, Maidenhead: Open University Press.

Goswami, U. and Bryant, P. (1990) *Phonological Skills and Learning to Read*, Hove: Psychology Press.

Gove, M. (2009) 'A comprehensive programme for state education'. Available online at http://www.conservatives.com/News/Speeches/2009/11/Michael_Gove_A_comprehensive_programme_for_state_education.aspx (accessed 8 February 2010).

Graff, H. J. (1987) *The Legacies of Literacies: Continuities and Contradictions in Western Society and Culture*, Bloomington: Indiana University Press.

Grainger, T., Goouch, K. and Lambirth, A. (2005) *Creativity and Writing*, London: Routledge.

Graves, D. (1981) 'Renters and Owners: Donald Graves on Writing', *English Magazine*, 8, Autumn.

— (1983) *Writing: Teachers and Children at Work*, London: Heinemann.

Greenbaum, S. and Nelson, G. (2002) *An Introduction to English Grammar*, London: Pearson Education.

Greenfield, S. (2000) *The Private Life of the Brain*, London: Penguin.

Greenleaf, C. L., Schoenbach, R., Cziko, C. and Mueller, F. L. (2001) 'Apprenticing adolescent readers to academic literacy', *Harvard Educational Review*, 71(1): 79–129.

Gregory, E. (1996) *Making Sense of a New World: Learning to Read in a Second Language*, London: Paul Chapman.

— (2004) '"Invisible" teachers of literacy: Collusion between siblings and teachers in creating classroom cultures', *Literacy*, 38(2): 97–105.

Gregory, E., and Williams, A. (2000) *City Literacies: Learning to Read across Generations and Cultures*, London and New York: Routledge.

Grossman, P. (1990) *The Making of a Teacher: Teacher Knowledge and Teacher Education*, New York: Teachers College Press.

Gunter, H. (1997). *Rethinking Education: The Consequences of Jurassic Management*. London: Cassell.

Hall, K. (2004) *Literacy and Schooling: Towards Renewal in Primary Education Policy*, Aldershot: Ashgate Publishing.

— (2006) 'How children learn to read and how phonics helps', in Lewis, M. and Ellis, S. (eds), *Phonics, Practice, Research and Policy*, London: Paul Chapman.

— (2007) 'To codify pedagogy or enrich learning: A Wengerian perspective on early literacy policy in England', in Goouch, K. and Lambirth, A. (eds), *Understanding Phonics and the Teaching of Reading: Critical Perspectives*, Maidenhead: Open University Press.

Halsey, A. H. (1998) 'Leagues Apart', *The Times Higher Education Supplement*, 6 February: 17.

Hammond, M., Crosson, S., Fragkouli, E., Ingram, J., Johnston-Wilder, P., Johnston-Wilder, S., Kingston, Y., Pope, M. and Wray, D. (2009) 'Why do some student teachers make very good use of ICT? An exploratory case study', *Technology, Pedagogy and Education*, 18(1): 59–73.

Hancock, C. (2009) 'How Linguistics can inform the teaching of writing', in Beard, R., Myhill, D., Riley, J. and Nystrand, M. (eds), *The Sage Handbook of Writing Development*, London: Sage, pp. 194–208.

Hansson, H. (2006) 'Teachers' professional development for the technology-enhanced classroom in the school of tomorrow', *E-Learning*, 3(4): 552–64.

Hardcastle, J. (2009) 'Vygotsky's enlightenment precursors', *Educational Review*, 61(2): 181–95.

Hardman, F. (2008) 'The guided co-construction of knowledge', in Martin-Jones, M., de Mejia, A. and Hornberger, N. (eds), *Encyclopaedia of Language and Education* New York: Springer Publishing, pp. 253–64.

Hardman, F. and Leat, D. (1998) 'Images of post-16 English teaching', *Teaching and Teacher Education*, 4(4): 359–68.

Hardman, F. and Mroz, M. (1999) 'Post-16 English teaching: From recitation to discussion', *Educational Review*, 51(3): 283–93.

Hardman, F. and Williamson, J. (1998) 'The discourse of A Level English teaching', *Educational Review*, 50(1): 5–14.

Hardman, F., Smith, F. and Wall. K. (2003) '"Interactive Whole Class Teaching" in the National Literacy Strategy', *Cambridge Journal of Education*, 33(2): 197–215.

— (2005) 'Teacher-pupil dialogue with pupils with special needs in the National Literacy Strategy', *Educational Review*, 57(3): 299–316.

Hardy, B. (1977) 'Narrative as a primary act of mind', in Meek M., Warlow, A. and Barton, G., *The Cool Web: The Pattern of Children's Reading*, London: The Bodley Head.

Hargreaves, D. (1967) *Social Relations in the Secondary School*, London: Routledge & Kegan Paul.

Harrison, B. T. (1994) *The Literate Imagination: Renewing the Secondary English Curriculum*, London: David Fulton.

Harrison, C. (2002) *Key Stage 3 National Strategy: Key Stage 3 English: Roots and Research*, London: HMSO.

Hart, S., Dixon, A., Drummond, M. J. and McIntyre, D. (2004) *Learning Without Limits*, Maidenhead: Open University Press.

Hartley, D. (2007) 'Personalisation: The emerging 'revised' code of education?', *Oxford Review of Education*, 33(5): 629–42.

Hattie, J. (2003) 'Teachers make a difference: what is the research evidence?', paper presented at the Australian Council for Educational Research Conference.

Hay Mcber (2000) *A Model of Teacher Effectiveness*, London: DfEE.

Heath, S. B. (1983) *Ways with Words: Language, Life, and Work in Communities and Classrooms*, Cambridge: Cambridge University Press.

Hillgate Group, The (1989) *Learning to Teach*, London: Claridge Press.

HMI (Her Majesty's Inspectorate) (1984) *English from 5 to 16*, London: HMSO.

Hobson, P. (2002) *The Cradle of Thought: Exploring the Origins of Thinking*, London: Macmillan.

Hogan, P. (2000). 'Virtue, vice and vacancy in educational policy and practice', *British Journal of Educational Studies*, 48(4): 371–90.

Holmes, B., Gardner, J. and Galanouli, D. (2007) 'Striking the right cord and sustaining professional development in information and communications technologies', *Journal of In-service Education*, 33(4): 389–404.

Holquist, M. (1990) *Dialogism: Bakhtin and His World*, London: Routledge.

House of Commons Children, Schools and Families Committee (2010) *Training of Teachers* [HC 275-I], London: The Stationery Office.

Huberman, M. (1993) *The Lives of Teachers*, London: Continuum.

Hudson, R. and Holmes, J. (1995) *Children's Use of Spoken Standard English*, London: School Curriculum and Assessment Authority.

Hughes, J. and Tolley, S. (2010) 'Engaging students through new literacies: The good, bad and curriculum of visual essays', *English in Education*, 44(1): 5–26.

Hunt, G. (2001) 'Democracy or a command curriculum: Teaching literacy in England', *Improving Schools*, 4: 51–8.

Hunt, K. (2006) '"Do you know Harry Potter? Well, he is an orphan": Every bereaved child matters', *Pastoral Care in Education*, 24(2): 39–44.

Ito, M., Horst, H., Bittanti, M., Boyd, D., Herr-Stephenson, B., Lange, P., Pascoe, C. and Robinson, L. (2008) *Living and Learning with New Media: Summary of Findings from the Digital Youth Project; The John D. and Catherine T. MacArthur Foundation Reports on Digital Media and Learning*, Chicago: MacArthur Foundation.

Jama, D. and Dugdale, G. (2010) *Literacy: State of the Nation A Picture of Literacy in the UK Today*, London: National Literacy Trust.

Jenkins, R. (2002) *Pierre Bourdieu* (2nd edn), London: Routledge.

Jimoyiannis, A. and Komis, V. (2007) 'Examining teachers' beliefs about ICT in education: Implications of a teacher preparation programme', *Teacher Development*, 11(2): 149–73.

Johnson, S. (1755) Preface to the English Dictionary. Available online at http://andromeda.rutgers.edu/~jlynch/Texts/preface.html (accessed 22 December 2009).

Jones, B. (1986) 'The search for a fairer way of comparing schools' examination results', *Research Papers in Education*, 1(2): 91–122.

Jones, K. (2003) *Education in Britain: 1944 to the Present*, Oxford: Polity Press.

Joyce, B. and Showers, B. (1995) *Student Achievement Through Staff Development: Fundamentals of School Renewal*, New York: Longman.

Karmiloff, K. and Karmiloff-Smith, A. (2001) *Pathways to Language: From Fetus to Adolescent*, Cambridge, MA: Harvard University Press.

Kearns, T. (2009) 'Problematizing Shakespeare in Curriculum English', *NALDIC Quarterly*, 6(3): 29–31.

Keith, G. (1990) 'Language study at KS3', in R. Carter (ed.), *Knowledge About Language*, London: Hodder & Stoughton, pp. 69–103.

Kelly, R. (2005) Speech to Specialist Schools Trust, BBC News. Available online at http://news.bbc.co.uk/1/hi/education/4649535.stm (accessed 1 August 2005).

Kendeou, P., Bohn-Gettler, C., White, M. J. and van den Broek, P. (2008) 'Children's inference generation across different media', *Journal of Research in Reading*, 31(3): 259–73.

Kintsch, W. (1988) 'The role of knowledge in discourse comprehension: A construction-integration model', *Psychological Review*, 95(2): 163–82.

Kneller, G. (1965) *The Art and Science of Creativity*, New York: Holt, Rinehart & Winston.

Koch, K. (1970) *Wishes, Lies and Dreams*, New York: Harper & Row.

— (1973) *Rose, Where Did You Get that Red?*, New York: Vintage.

Koz7iminsky, E. and Koziminsky, L. (2001) 'How do general knowledge and reading strategies ability relate to reading comprehension of high school students at different educational levels?', *Journal of Research in Reading*, 24(2): 187–204.

Kozulin, A., Gindis, B., Ageyev, V. and Miller, S. (eds) (2003) *Vygotsky's Educational Theory in Cultural Context*, Cambridge: Cambridge University Press.

Kress, G (1997) *Before Writing: Rethinking the Paths to Literacy*, London: Routledge.

— (1988) *Communication and Culture*, Kensington: University of New South Wales.

— (2010) *Multimodality: A Social Semiotic Theory of Contemporary Communication*, Abingdon: Routledge.

Kress, G., Jewitt, C., Bourne, J., Franks, A., Hardcastle, J., Jones, K. and Reid, E. (2004) *English in Urban Classroom*, London: RoutledgeFalmer.

Kress, G. and van Leeuwen, T. (1996). *Reading Images: The Grammar of Visual Design*. London: Routledge.

Kyriacou, C. (1997) *Effective Teaching in Schools: Theory and Practice*, London: Nelson Thomas.

Lacey, C. (1970) *Hightown Grammar*, Manchester: Manchester University Press.

Lambirth, A. (2007) 'Social class and the struggle to learn to read: Using Bernstein to understand the politics of the teaching of reading', in Goouch, K. and Lambirth, A. (eds), *Understanding Phonics and the Teaching of Reading*, Maidenhead: Open University Press.

Laming Report (2003) *Victoria Climbié Inquiry Chaired by Lord Laming Presented to Parliament by the Secretary of State for Health and the Secretary of State for the Home Department by Command of Her Majesty*, January 2003, London: HMSO.

Lankshear, C. (1987) *Literacy, Schooling and Revolution*, London: Falmer Press.

Lankshear, C., Gee, P. J., Knobel, M. and Searle, C. (1997) *Changing Literacies*, Buckingham: Open University Press.

Lankshear, C. with Lawler, M. (1987) *Literacy, Schooling and Revolution*, London: Falmer Press.

Lave, J. and Wenger, E. (1991) *Situated Learning: Legitimate Peripheral Participation*, Cambridge: Cambridge University Press.

Lawlor, S. (1990) *Teachers Mistaught: Training in Theories or Education in Subjects?*, London: Centre for Policy Studies.

Leavis, F. R. (1948) *The Great Tradition*, London: Peregrine Press.

Leavis, F. and Thompson, D. (1933) *Culture and Environment*, London: Chatto & Windus.

Levine, J. (1996) *Developing Pedagogies in the Multilingual Classroom*, Stoke on Trent: Trentham.

Locke, J. (1690) *An Essay Concerning Human Understanding*, Hayes Barton Press, VitalBook.

Locke, J. (1690) *An Essay Concerning Human Understanding in Four Books*, London: The Baffet.

Lord, A. (1960) *The Singer of Tales*, Cambridge, MA: Harvard University Press.

Loveless, A. (2002) 'Report 4: Literature review in creativity, new technologies and learning', *Futurelab*. Available online at http://www.futurelab.org.uk/research/lit_reviews.htm (accessed 14 April 2010).

Lupton, R. (2004) *Do Poor Neighbourhoods Mean Poor Schools?*, London: Centre for Analysis of Social Exclusion/ESRC.

MacArthur Report (2008) *Living and Learning with New Media: Summary of Findings from the Digital Youth Project. The John D. and Catherine T. MacArthur Foundation Reports on Digital Media and Learning*, November 2008, Cambridge: MIT Press.

Macarthur, T. (1992) *The Oxford Companion to the English Language*, Oxford: Oxford University Press.

MacDonald, H. (1995) 'Why Johnny can't write – teaching grammar and logic to college students', *Public Interest*. Available online at http://course1.winona.edu/pjohnson/e511/macdonald.htm (accessed 10 January 2010).

McKernan, James (1996) *Curriculum Action Research: A Handbook of Methods and Resources for the Reflective Practitioner* (2nd edn), London: Routledge.

McLaren, P. and Lankshear, C. (eds) (1994) *Politics of Liberation: Paths from Freire*, London: Routledge.

MacSwan, J. and McLaren, P. (1997) 'Basil Bernstein's sociology of language', *Bilingual Research Journal*, 21(4): 334–40.

Marenbon, J. (1987) *English Our English*, London: Centre for Policy Studies.

Marsh, J. (2005) *Popular Culture, New Media and Digital Literacy in Early Childhood*, Abingdon: RoutledgeFalmer.

Marsh, J. and Millard, E. (2000) *Literacy and Popular Culture*, London: Paul Chapman.

Marshall, B. (2000) *English Teachers – the Unofficial Guide: Researching the Philosophies of English Teachers*, London, Routledge.

— (2001) 'Creating danger: The place of arts in education policy', in Craft, A., Jeffrey, B. and Leibling, M. (eds), *Creativity in Education*, London: Continuum, pp. 116–25.

Massey, A. J., Elliott, G. L. and Johnson, N. K. (2005) 'Variations in aspects of writing in 16+ English examinations between 1980 and 2004: Vocabulary, spelling, punctuation, sentence structure, non-standard English', *Research Matters: Special Issue 1*, Cambridge: University of Cambridge Local Examinations Syndicate.

Mathieson, M. (1975) *The Preachers of Culture*, London: Allen & Unwin.

McDougall, J (2006) *The Media Teacher's Book*, London: Hodder Education.

Meek, M. (1988) *How Texts Teach what Readers Learn*, Stroud: Thimble Press.

Mercer, N. (1995) *The Guided Construction of Knowledge*, Clevedon: Multilingual Matters.

Mercer, N, and Hodgkinson, S. (2008) (eds) *Exploring Talk in Schools*, London: Sage.

Mercer, N. and Littleton, K. (2007) *Dialogue and the Development of Children's Thinking: A Sociocultural Approach*, London: Routledge.

Mercer, N., Wegerief, R. and Dawes, L. (1999) 'Children's talk and the development of reasoning in the classroom', *British Educational Research Journal*, 25(1): 95–111.

Mertzman, T. (2008) 'Individualising scaffolding: Teachers' literacy interruptions of ethnic minority students and students from low socioeconomic backgrounds', *Journal of Research in Reading*, 31(2): 183–202.

Millard, E. (1997) *Differently Literate: Boys, Girls and the Schooling of Literacy*, London: Routledge.

Miller, J. (1983) *Many Voices: Bilingualism, Culture, and Education*, London: Routledge & Kegan Paul.

Misson, R. and Morgan, W. (2006) *Critical Literacy and the Aesthetic: Transforming the English Classroom*, Urbana, IL: NCTE.

Mitchell, C. and Weiler, K. (1991) *Rewriting Literacy: Culture and the Discourse of the Other*, New York: Bergin & Garvey.

Moll, L. C. (2000) 'Inspired by Vygotsky: Ethnographic experiments in education', in Lee, C. D. and Smagorinsky, P. (eds), *Vygotskian Perspectives on Literacy Research*, Cambridge: Cambridge University Press, pp. 256–68.

Moran III, J. D. (1988) 'Creativity in young children', *Eric Digest*, identifier 53 ED306008. Available online at http://www.nagc.org/index.aspx?id=326 (accessed 24 March 2010).

Moss, G. (2007) *Literacy and Gender: Researching Texts, Contexts and Readers*, London: Routledge.

Moss, G., Jewitt, C., Levacic, R., Armstrong, V., Cardini, A. and Castle, F. (2007) *The Interactive Whiteboards, Pedagogy and Pupil Performance Evaluation: An Evaluation of the Schools Whiteboard Expansion (SWE) Project: London Challenge*, Nottingham: DfES.

Moyles, J., Hargreaves, L., Merry, R., Paterson, F. and Esarte-Sarries, V. (2003) *Interactive Teaching in the Primary School*, Maidenhead: Open University Press.

Mroz, M., Smith, F and Hardman, F. (2000) 'The discourse of the Literacy Hour', *Cambridge Journal of Education*, 30(3): 379–90.

Mullis, I. V. S., Martin, M. O., Kennedy, A. M. and Foy, P. (eds) (2006), *PIRLS 2006 International Report: IEA's Progress in International Reading Literacy Study in Primary Schools in 40 Countries*. Available online at http://timss.bc.edu/pirls2006/intl_rpt.html (accessed 28 August 2010).

Myhill, D. A. (2008) 'Towards a linguistic model of sentence development in writing', *Language and Education*, 22(5): 271–88.

—— (2009) 'Becoming a designer: Trajectories of linguistic development', in Beard, R., Myhill, D., Riley, J. and Nystrand, M. (eds), *The Sage Handbook of Writing Development*, London: Sage, pp. 402–14.

Nassaji, H. and Wells, G. (2000) 'What's the use of "Triadic Dialogue"? An investigation of teacher-student interaction', *Applied Linguistics*, 21(3): 376–406.

NATE (National Association for the Teaching of English) (2007) *ICT in English: A Position Paper; NATE English and ICT Committee*. Available online at http://www.nate.org.uk/cmsfiles/ict/Seconday_English_entitlement_document_2009.pdf (accessed 28 August 2010).

—— (2009) *Entitlement to ICT in Secondary English*. Available online at http://www.nate.org.uk/index.php?page=44 (accessed 28 August 2010).

NACCCE (National Advisory Committee on Creative and Cultural Education) (1999) *All Our Futures: Creativity, Culture and Education. Report to the Secretary of State for Education and Employment and the Secretary of State for Culture, Media and Sport.* Available online at http://www.cypni.org.uk/downloads/alloutfutures.pdf (accessed 25 March 2010).

NAWE (National Association of Writers in Education Higher Education Committee) (2008) *Creative Writing Subject Benchmark Statement*, New York: NAWE.

NICHD (National Institute of Child Health and Human Development) (2000) *Report of the National Reading Panel. Teaching children to read: An evidence-based assessment of the scientific research literature on reading and its implications for reading instruction*, Washington, DC: US Government Printing Office.

New Media Consortium and Educause, The (2008) *The Horizon Report.* Available online at http://www.nmc.org/publications/2008-horizon-report (accessed 18 September 2008).

— (2009) *The Horizon Report.* Available online at http://www.nmc.org/publications/2009-horizon-report (accessed 20 September 2009).

— (2010) *The Horizon Report.* Available online at http://www.nmc.org/publications/2010-horizon-report (accessed 11 May 2010).

New Zealand Ministry of Education (1996) *Te Whāriki, Early Childhood Curriculum*, Wellington: Learning Media.

Nicholls, J. (1990) 'Verse and verbiage', *The Times Educational Supplement*, 11 May: B27.

Norwood, C. (1943) *The Norwood Report: Curriculum and Examinations in Secondary Schools*, London: HMSO.

Nystrand, M., Wu, L. L., Gamoran, A., Zeiser, S. and Long, D. A. (2003) 'Questions in time: Investigating the structure and dynamics of unfolding classroom discourse', *Discourse Processes*, 35(2): 135–98.

O'Hear, A. (1988) *Who Teaches the Teachers?*, London: Social Affairs Unit.

Ofcom (Office of Communications) (2008) *Media Literacy Audit: Report on UK Children's Media Literacy*, London: Ofcom.

Ofsted (Office for Standards in Education) (2005) *English 2000–2005: A Review of Inspection Evidence*, London: Ofsted.

— (2009) *English at the Crossroads*, London: Ofsted.

— (2010) *Learning: Creative Approaches that Raise Standards.* HMI: 080266, Ofsted. Available online at http://www.ofsted.gov.uk/Ofsted-home/Publications-and-research/Browse-all-by/Documents-by-type/Thematic-reports/Learning-creative-approaches-that-raise-standards (accessed 12 April 2010).

Ong, W. J. (1982) *Orality and Literacy: The Technologising of the Word*, London: Routledge.

OECD (Organisation for Economic Co-operation and Development) (1997) *Literacy Skills for the Knowledge Society: Further Results from the International Adult Literacy Survey*, Paris: OECD.

— (2006) *Starting Strong 11, Early Childhood Education and Care*, Paris: OECD.

Pachler, N., Bachmair, B. and Cook, J. (2010a) *Mobile Learning: Structures, Agency, Practices*, New York: Springer.

Pachler, N., Daly, C. and Turvey, A. (2010b) 'Teacher professional development practices: The case of the Haringey Transformation Teachers Programme', in Lindberg, O. and Olofsson, A. (eds), *Online Learning Communities and Teacher Professional Development*, Hershey, PA: IGI Global, pp. 77–95.

Pahl, K. (1999) *Transformations, Meaning Making in Nursery Education*, Stoke on Trent: Trentham.

Palmer, D. (1965) *The Rise of English Studies*, Oxford: Oxford University Press.

Park, C. C. (2001) *Exiting Nirvana: A Daughter's Life with Autism*, London: Aurum.

Park, E. and King, K. (2003) 'Cultural diversity and language socialization in the early years', *Eric Digest*. Available online at http://www.cal.org/resources/Digest/0313park.html (accessed 28 January 2010).

Parry, M. (1930) *The Making of Homeric Verse*, Cambridge, MA: Harvard University Press.

Patel, P. (2007) 'Every Child Matters: The challenge of gender, religion and multiculturalism', *Forum*, 49(3): 261–76.

Patten, J. (1992) Speech to Conservative Party Annual Conference, 7 October.

— (1993) *Literacy in the Opportunity Society*, London: Conservative Party Information Office.

Perera, K. (1984) *Children's Writing and Reading: Analysing Classroom Language*, Oxford: Blackwell.

Peters, M. and Lankshear, C. (1994) 'Education and hermeneutics: A Freirean perspective', in McLaren, P. and Lankshear, C. (eds), *Politics of Liberation: Paths from Freire*, London: Routledge.

Philpot, D. (2005) 'Children's metafiction, readers and reading: Building thematic models of narrative comprehension', *Children's Literature in Education*, 36(2): 141–59.

Pinker, S. (1994) *The Language Instinct: How the Mind Creates Language*, New York: Morrow.

Pound, T. (1996) 'Standard English, standard culture?', *Oxford Review of Education*, 22(2): 237–42.

Powell, S. (2010) 'Not allowed to kiss the babies: Complexities and contradictions in baby room policies and practice', paper presented to OMEP conference, Chester.

Preston, C. (2004) *Learning to Use ICT in Classrooms: Teachers' and Trainees' Perspectives. An Evaluation of the English NOF ICT Teacher Training Programme 1999–2003*, London: MirandaNet and the Teacher Training Agency.

Price, C. J. (2000) 'The anatomy of language: Contributions from functional neuroimaging', *Journal of Anatomy*, 197(3): 335–9.

Protherough, R. (1989) *Students of English*, London: Routledge.

Protherough, R. and Atkinson, J. (eds) (1991) *The Making of English Teachers*, Buckingham: Open University Press.

— (1994) 'Shaping the image of an English teacher', in Brindley, S. (ed.), *Teaching English*, Buckingham: Open University Press.

Protherough, R., Atkinson, J., Fawcett, J. (1989) *The Effective Teaching of English*, London: Longman.

Pullman, P. (2005) 'Common sense has much to learn from moonshine', *The Guardian* 22 January. Available online at http://www.guardian.co.uk/education/2005/jan/22/schools.wordsandlanguage (accessed 22 January 2010).

Purewal, S. and Simpson, J. (2010) *EAL Reading: Research and Policy*, NALDIC Occasional Paper 23 (Feb 2010), Reading: NALDIC (National Association for Language Development in the Curriculum).

QCA (1999) *Improving Writing*, London: QCA.

— (2005a) *English 2*, London: QCA.

— (2005b) *Playback*, London: QCA.

— (2005c) *Taking English Forward*, London: QCA.

— (2006a) *A Level Criteria: English Literature Subject Criteria*, London: QCA. Available online at http://www.ofqual.gov.uk/component/search/english%2Blit erature/%252F?ordering=&searchphrase=all (accessed 28 August 2010).

— (2006b) *A Level English Language Subject Criteria*, London: QCA. [This document is no longer available on the web but can be retrieved from http://www.phon.ucl. ac.uk/home/dick/ec/gce.htm (accessed 13 June 2010).]

— (2006c) *A Level Criteria: English Language and English Literature Subject Criteria*, London: QCA. Available online at http://www.ofqual.gov.uk/component/search/ english%2Bliterature/%252F?ordering=&searchphrase=all (accessed 28 August 2010).

— (2007a) *National Curriculum English Key Stage 3 Programme of Study*, London: QCA. Available online at http://curriculum.qcda.gov.uk/key-stages-3-and-4/sub-jects/key-stage-3/english/index.aspx (accessed 13 June 2010).

— (2007b) *National Curriculum English Key Stage 4 Programme of Study*, London: QCA. Available online at http://curriculum.qcda.gov.uk/key-stages-3-and-4/sub-jects/key-stage-4/english/index.aspx (accessed 13 June 2010.)

— (2007c) *The National Curriculum*. Available online at http://curriculum.qcda.gov. uk/key-stages-3-and-4/About-the-secondary-curriculum/equalities-diversity-and-inclusion/inclusion-guidance/index.aspx (accessed 9 March 2010).

QCDA (Qualifications and Curriculum Development Agency) (2010a) 'Creativity and critical thinking'. Available online at http://curriculum.qcda.gov.uk/key-stages-3-and-4/cross-curriculum-dimensions/creativitycriticalthinking/index.aspx (accessed 8 March 2010).

— (2010b) 'New primary curriculum: Learning and thinking skills'. Available online at http://curriculum.qcda.gov.uk/new-primary-curriculum/essentials-for-learning-and-life/learning-and-thinking-skills/index.aspx (accessed 30 March 2010).

Raban-Bisby, B. (Ed) with Brooks, G and Woolfendale, S. (1995) *Developing Language and Literacy*. Staffordshire: Trentham Books/UKRA.

Rae, A. and O'Brien, J. (2007) 'Information and communications technologies and teacher professional learning policy in Scotland: Some primary school perspectives', *Journal of In-service Education*, 33(4): 425–41.

Rampton, B. (2006) *Language in Late Modernity: Interaction in an Urban School*, Cambridge: Cambridge University Press.

Ray, R. (1999) 'The diversity of poetry: How trainee teachers' perceptions affect their attitudes to poetry teaching', *Curriculum Journal*, 10(3): 403–18.

Reiss, M. (2008) 'Science lessons should tackle creationism and intelligent design'. Available online at http://www.guardian.co.uk/science/blog/2008/sep/11/ michael.reiss.creationism (accessed 10 February 2010).

Robinson, K. (2006) 'Ken Robinson says schools kill creativity', TED talks [blog]. Available online at http://www.ted.com/talks/lang/eng/ken_robinson_says_ schools_kill_creativity.html (accessed 24 March 2010).

Rodgers, C. and Scott, K. (2008) 'The development of the personal self and profes-sional identity in learning to teach', in Cochran-Smith, M., Feiman-Nemser, S. and Mcintyre, D. (eds), *The Handbook of Research on Teacher Education*, New York: Routledge.

Rogoff, B. (1990) *Apprenticeship in Thinking: Cognitive Development in a Social Context*, New York: Oxford University Press.

Rose, J. (2006) *Independent Review of the Teaching of Early Reading*, London: DCSF.

Rosen, H. (1988) *Stories and Meanings*, NATE Papers in Education, National Association of Teachers in English.

Rosenblatt, L. (1978) *The Reader, the Text, the Poem*, Carbondale, IL: Southern Illinois University Press.

Runnymede Trust (2009) *Who Cares about the White Working Class?*, London: Runnymede Trust.

Salen, K. and Zimmerman, E. (2004) *Rules of Play: Game Design Fundamentals*, Cambridge: MIT Press.

Sampson, G. (1921) *English for the English*, Cambridge: Cambridge University Press.

— (1924) *The Problem of Grammar*, London: English Association.

Saskatchewan Education (1998) 'Writing', *English Language Arts 20: A Curriculum Guide for the Secondary Level*, Regina, SK: Saskatchewan Education. Available online at http://www.sasked.gov.sk.ca/docs/ela20/copyright.html (accessed 17 May 2010).

Scarratt, E. and McInnes, R. (2009) 'Media education and ICT', in Davison, J. and Dowson, J. (eds), *Learning to Teach English in the Secondary School* (3rd edn), Abingdon: Routledge.

Scholes, R. (1998) *The Rise and Fall of English*, New Haven and London: Yale University Press.

Schon, D. A. (1983) *The Reflective Practitioner: How Professionals Think in Action*, New York: Basic Books.

— (1987) *Educating the Reflective Practitioner*, San Francisco: Jossey-Bass.

Scott, K. (2010) 'Lost in translation', *The Guardian*, 19 January: 1–2.

Searle, C. (ed.) (1971) *Stepney Words*, London: Reality Press.

— (1995) *Heart of Sheffield*, Sheffield: Earl Marshall School.

Shannon, P. (2007) *Reading Against Democracy: The Broken Promises of Reading Instruction*, Portsmouth, NH: Heinemann.

Showers, B., and Joyce, B. (1996) 'The evolution of peer coaching', *Educational Leadership*, 54(3): 12–16.

Shulman, L. S. (1986) 'Those who understand knowledge growth in teaching', *Educational Researcher*, 15(2): 4–14.

— (1987) 'Knowledge and teaching: Foundations of the new reform', *Harvard Educational Review*, 57(1): 1–22.

— (2004) *The Wisdom of Practice: Essays on Teaching, Learning and Learning to Teach*, New York: Jossey-Bass.

Sinclair, J. and Coulthard, M. (1975) *Towards an Analysis of Discourse: The English Used by Teachers and Pupils*, Oxford: Oxford University Press.

Siraj-Blatchford, I. and Sylva, K. (2004) 'Researching pedagogy in English pre-schools', *British Educational Research Journal*, 30(5): 713–30.

Skidmore, D., Perez-Parent, M., and Arnfield, S. (2003) 'Teacher-pupil dialogue in the guided reading session', *Reading: Literacy and Language*, 37(2): 47–53.

Smith, F. (1994) *Writing and the Writer* (2nd edn), Hillsdale, NJ: Lawrence Erlbaum.

Smith, F., Hardman, F. and Higgins, S. (2006) 'The impact of interactive whiteboards on teacher-pupil interaction in the National Literacy and Numeracy Strategies', *British Educational Research Journal*, 32(3): 437–51.

— (2007) 'Gender inequality in the primary classroom: Will interactive whiteboards help?', *Gender and Education*, 19(4): 455–69.

Smith, F., Goelman, H. and Oberg, A. (eds) (1984) *Awakening to Literacy*, London: Heinemann.

Smith, L. (2008) 'An investigation into the effect of a NATE/Becta training programme on the use of interactive whiteboards in teaching and learning in Secondary English', *English in Education*, 42(3): 269–82.

— (2010) 'An investigation into the effective design of the ICT component of PGCE English courses', paper presented at the National Association for the Teaching of English conference, July.

Smith, L. and Henderson, M. (2008) 'Royal Society's Michael Reiss resigns over creationism row', *The Times*, 17 September. Available online at http://www.timesonline.co.uk/tol/news/science/article4768820.ece (accessed 10 February 2010).

Smithers, A. (2000) 'Woodhead sparks row over value of degrees', *The Independent*, 3 March.

Smyth, J. and Shacklock, G. (1998) *Re-making Teaching*. London: Routledge

Snapper, G., Dymoke, S. and Cliff Hodges, G. (2008) 'Transitions and transformations – exploring creativity in everyday and literary language', *English Drama Media*, (12), October: 8–9.

Soler, J. and Openshaw, R. (2007) '"To be or not to be": The politics of teaching phonics in England and New Zealand', *Journal of Early Childhood Literacy*, 7(3), December: 333–52.

Solity, J. (2006) 'An instructional perspective on the Rose Review', in Lewis, M. and Ellis, S. (eds), *Phonics, Practice, Research and Policy*, London: PCP/UKLA.

Squires, G. (1999) *Teaching as a Professional Discipline*, London: Falmer Press.

Stannard, J. and Huxford, L. (2007) *The Literacy Game: The Story of the National Literacy Strategy*, London: Routledge.

Stanovich, K. E. (1986) 'Matthew effects in reading: Some consequences of individual differences in the acquisition of literacy', *Reading Research Quarterly*, 21: 360–407.

— (2000) *Progress in Understanding Reading: Scientific Foundations and New Frontiers*, London: Guildford Press.

Stern, Julian (2007) 'Mattering: What it means to matter in school', *Education 3–13*, 35(3): 283–93.

Stibbs, A. (1981) 'Teaching poetry', *Children's Literature in Education*, 12(1): 39–50.

Strauss, S. L. and Altwerger, B. (2007) 'The logographic nature of English alphabetics and the fallacy of direct intensive phonics instruction', *Journal of Early Childhood Literacy*, 7(3) December: 299–321.

Street, B. (1984) *Literacy in Theory and Practice*, Cambridge: Cambridge University Press.

— (1995) *Social Literacies: Critical Approaches to Literacy in Development, Ethnography and Education*, London: Longman.

— (1999) 'The meanings of literacy', in Wagner, D., Venezsky, R. and Street, B. (eds), *Literacy: An International Handbook*, Boulder: Westview Press.

— (ed.) (2001) *Literacy and Development: Ethnographic Perspectives*, London and New York: Routledge.

Stubbs, M. (1989) 'The State of English in the English State: Reflections on the Cox Report', *Language and Education*, 3(4): 235–50.

Swift, Jonathan, (1712) 'Dr Swift's letter to the Lord High Treasurer: A proposal for correcting, improving and ascertaining the English tongue: in a letter to the Most Honourable Robert Earl of Oxford and Mortimer, Lord High Treasurer of Great Britain', London: printed for Benj. Tooke, p. 48.

TDA (Training and Development Agency for Schools) (2007) *Professional Standards for Teachers: Why Sit Still in Your Career?*, London: TDA.

Tharp, R. G. and Dalton, S. S. (2007) 'Orthodoxy, cultural compatibility, and universals in education', *Comparative Education*, 43(1): 53–70.

Thomson, P., Hall, C. and Russell, l. (2006) 'An arts project failed, censored or . . .? A critical incident approach to artist-school partnerships', *Changing English*, 13(1): 29–44.

Times Educational Supplement, The (1915) 'Report of Lancashire Headteachers' Report', London: Times Newspapers.

Tomasello, M. (1999) *The Cultural Origins of Human Cognition*, Cambridge and London: Harvard University Press.

Trudell, B. (2009) 'Local language literacy and sustainable development in Africa', *International Journal of Educational Development*, 29(1): 73–9.

Trudell, B. and L. Schroeder (2007) 'Reading methodologies for African languages: Avoid linguistic and pedagogical imperialism', *Language, Culture and Curriculum*, 20(3): 165–80.

Trudgill, P. (1974) *Sociolinguistics: An Introduction to Language and Society*, London: Penguin Books.

— (1995) *Sociolinguistics: An Introduction to Language and Society*, London: Penguin.

— (2001) *Sociolinguistic Variation and Change*, Edinburgh: Edinburgh University Press.

Turner-Bisset, R. (2001) *Expert Teaching: Knowledge and Pedagogy to Lead the Profession*, London: David Fulton.

Turvey, A. (2005) 'Who'd be an English Teacher?', *Changing English*, 12(1), April: 3–18.

Twist, L., Sainsbury, M., Woodthorpe, A. and Whetton, C. (2003) *Reading All Over the World: Progress in International Reading Literacy Study. National Report for England*, London: DfES and NFER.

UNESCO (United Nations Educational, Scientific and Cultural Oganization) (2003) *Education for All: United Kingdom Perspectives*, Paris: UNESCO.

— (undated/2007/tbc) *Literacy Initiative for Empowerment LIFE 2006–2015 Vision and Strategy Paper* (3rd edn), UNESCO Institute for Lifelong Learning, p. 15.

— (2010) *EFA Global Monitoring Report*, Paris: UNESCO.

Van der Veer, R., and Valsiner, J. (1991) *Understanding Vygotsky: A Quest for Synthesis*, Oxford: Blackwell.

Vygotsky, L. (1962) *Thought and Language*, 1986 edition, Cambridge, MA: MIT.

— (1987) *Problems of General Psychology, Including the Volume Thinking and Speech*, New York and London: Plenum.

— (1992) *Thought and Language*, Cambridge, MA: MIT Press.

— (1998). *Collected works*, New York: Plenum.

Waugh, E. (1928) *Decline and Fall*, London: Chapman & Hall.

Webster, Noah (1806) *A Compendious Dictionary of the English Language*, Boston and New Haven: Hartford & Increase-Cooke.

Wee, L. (2005) 'Intra-language discrimination and linguistic human rights: The case of Singlish', *Applied Linguistics*, 26(1): 48–69.

Wells, G. (1986) *The Meaning Makers: Children Learning Language and using Language to Learn*, London: Hodder & Stoughton.

— (1999) *Dialogic Inquiry: Towards a Sociocultural Practice and Theory of Education*, Cambridge: Cambridge University Press.

Westbrook, J. (2007) 'Wider reading at Key Stage 3 – happy accidents, bootlegging and serial readers', *Literacy*, 41(3): 147–54.

— (2008) 'Finding the plot: A study of wider reading', *Journal of Reading, Writing and Literacy*, 3(3): 1–20.

— (2009) 'Narrative reading processes and pedagogies in the secondary school', unpublished EdD thesis, Brighton: University of Sussex.

Westbrook, J., Robertson, C. and Todd, J. (1998) *Factors Affecting the Attainment of Pupils at KS3 in English*, London: QCA.

Whitehead, M (1999) 'A Literacy Hour in the nursery? The big question mark', *Early Years*, 19(2), Spring: 38–62.

— (2009) *Supporting Language and Literacy Development in the Early Years* (2nd edn), Maidenhead: Open University Press.

Williams, R. (1958) 'Culture is ordinary', in MacKenzie, N. (ed.), *Conviction*,

— (1961) *The Long Revolution*, London: Chatto & Windus.

— (1977) *Marxism and Literature*, Oxford: Oxford University Press.

Willis, P. (1977) *Learning to Labour: How Working Class Kids Get Working Class Jobs*, Sheffield: Saxon Press.

— (1981) 'Cultural production is different from cultural reproduction . . .', *Interchange*, 12(2–3): 48–67.

Wilson, T. (1553) *The Arte of Rhetorique* (1969 edn), Amsterdam: Da Capo Press.

Winnicott, D. (1971) *Playing and Reality*, London: Tavistock.

Wittner, J. and Renkl, A. (2008) 'Why instructional explanations often do not work: A framework for understanding the effectiveness of instructional explanations', *Educational Psychologist*, 43(1): 49–64.

WJEC (2009) *GCE Examinations from 2009: English Language*. Available online at http://www.wjec.co.uk/index.php?subject=51&level=21 (accessed 12 April 2010).

Wolfe, M. and Mienko, J. (2007) 'Learning and memory of factual content from narrative and expository text', *British Journal of Educational Psychology*, 77: 541–64.

Wolfram, W. (1998) 'Language ideology and dialect: Understanding the Ebonics controversy', *Journal of English Linguistics*, 26: 108–21.

Woodhead, C. (2000) 'Teenage culture harming pupils, says Woodhead', *The Guardian*, 12 February.

— (2008) 'A GCSE in Jade', *Daily Mail*, 19 April.

Wray, D. (2006) 'Poor Mr Rose!', in Lewis, M. and Ellis, S. (eds), *Phonics, Practice, Research and Policy*, London: Paul Chapman.

Wright, L. (2000) *The Development of Standard English 1300–1800: Theories, Descriptions, Conflicts*, Cambridge: Cambridge University Press.

Yandell, J. (2008) 'Embodied readings: Exploring the multimodal social semiotic resources of the English classroom', *English Teaching: Practice and Critique*, 7(1): 36–56.

Yandell, J. and Franks, A. (2009) 'Approaching Shakespeare', in Davison, J. and Dowson, J. (eds), *Learning to Teach English in the Secondary School*, London and New York: Routledge.

Yates, C. (1999) *Jumpstart: Poetry in the Secondary School*, London: Poetry Society.

Index

A level 14, 20–1, 26, 34, 148, 151–5
accountability 31, 78, 86, 96, 184–5
achievement 82–3, 149, 159; academic
    79, 183; in 11-plus examination 172;
    creative 153; literacy 86, 89, 94, 97,
    99 *see also* underachievement
acquisition: of English 163, 165; of
    information 160; of literacy 164;
    of social 'goods' 182; of university
    degree 170; of vocabulary 107–8; of
    world view 180
African American Vernacular English
    (AAVE) *see* Ebonics
Aiming High 95
Alexander, R. 4, 7, 36, 43, 45–6, 78,
    80
All Our Futures 143–4
Altwerger, B. 80
Anderson, H. 72
Appleyard, J. A. 22, 26
apprenticeship 28–9, 53, 181
assessment: agencies 13; choices 154;
    comments in 95; control of 15; of
    creativity 14, 146; of curriculum 16;
    formative 103; framework 142, 153,
    155; internal 151; methodology 177;
    model of 33; objectives 93, 151,
    154; processes 13; schemes 14, 60–1;
    summative 153; of writing 56, 147,
    151–2
Assessment and Qualifications Alliance
    150, 153
Assessment Focuses 93, 96–7
Atkinson, J. 34, 152
attainment: academic 169; educational
    16; of fluency 153; of literacy 9, 87,
    94–5, 97; and reading 108; of skill 79;
    targets 115; and writing 76

audiences: and creativity 147, 151, 153;
    and media 121–6, 128, 130
Australia 17, 21, 33–4
authority: adult 158; crisis of 158;
    polarised 177–8; of policy makers
    1–4, 8; shared 17; of teachers 3, 9,
    46, 134, 182–3; and technology 12,
    140
autonomy 31, 84, 91, 138, 145, 156

Bakhtin, M. 4, 37, 47, 82
Ball, S. 24, 33, 90, 172–3, 177–80
Bennett, A. 153, 173
Bernstein, B. 172–3
best practice 28, 30, 60 *see also* good
    practice
bilingualism 118, 163–5
Black Pupils' Achievement Programme
    95
Blake, J. 21
Blake, R. 73
Bleiman, B. 151
Board of Education 173–4
Boden, M. 143–4
Boocock, S. 173
boundaries 11, 17, 52, 56, 90, 117, 139
Bourdieu, P. 170–1
Bowles, S. 171
boys 80, 95, 110, 116, 172, 175
Brown, L. 142
Brown, R. 171
Bruner, J. 144
Buckingham, D. 117, 123
Bullock Report 133, 162–3, 167, 176

Cameron, D. 65, 74
Cameron, David (Prime Minister) 169
Canada 21, 148

Carter, Ronald 68, 76, 147
cinema *see* film
class *see* social class
classroom management 25, 157
Clifton, J. 63
Cogill, J. 135
colloquial language 71
communication 37, 48, 50–9, 61, 63, 67, 104, 108, 133, 139, 184; skills 133; technology 131–2 *see also* ICT
communities of practice 3–4, 17, 29–30, 32
composition 5–6, 49–51, 53–61, 75, 127, 148
computer games 22, 99, 107, 118–19, 121, 123–8, 132, 176; design of 123–5, 127
continuing professional development (CPD) *see* professional development
correctness in language 25, 73–4, 171, 177, 179
Cox, B. 33, 72, 99
Cox Report 95, 118, 135, 177, 180
Craft, A. 143–5
creative: act 53, 143, 145–6, 148; approach 61, 96–7, 145–6, 149; production 117, 130 *see also* production; response 15, 153, 155; writing 21, 93, 146, 148–55 *see also* writing development
Creative Partnerships 149
creativity: and curriculum 96, 117, 129; definitions of 142; in education 13–14, 33, 126; in English 13–14, 127, 136, 142–55, 180; of students 127; of teachers 91
Cremin, T. 103, 149
cultural: capital 170–1, 183; reproduction 15–16, 170–1
culture 11, 27, 32, 51, 73, 81, 84, 86, 95, 99, 104, 108–9, 117–20, 127, 131–3, 143–5, 160, 162–5, 167, 176, 180, 183; of schools 85, 88, 96, 171, 173, 186; *see also* popular culture
curriculum: and assessment 15, 97, 142; control of 20, 83–4, 92, 121; and creativity 13–14, 129, 141, 145–7; design 17, 61, 63, 72, 75–6, 79, 86, 88, 92, 96–7, 102, 109, 114, 118, 129, 134, 147–8, 154, 164, 166, 170, 181; and development of children 7–8, 45–6, 161, 167,

171, 186; knowledge 25; and media 11–12, 117; primary 102, 147, 155, 160–1, 164, 166–71, 177, 181, 186; secondary 92; teaching of 15; university 21 *see also* National Curriculum
Cutler, C. 73

Dalton, S. S. 45
Denmark 19, 80
descriptive: approach 6, 23, 120, 139, 152, 163; grammar 68, 73–6
dialect 6, 15, 63, 65, 68, 70, 72–3, 76
digital media 23, 54–5, 61–2, 117, 127, 131–3
Dillon, J. 43, 45
diplomas, creative and media 154
discourse: academic 182; alternative 186; and approaches to teaching and learning 6; awareness of 182–3, 186; classroom 36, 42–3, 46, 114, 181–2, 184; communities 181, 184–5; competing 11; contribution to 1; and creativity 13; and culture 11, 181, 183; and curriculum 15–16, 173; definition of 1; dialogic 4, 17, 37, 41, 181; dichotomous 7, 78; dominant 9, 185–6; and early learning 8; educational 37, 159, 182; and grammar 74–6; hegemonic 72; knowledge of 186; and language 6, 68, 71, 185; and literacy 7–9, 83–4, 99, 173, 177, 179; and literary theory 9; and media 11; meta- 185; patterns 41, 45; and pedagogy of talk 4; and policy 2, 8, 17, 85, 98, 163; political 68, 73; primary 8, 16, 180–5, 187; public 68; and pupils 2, 41, 170; and reading 10; recitational 4; religious 65; and schooling and society 12, 15, 73, 173, 180; secondary 8, 16, 181, 183–7; and social construction of knowledge 2; strategies 36, 43, 45; style 38; and subject teaching 2–3, 8, 14–17, 42, 181; and teachers 2–4, 8, 12, 14, 17, 42, 184; and technology 12; and texts 11; theory 15–16; and writing 5, 50
Dixon, J. 22, 180
Douglas, J. 172
drama 21, 118–20, 124, 127, 152, 165

Eagleton, T. 22
Ebonics 72–3
Economic and Social Research Council
    (ESRC) 131, 155
Eisner, E. W. 27, 186
emotion 5, 27, 46, 48, 54, 59–60, 63,
    79, 124, 154, 175
English Association 34
English department, role of 25, 92, 109,
    131, 134, 137, 139, 155
epistemology 45, 90, 163
Eraut, M. 31
evaluation 4, 36, 38, 41–3, 46, 60–1,
    73, 82, 114, 184 see also self-
    evaluation
Every Child Matters 15, 145, 158–60, 163
examinations 14, 71, 97, 146, 150–5,
    159, 169, 172, 177, 180, 182–3 see
    also GCSE
expertise 12, 18, 27, 29, 78, 106,
    137–40, 151, 153, 163–4

Farrel, T. C. 73
feedback 5, 36, 38, 42–5
film 20, 22, 92, 99, 107, 113, 115,
    118–21, 123–8, 132–4, 165, 176
Finland 80, 87, 108
flexibility 44, 61, 92, 101, 109, 137,
    139–40, 142–3, 145
Floud, H. 172
framework: conceptual 122–4;
    pedagogical 133, 138; of players 138
Framework for English, The 34
'framing' 5, 49, 51–2, 54–8, 61
Freire, Paolo 81–2, 154, 181
Furedi, Frank 158–60

GCSE 71, 92, 96, 148, 150–5, 157,
    164, 169 see also examinations
Gee, J. P. 173, 180–1, 183–7
genre 5, 38, 48, 51–2, 59, 76, 93, 103,
    113, 119, 128, 152
Gintis, H. 171
girls 100–1, 116, 127–9, 172, 175,
    182–3
good practice 1, 14, 16, 60, 92, 95 see
    also best practice
Goodson, I. 33
Gossman, L. 173
grammar 6–7, 18, 24–5, 63, 65–9,
    73–7, 93, 105, 122, 124–5, 130, 171,
    179; schools 172

Graves, Donald 148
Greenbaum, S. 67–8
group-based approaches: and guided
    reading 93, 98, 107, 109, 111–14;
    and literacy 40, 97, 102; in
    professional development 45–6; to
    talk 36–7; and teaching assistants 98;
    as teaching strategy 40, 44, 96
guided construction of knowledge 45,
    183
guided reading 93, 98, 107, 111–12 see
    also reading

Hansson, H. 135
Hargreaves, L. 172
headteachers 8–9, 81, 93–4, 102, 135,
    138
Hodgkinson, S. 46
Holmes, B. 137
Holmes, J. 70–1
Horizon Reports 131
Hudson, R. 70–1
Hughes, J. 133, 136

ICT (Information and Communications
    Technology) 132–5, 137–8, 140
identity 2–4, 6, 11, 18–22, 24–5,
    27–30, 32–5, 55, 64–5, 72, 99, 118,
    120, 133, 159, 181; conflict 24, 30;
    national 63, 65, 72, 179; professional
    2–3, 18, 23, 31, 34–5, 84, 138
informal: language 71–2, 76; learning
    7–8, 13, 26, 50, 83–4, 87, 99, 107,
    113, 131, 137, 140
initial teacher education 1, 133, 135,
    157
initiation-response-feedback (IRF) 38,
    45
inspection 30, 79, 86, 144, 158
interpretation 14–15, 27, 37, 54–5, 81,
    90, 99–100, 106, 125, 165–6

Japan 108
Johnson, Boris 169
Jones, B. 182–3

King, K. 73
Kingman Report 24, 71
knowledge 2, 14–15, 17, 24–5, 28–31,
    33, 37, 42, 45–6, 54, 64, 72–3,
    75, 77, 80–3, 85–8, 90, 99, 104–8,
    114–15, 129, 133, 135–6, 138–9,

143, 145, 147, 152–3, 157, 160–5, 170–2, 177, 180, 186; construction of 2, 17, 37, 45–6, 170, 179–80, 183; of subject 15, 20–1, 24–5, 89–90, 94, 102, 133, 157–8, 160, 162
Koch, K. 148
Kress, G. 52, 82, 145, 182

Lacey, C. 172
Laming Report 158
language: oral 92, 105; register 67, 153, 172, 183; spoken 108, 147, 175; teaching 6, 24, 41, 63–77; use of 37, 50, 64–5, 68–9, 76–7, 99, 153, 172, 180–1, 183, 185–6; written 50, 54, 108
Lankshear, C. 171–3, 177, 179–83, 186
Lave, J. 29–30, 33
Leavis, F. R. 22, 99, 117–19
LeCompte, M. D. 173
libraries 92, 98, 109–13
listening 14, 21, 57–8, 91, 93, 100, 105, 113, 132, 147, 150
literacy: critical 9, 11, 15–17, 33, 99, 124, 126, 177–8, 180; early 7–8, 78, 80–1, 85, 87–8
literary canon 19–20, 72, 99, 118–19, 165, 179
literature 21–4, 33, 88, 115, 119–24, 132, 137, 146, 151, 153, 156, 159, 166, 174–5, 180
Littleton, K. 37, 47
Local Authorities 96, 134, 136, 138, 140

MacArthur Report 12, 67, 131, 139
McCarthy, M. 68
McInnes, R. 133–4
McKinsey Report 27, 32
Marenbon, J. 63, 75, 179
Marshall, B. 21–2, 32–3, 154
mass media 117, 119, 180
Massey, A. J. 71
Mathieson, M. 32
media 11–12, 19, 21–2, 30, 32, 52, 61–2, 72, 78, 84, 100–1, 117–27, 129–32, 139, 154, 167, 176, 180; culture 117, 120, 132; education 11–12, 117–30, 176; studies 21, 117–18, 123, 176
Media Literacy Audit 132
memory 24, 81, 86, 105, 108, 114, 161

Mercer, N. 37, 46–7, 181, 183–6
Mission, R. 146
MissionMaker software 124, 127
mobile devices 52, 132, 139
Morgan, W. 146
Motion, A. 145
Moyles, J. 45–6
multimedia 52

NACCCE (National Advisory Committee on Creative and Cultural Education) 143–4
narrative 53, 71, 82, 100, 104, 108, 118–22, 124–5, 128–9, 153
Nassaji, H. 44
National Association for the Teaching of English (NATE) 34–5, 133
National Curriculum 11, 13–14, 22, 24, 33, 63, 71–2, 75, 94–6, 100, 109, 119, 132, 145–7, 150, 155, 159, 170, 172, 174, 177 *see also* curriculum
National Literacy Strategy (NLS) 8–9, 28, 34, 38, 40, 89–96, 102–3, 149, 178–9, 186
Nelson, G. 67–8
New Zealand 7, 21, 33, 85–6, 182
Newbolt Report 22, 65, 174–5
Nicholls, J. 149
Norwood Report 65
novels 22, 26, 55, 76, 108–12, 114–15, 120–3, 152, 165
Nystrand, M. 40–1, 43

Ofsted (Office for Standards in Education) 21, 67, 98–9, 109, 144–5, 155
one-to-one approaches: to talk 36; as teaching strategy 40, 46, 98, 100, 180
Osborne, G. 169

pairs, learning in 44, 114
parents 7, 25, 27, 31, 37, 55, 78, 87, 98–9, 102, 109, 125, 131, 170, 183
Park, C. C. 162–3
Park, E. 73
Patten, John 176–7, 179
pedagogy: and creativity 13–14, 149; dialogic 4–5, 36, 41, 43, 45–7; and English teaching 14–16, 24, 36, 157, 160, 162; of language teaching 6; and literacy 8–9, 34, 79, 83, 101; of primary mathematics 90;

pedagogy: and creativity (*continued*)
and professional development 13;
radical 117, 123; and reading 10,
109; scripted 83; and talk 4, 37; and
technology 132, 134–5; and textual
production 11; universalistic 45; and
writing development 5
personal growth 3, 15–16, 33, 177,
180
philosophy 56; of English teaching 1–3,
8–9, 14–16; of language teaching 6
phonics 7, 80–1, 84–6, 101, 105
planning 28, 96, 134, 140, 147, 155
play, children's 80, 82–3, 87–8, 127
pluralist approach 6, 76
poetry 26, 55, 103, 105, 108, 118–22,
125–6, 128, 130, 142–3, 145,
148–52, 154, 174
policy 2–4, 6–10, 12, 15–17, 32, 46,
61–2, 72–3, 77, 83–8, 90–1, 98,
102–3, 121, 131–2, 135, 139, 141–2,
145, 148, 155, 157–60, 163, 173–5
policy makers 2, 15–16, 46, 72, 98,
144, 155, 160, 173–5
political: authorities 12, 17; context
of reading 84; drivers of educational
practice 5, 19; imperatives 86;
intervention 78; language 87;
messages 179; opinion 94
politics: of English teaching 1, 16, 20,
24–5, 27–8, 31–4, 72, 74–5, 86–90,
95–6, 99–100, 122–3, 132, 142, 157,
166, 180; and Standard English 71
popular culture 15, 118, 121, 129, 131,
175–6, 181, 186 *see also* culture
power 2, 6, 12–13, 50–1, 54, 64, 69,
72–3, 75–6, 82, 84, 88, 90, 109, 120,
139, 142, 154–5, 164, 172, 174,
177–83; of talk 36, 46
prescriptive: approach 6, 25, 28, 30,
34, 84–5, 91, 96, 178–9, 182, 186;
grammar 68, 73–6
production: task 153; of text 11, 123 *see
also* creative: production
professional development 4, 9, 12–13,
29, 31–2, 34, 36, 43, 45–6, 83, 91,
112, 129, 132, 134–40, 149
Pullman, P. 74–5

questioning 36, 38–46; closed 42, 107;
open 40, 42, 107; probing 38–9,
42–4; uptake 40–1, 45

radio 118, 176
reading: development 10, 22;
independently 22, 91, 104, 108,
112, 115; skills 100, 104, 108,
114–15, 117; strategies 101, 108,
111; widely 99, 104, 109, 112,
114; *see also* guided reading; silent
reading
recall 39, 43, 49, 85, 105
reflection 24–5, 27–8, 45–6, 89, 129,
142, 149, 155–6, 181; critical 124,
140
reflective: dialogue 46; practice 2, 27;
practitioner 28
Re-framing Literacy 56
relevance 37, 39–40, 46, 116, 138
*Report of the Task Group on Assessment
and Testing* (TGAT) 172
research: and creativity 14, 142–4, 146;
and curriculum 7; and language 73,
80; and literacy 7–8, 95, 97, 101,
108, 182–5; and pedagogy 7, 16,
36, 43–6, 79–83, 87–8, 95, 161,
173; and policy 1–2, 17; and subject
teaching 1–2, 16–17, 20–1, 23–4, 28,
30, 33–4, 40–1, 148–9; and writing
development 6, 49, 60–1
responsibilities: of schools 132, 158–9;
of students 46; of teachers 15, 65, 84,
97, 155, 158, 160, 183
rhetoric 5, 49–51, 53–8, 60–1, 85, 95,
117, 122–3
Robinson, Sir Ken 143–4, 146
Rose Review 78, 80, 85, 87
Rosenblatt, L. 148

Sampson, George 65, 175
SAT (Standard Assessment Tasks) 33,
92, 97–8, 186
Scandinavia 7
Scarratt, E. 133–4
Scholes, R. 166
Searle, C. 180
self-evaluation 21, 45–6
semiotics 56, 120, 123, 125–6, 130,
161, 165
'serial reading' 22, 107
Shakespeare, William 20, 64, 69, 92,
118–19, 127–8, 158, 164–6, 176
'shaping' 55
short story 112–13, 152
Shulman, L. S. 20–1, 25

silent reading 92, 108, 111–13 *see also* reading
Singapore 72–3
Smith, F. 38, 48, 142
Smith, L. 136, 167
social class: middle 75, 109, 170, 172, 174–5, 182; working 65, 95, 170, 172–6, 181–2, 186
social networking 48, 76, 109, 132, 139
socio-cultural approach 37, 47, 75, 139, 161
socio-economic factors 86, 95, 109, 125, 132 *see also* class
speaking 14, 21, 44, 76, 93, 132, 147, 150, 183
spelling 18, 25, 55, 93, 150–1
Squires, G. 27, 31
stakeholders, in teaching English 1, 17, 31, 134, 136
Standard English 6, 15, 63, 65–73, 75–6, 99, 174–5, 177, 179
Stibbs, A. 149
strategies: coping 30; feedback 36, 45; learning 45; reading 101, 108, 111, 116; teaching 4, 7, 10, 43, 45–6, 95, 97, 112, 138
Strauss, S. L. 80
subject knowledge: acquisition of 162; audit of 21; corpus of 102; disparity of 94; as educational aim 157–60; English 133; high-status 15; literacy 89–90; and National Literacy Strategy 90; and novice teachers 24; and relationship to teaching 25; secure 135
subject pedagogical knowledge (SPK) 20, 25–6
Sweden 80
syllabus 14, 118, 152, 156, 177

talk 4, 16, 36–7, 43–8, 67, 76, 82–3, 88, 107, 111–14, 147, 184–5
Tan Kiat Kun, T. 73
Tebbit, Norman 25, 74
technology 11–13, 30, 99, 131–7, 139–41, 143, 179
television 52, 100, 118, 132, 176
testing 6, 25, 33, 42, 59, 72, 77, 79, 94, 103, 128, 144, 146, 159, 172, 185

Tharp, R. G. 45
Thought and Language 37
Tolley, S. 133, 136
Trudgill, P. 67–8
Turner-Bissett, R. 27

UK (United Kingdom) 34, 74, 78–80, 94, 100, 102, 106, 113, 131–3, 135, 139, 148, 155, 169, 172, 178, 183
underachievement: educational 170–1; literacy 102; and social class 172–3, 181 *see also* achievement
United Kingdom Literacy Association (UKLA) 34
United Kingdom Reading Association (UKRA) 34
university degree 21–3, 26, 115, 148, 157, 162, 170

values 15, 25, 33, 76, 79, 102, 118, 120–2, 137, 159, 163, 166, 171, 174, 177, 180–6
video 4, 46, 127, 176
viewing 21, 114, 125
vocabulary 25, 32, 56, 64, 66–7, 69–70, 85, 93, 97, 101, 105–8, 114, 150, 172
vocation 2, 18–19, 23, 28, 31, 33, 181
Vygotsky, L. 4, 37, 47, 99, 127, 161–2, 167

Wee, L. 73
Wells, G. 44, 47, 83
Wenger, E. 29–30, 33
whole-school approaches 10, 92, 110, 140
Williams, R. 33, 118–19, 127, 167
Winnicott, D. 144
Wolfram, W. 72–3
Woodhead, Chris 176
Wright, L. 67, 69
writing: development 5–6, 48–61, 76 *see also* creative writing; as political act 5, 48–9, 51, 54, 60

Yates, C. 149

zone of proximal development 37